We Are The People

Also by Geoffrey Beattie

Survivors of Steel City
Making It: The Realities of Today's Entrepreneurs
All Talk
England After Dark

GEOFFREY BEATTIE

We Are The People

Journeys through the
heart of Protestant Ulster

HEINEMANN : LONDON

William Heinemann Ltd
Michelin House, 81 Fulham Road, London SW3 6RB
LONDON   MELBOURNE   AUCKLAND

First published 1992
Copyright © Geoffrey Beattie 1992

A CIP catalogue record for this book
is held by the British Library
ISBN 0 434 04964 6

Printed in England by
Clays Ltd, St. Ives PLC

For Carol

Contents

Acknowledgements

I would like to express my sincerest gratitude to John Course, Northern features editor of the *Guardian*, who encouraged me to write several pieces about my Belfast childhood for that paper. I was moved by the response to those articles. *New Statesman and Society* published several other articles which I wrote about Northern Ireland, and I would like to extend my thanks to Steve Platt, editor of *NSS*. Lisa Glass, my editor at Heinemann, suggested that I might like to write a book about the Protestants of Ulster, and proved to be very sensitive in providing feedback about the whole enterprise. Her genuine enthusiasm for the project meant that my interest could not dim – no matter what, as the writing on the gable wall subsequently said. I would also like to thank Weidenfeld and Nicolson for permission to use in a modified form certain chapters that I had written in two books which I did for them. The chapters were on two of the entrepreneurs featured in this book, namely Tom Pierce and Bryan West, which first appeared in *Making It: The Reality of Today's Entrepreneurs* (Weidenfeld and Nicolson, 1987), plus chapters on the Maze and my education in Belfast, which first appeared in *All Talk: Why it's important to watch your words and everything else you say* (Weidenfeld and Nicolson, 1988). I would also like to express my gratitude to Martin Dillon, author of *The Shankill Butchers* (Hutchinson, 1989) for permission to use certain extracts of coroner's reports and confessions of members of that gang, which were first printed in his book, in Chapter 15 of this one. These days I do nearly all of my own typing, but Anne Clifton helped out with typing when the going got tough, and I took off to do yet another interview. She can now almost understand someone with a Belfast accent. Almost. Lastly, I would like to thank all the people of Ulster, who gave me their time so freely. A hospital consultant in the book describes them as the warmest people on God's earth. I am inclined to agree.

My mother always felt that she deserved a medal for putting up with me. With hindsight I think she may have been right, and she deserves a very special thank you.

1

Going Home

Sights and Smells

I always find it a little strange flying to Belfast at night. You miss the sight of those great water-logged green fields. All that dank greenery. But you can smell that air as soon as you touch down. It's all so familiar. I dialled a number that my mother had given me some time ago. 'It's a local taxi firm,' she had said on the telephone. That meant that it was Protestant. The taxi came quickly. There were no markings on the cab to identify it, there was no number to ring. The driver, however, seemed to recognise me, or rather acted as if he did. 'How's it goin'?' he said. I didn't recognise him. I find that kind of friendliness disconcerting. I have, you see, been living in England for a number of years. The taxi moved out of the Harbour airport onto the Sydenham by-pass. I remembered that road from day trips to Bangor, not as a short cut from the new airport. We drove past Shorts and towards town. We reached North Street and there we reached a critical choice point – the loyalist Shankill Road or the more ambiguous Crumlin stretched out before us equally invitingly.

We accelerated up the Crumlin. 'Quicker at this time of night,' said the taxi driver as if having to explain his action.

The taxi took me up past Ardoyne Chapel silhouetted against the iron grey sky. It still looks formidable. It stirs up images of nuns and priests with ruddy complexions and the St Christopher my uncle kept in his Ford Anglia. It was an ivory colour. My aunt – my mother's sister – married a Catholic. He was my favourite uncle but I hated that car. He would park it in the street. My friends would notice it. 'That's not a St Christopher in your uncle's car, is it?' they would say, as they circled round the car viewing it from slightly different angles, as if the little religious statue would suddenly turn into something else when viewed from the side. There was no point in denying it. 'It was in the car when he bought it. He just keeps forgetting to take it out. I'll have to remind him . . . again,' I'd say. 'Just as long as your Uncle Terence isn't a Fenian fucker,' they'd say. 'Now that would be bad news.'

The taxi driver saw me looking up at the chapel. 'Still there,' he said. 'Solid as a rock.' I always hum when I pass that great monolith. It reminds me of all the nights when I was young following the Orange band down past the chapel. The band would play louder as it passed. Those warm, balmy nights of youth. The Catholics, or Roman Catholics as my mother would insist on calling them – 'We're all Catholics, Geoffrey. They're just the Catholics of Rome', – would stay indoors, despite the heat.

I started to sing in a low, inaudible murmur. 'If the Pope says no, then we'll have another go . . .' Nobody could have made out the words, but the tune was unmistakable, even in a murmur. The taxi driver laughed. 'You're obviously a local lad, although you've got a bit of an English accent.' The taxi driver was a Protestant, I know that, because his was a Protestant firm. He started to sing with me. 'On the twelfth of July in the m-o-r-n-i-n-g.' He laughed again. 'I like your choice of music.'

I commented on the fact that there were no identification markings on the cab. 'We had to take them all off because we kept getting stoned as we drove past the New Lodge,' he said. 'Well I suppose it's fair enough, our lads stone their taxis up our way, they stone ours down theirs. But there's been a few fatalities. Taxi drivers are very easy targets. You can lure them out just by making a call. I've been hijacked twice in the past year, but I'm still alive. Thank God. But our lads hijack them. One side's as bad as the other.'

I said that I could understand the fairness in the whole

2

thing, the perfect symmetry of it all, conflict in equilibrium – balanced, still, permanent.

'How long have you been away across the water?' he asked me. 'Eighteen years. Jesus, that's a long time. Things have changed around here, since you left. Then it was all about religion, now it's not. It's all about something else.'

I surveyed the streets and the silhouettes of the hills of my childhood. Those ancient hills, imprinted on my ancient memories. The hills of my forefathers for what . . . three, four hundred years? I don't know when my family left Scotland, but my ancestors have been looking up at Divis and Black Mountain and Cavehill for years. I know that. I can feel it in my bones. Eighteen years hasn't weakened that feeling.

I returned to the present. 'What do you think it's all about then?' I asked. 'It's all history really, and the prejudices of history, isn't it? Three or four centuries of it.'

The taxi driver took a long pull on his cigarette. 'Baaaaaaallicks. Who told you that? You've been reading too many books in England. It's all about money, now. Money, money, money. Everybody wants their whack. Everybody has to have their cut. That's all anybody's interested in around here.'

The taxi driver glanced over his shoulder to see what effect this pronouncement of his had had.

I must have looked taken aback. I'd been away from the Troubles all right. I hadn't heard anyone say 'baaaaalicks' in that kind of way for years. I myself had been saying 'bollocks' for as long as I could remember. I was shocked, brought down to earth by this revelation. They made that 'a' sound last forever.

I went back to counting the street lights. It gets dark early there – something to do with the smoke in the air. This isn't Los Angeles, there the smog clings to the valleys, here it clings to the mountain tops, and the hill tops and the wide open fields strewn with litter. The damp, grey little streets in the middle of them all haven't got a chance. The nights are long, very long. Long and smoky. That smoke evoked lots of memories.

'I was in Los Angeles recently, you know,' I said trying to restart the conversation.

3

'Did you go to Hollywood?' asked the taxi driver.

'No I missed that.'

'Oh. I'd love to go to Hollywood. My morrrrr says I smile just like John Wayne. A big fruity smile. Big Wanky Wayne. Well you never know your luck. I might be discovered over there.'

I felt myself freeze once more. It had happened again. For years I had been calling my mother 'mother' or 'mum'. My mother said that I sounded 'awful swanky'. I thought that she was exaggerating again. In my romantic memory of my working-class past, I remembered that I had sometimes called her 'mammy'. But never 'morrrr', rolling that 'r' to infinity. It sounded so harsh, so unloving and I had forgotten it completely. It sounded like 'morrrrder'. Or how they might say it. It was starting to rain.

'It's spittin' a wee bit now,' said my driver. 'They call me Bucky, by the way.' Bucky put his wipers on. I could see the rain staining the tarmac. I remembered the night that my father died. The stains on the tarmac and that smell in the air dragged it all back. He had lain in a coma for a week. Every day I prayed that the blinds on my house wouldn't be pulled down. As the bus turned towards Ligoniel, I would have that one look. Every day the blinds had been up. There was still some hope, and I prayed. Every night, every day, I prayed and prayed. On the Sunday, my Uncle Terence was to take my aunt and me to the Royal. He was late. It was spitting that night as we got on the bus. My aunt was angry because my uncle was late. We saw him on the tarmac of the Royal's car park. I slowed down as I saw him come out. I wasn't expecting to see him there. I wanted to avoid the unexpected. 'Billy's . . .' The sentence was never finished, but my aunt burst into tears. I froze in that rain that stung. We were never poor, not until that moment. We had everything. A nice wee house, a wee car. I can still remember all the registration numbers – 'NKF 148', 'DZ 1135', 'SAO 277'. They used to get me to recite them. 'Our Geoffrey forgets nothing,' they'd say. The last car we owned as a family was a Morris Minor. Black and shiny. But that night at the Royal, it was all taken away. After that the house got worse, the car went. The toilet out the back stank. The slugs grew bigger, thicker and juicier. But I was past all that now. Bucky pulled up at the door.

I could see my morrrrr as I got out of the taxi. She was sitting with her face lit up by the light of the television. The front gate was open, and the curtains open, as if she was waiting for the visitors that would never come. 'Nobody goes out around here at nights, nobody,' she always liked to say. I was half way through the open door before she noticed me.

'It's lovely to see you, son. I'll get the kettle on. You know that I can make tea like nobody else, and you don't drink enough of it. All that coffee isn't good for you.'

I had been there less than three seconds and already my lifestyle and my manners were being criticised. Coffee was foreign, coffee was English. More English than tea. Ulster had taken tea to its bosom, and filled it with sugar and milk – lots of both. Sweet, milky tea was Northern Irish. My mother still thinks that you make coffee with milk. We used to drive to Nutt's Corner on a Sunday evening to watch the planes take off, and to drink the coffee which was indeed made with milk. When we still had a car.

'This place will seem very quiet to you after what you're used to across the water.'

My mother allowed time for a response, but there was no point. She was hinting at the debauchery and wild times that are to be had across the water. I didn't want to have to defend it, and, anyway, she was just jealous. But I knew what was coming next.

'People don't go out at nights around here anymore. I'm on my own here every bloody night.'

She still hadn't forgiven me for leaving home to go to university. She used to like to point out that boys stayed with their mothers in Belfast until they got married, and even then the married couple would move in with their mothers (or heaven forbid their mother-in-law). She and my father, and my brother and me, had lived with her mother, and she never tired of telling me how cozy it was with all of us living in a two-up, two-down. 'There was plenty of room, plenty,' she would say. That's how life could have been. Now she was alone. I had deserted her for the university, all those years ago. Now she talked to herself.

She looked out of the window at the public library that had once been the Public Baths. 'It's far too dangerous to walk around here at nights, you know,' she said. 'After about six o'clock you don't see a soul until the next morning. I have a couple of friends who visit me, but only during the day. You're the first person that I've seen at night for ages.'

My mother served tea in her best china cups. Her china cup was cracked, mine wasn't. I felt a huge surge of remorse – how could I ever criticise her? How could I ever have left her?

The TV was on the blink again, it was spitting and spluttering in the corner of the dark room. She saw me looking at it. 'The set was bought four years ago off a man I knew who used to fix up broken televisions. It only cost forty pounds. It worked for a while, but as the man said recently when I bumped into him: 'This new technology isn't designed to work for ever, you know, love.' I told him that nothing lasts forever, and that he shouldn't worry about it. I got my money's worth. It was worth every penny.'

My mother explained that if I squinted my eyes, the picture would be clearer. 'It tires your eyes, though,' she added as an afterthought. We both sat squinting at that unreliable lined box in the corner. She brought me in a plate of digestives.

The house had been cleaned for my return. She insisted on giving me yet another tour of it. She was very proud of her home. 'I managed to furnish this new house with things which were secondhand, or with what people gave me. You know, the neighbours are very good around here. The cooker cost fifteen pounds seven years ago and that still works, well most of the time. The fridge was given to me by Betty from number forty-six, she's a very good friend. It works well except the ice keeps melting. But I've nothing to put the ice in anyway.'

The message here was only slightly veiled.

'The off-licence by the way closes at nine o'clock, if you want to buy a drink. I know the English are mean, but I hope you haven't picked up that characteristic as well.'

I said that I didn't want a drink. 'But it's nothing to do with being mean. I just don't fancy a drink at the moment. I'm tired

6

travelling. If I have a drink, I'll fall asleep. And if I don't want a drink, I don't see why I should have to go to the off-licence, like some kid going on a message.' She ignored this.

She led me upstairs to the back bedroom. 'I've recently got a new wardrobe of clothes from Lena. You remember Lena. We used to go to the International Hotel every Boxing Day with her and her sister Lily. You and your dad and me and your brother and your Aunt Agnes and Uncle Terence. She was a very good friend. She had cancer, you know. It's funny that all of my friends have cancer. Jean Reynolds – you remember her – she had her two breasts removed. Both at the same time. But that didn't save her. I'd just tell them to leave my boobs alone, if that happened to me, but I always had a better bust than Jean.'

She sat there patting her bust, presumably trying to imagine life without them. I averted my gaze. 'If they haven't got cancer round here, then they have a heart attack. One or the other gets you here. Lily, Lena's sister had a heart attack.'

'How serious was it?' I asked, desperately trying to remember which was Lena and which was Lily, two sisters that I always confused. When I was young, I always thought that they both looked like witches. One looked slightly more sinister than the other, but I couldn't remember who was the sinister one, and who was the very sinister one.

'You're asking me how serious was her heart attack? It was very serious, son. She died in fact,' said my mother. 'She had a corony – that means sudden death.'

'Do you mean a coronary?' I asked.

'Don't you correct me.' She proceeded to spell it out – 'C O R O N A R Y', until it lay there in space in front of her. Then she tried to read it off this imaginary page – 'A corony, a corony.' She was still getting it wrong.

'You've got me so that I don't know what I'm saying. Don't start being clever with me. Just remember I didn't have your education. We can't all be smart alecs like you. I might not be able to say it, but I know what it means – it means a clot, and the clot travels over your heart and kills ye.'

'Oh,' I said, and picked up my tea cup, not wishing to get into a dispute about the medical implications of a coronary. 'I see.'

'But it's marvellous what they can do for ye these days in hospitals. I have a friend just over from Canada and she's had a new valve put in. A completely new valve. It was a pig's valve. The way that I know that it was a pig's valve, is that our churchwarden Harry was telling her that he loved Canada. He had a holiday over there, you see, and he loved the place. He loved it. He also said that he loved the pigs that he saw on the farm there, and she told him that it was a pig's valve that she had put inside her. She says that some morning she'll not say "hello", she'll just grunt instead. I suppose that you have to try to make a joke of it sometimes. If you didn't have a laugh around here, then you'd go daft.'

My mind was racing. I had never associated Canada with pigs before. It would only be an Irishman who would go to Canada and above all else notice the pigs. The great pigs of Canada.

But my mother was now moving away from the pig's heart transplants.

'I've always liked style, you know, and so did my friend, Lena. I miss her terribly, but she had some great clothes. All the style.'

My mother always likes to keep me up on which of her friends had died recently, and what clothes she'd managed to get from their wardrobe, after they'd passed on. She also likes to tell me which pieces of jewellery she was going to pass on to my daughter, Zoe. 'Zoe will get this gold chain off me when I'm dead. It cost eight pounds seven years ago, so it must be worth more than that now.' The gold chain had been promised to my wife for years, but now it was intended for someone else.

'I hope that you brought your cheque book home with you to write me out a wee cheque. I can get it cashed in the chemist's. Do you know that I get forty-one pounds ninety-seven pence pension a week, and thirty-two pounds sixty pence a month from your father's superannuation. The rent's six pounds eighteen a week, the coal – eight pounds forty for a bag. In winter I have to use two bags a week.'

She continued describing her weekly budget, continued counting out every penny – 'One pound a week goes in the church envelope. I don't begrudge them it mind. Our church has to be kept, our church isn't well off like the *Roman* Catholic church.

'And then, two pounds twenty-two pence a month goes on insurance – to bury me. It costs more than you think these days. You can't expect anyone else to pay for ye. I'm ready to go. I can tell you that.'

My mother is sixty-eight, but looks much younger, which makes her constant preoccupation with death that much more incongruous. Objectively speaking, you could say that she'd got a lot of life left in her.

She would disagree. 'There's not much to look forward to here, nothing to live for, anything has to be better than this.'

I told her not to be so silly.

'You're all right. You're away from it all. You don't know what it's like. Some of the lads around here have never worked, and probably never will. There's no work. Mind you, some of them are right lazy so-and-so's and they wouldn't work if you forced them. They wouldn't know how. But I miss my work, and all my friends up in the mill. We always had a good laugh.'

I remembered that the last time I'd passed Ewart's mill where she used to work, I noticed that the 'E' in Ewart's had fallen off the large sign on the front of the building. I didn't dare mention this.

'There's no work here, now. They made me retire at sixty. I'd worked all my life and I'd got nothing to show for it. I didn't want to retire. Who would want to retire around here with nothing to do? I was still in the old house when they kicked me out of work. Do you remember the old house?'

Did I remember the old house? That house was imprinted on my brain. The root of every insecurity and anxiety. Did she really think that I could have forgotten it? I had grown up in that little mill house with the outside toilet, full of slugs, learning over the years to go to the toilet quickly before one of them got the opportunity to slide over my backside. The wallpaper on the kitchen walls would never stay on, because the walls were so damp. And when my father died when I was thirteen, and laid out in the front room, I would have to go

9

down the stairs and past the coffin, illuminated by the street light outside, and then face the slugs.

I hated that house, but I never dared criticise it – lest it set off another argument. 'You're a wee snob, that's your problem. Only snobs are ashamed of where they grew up.' But I wasn't ashamed of where I grew up – I just hated that squalor of the place, and got angry that others saw nothing wrong with it.

When I brought my first girlfriend to the house I put red light bulbs in all the electric sockets, not because I wanted the place to look like a brothel, but because I didn't want her to see the state of the place. And besides all that, our next-door neighbour was vicious. When I or my girlfriend, or even the local Minister for that matter, tried to go to the toilet outside, the next-door neighbour would hurl half-bricks over the yard wall.

'Whoremaster,' she would shout – at me or the Minister. 'Whore' – pronounced 'whoer', at my mother or girlfriend.

Our next-door neighbour seemed to be able to discriminate man, woman or beast, on the basis of how long they spent on the toilet. The insults and the bricks only started on the way back. She obviously listened the whole time the toilet was occupied. How could I forget that house?

My mother always talked fondly of it, in a strange kind of way. 'The house was due for demolition, as you know. Not before bloody time. It had been condemned years ago. I was the last one in the street, because I was waiting for the new house to be finished. The rain was coming in through the roof, the living room ceiling collapsed. I was sleeping in a wet bed.'

She knew how to make me feel guilty all right. While I was living it up in college at Cambridge University no less, she was sleeping in a wet bed. It didn't matter that I'd served eighteen years in just such a wet bed. No, at the end when it really mattered I'd taken myself off to skive at university whilst she was suffering.

'The paper used to hang off the walls. Do you remember that? And then to cap it all, the slates fell off the house next door and just missed me one night when I was going out to the toilet.' She laughed – 'I wish they'd hit me a wee crack, not enough to do me any real damage, just so that I could have got a claim in. I know people, from both sides, who have got

10

some good money in compensation from claims from the Troubles. It's as good as winning the pools, some people say. But the Catholics, sorry I mean the Roman Catholics – the RCs are better at claims than us Protestants. That's what they say anyway. They know the ins and outs of all the forms. It's because they're so good at collecting the social security. This is what you hear. They get plenty of practice at it. They're brought up on official forms. Mind you, some of our own lot aren't so bad at it either. They're catching up all right.

'The funny thing is that I still miss the old house. Silly isn't it? I suppose it was because I was born in it. But this new house is something else. It's nearly on the exact spot where the old one used to be. Well, it's up closer to the park than the old one. The Housing Executive did a great job of keeping the local community together, and that's very important. But nearly all the locals are getting on a bit now. But this new house, what a difference to the old one. It's a palace.'

I looked out of the window. The front garden, lit up by the street light, was about six foot by three feet. She had flowers planted in every corner of it. But it looked so small and cramped.

'Just room enough to bury me in, eh? You could save yourself a bit of money and just lay me in the front garden. But I've got my grave all arranged in Roselawn with your father. We had to buy a new grave up there. Your grand-parents are buried in the City Cemetery up the Falls Road near the bus depot where your dad used to work. But Protestants would be a bit worried about going up there these days. The vandals have got the graves wrecked anyway. We wanted somewhere away from all that – away from the Troubles. Somewhere nice and quiet like Roselawn.'

She leaned back and gazed out at the street light.

'The only problem with Roselawn is that it's not very easy to get to without a car. So I have to wait on your Uncle Terry to come over from England to take me up there. It used to be lovely when it first opened, but like everything over here it gets shabby very quickly.'

I felt guilty again that I hadn't been to the grave for years. There was still no gravestone, just a black bowl for flowers

11

with 'Beattie' written on it. This makes me feel more guilty than anything. 'We hadn't the money when your father died,' my mother always said.

'Nobody cares about you. Nobody remembers you when you've gone. But I wouldn't care if I died tomorrow and that's the truth. Who wants to get old. There's an old woman down the street, who's eighty-three and she gets all her instructions about what to do from the television. Presumably her set is in better condition than mine.'

She laughed again. 'You can hardly make out what they say on mine. When this old neighbour of mine saw the photographs of the victims of the Lockerbie air crash in the *Belfast Telegraph*, row after row of them all smiling, she thought that it was marvellous them all smiling like that and dead as well. That's how far gone she is. Who wants to end up like that.'

I was reminded that up here in North Belfast, there was no such thing as growing old gracefully. No, the cumulative deprivation of all the years just produced one end-product and this was it, sitting in front of a telly on the blink wondering what it was trying to say to you, and thinking about your final resting place and how peaceful it was, if you could only just cadge a lift out to it.

'And there's so much bitterness about. The Troubles have made everyone bitter. So many young lives wasted. One or two making money out of it all as usual. But then they'd make money out of any situation. There was a shooting at Our Lady of Mercy school earlier today. Some man waiting for his daughter was shot at by some cowboy on a motorbike. The cowboy missed. My neighbour says that the Protestants always miss or the gun backfires – one or the other. But, there are a lot around here who say that nobody ever gets it for nothing. They must have done something, or why would they be after him? Don't ask me what this girl's father had done, but it must have been something. At least that's what I believe. That's what you have to believe, or it would drive you nuts.'

Through the noise of the television, now stuttering as well as blinking, you could hear the noise of an army helicopter circling overhead. 'There must be trouble some place close-by. I feel sorry for the young soldiers over here. But they're doing a good job. They don't really come round here anymore on foot patrol, some of my neighbours used to give them tea. I remember once waving at some soldiers from a Scottish regiment leaving our factory to go back across the water, and do you know what they did back? They gave us the V-sign, that's what. And not for victory. I suppose they were just a bit fed up with the whole thing, cooped up in a factory for weeks on end.'

'I suppose we're all Paddies from their point of view,' I said.

'What did you say? We're not Paddies, as you call them. We're Ulstermen.'

'And women . . .'

'Yes certainly and women. Some of the staunchest Loyalists are women. We're certainly not Paddies, and nobody on God's earth could mistake us for them. Sometimes the army mount a roadblock just opposite here, and to be honest it's one of the few bits of excitement around here. Something to watch, because you never see a soul walking about here late at night. They're too afraid. But at least everyone knows that all of us pensioners around here aren't going to be any trouble to anyone. At least not usually. But I did see this pensioner at the bus stop yesterday shooting at a passing army Land Rover with his walking stick. He was holding it as if it was a gun. He was a Catholic by the way, he's not from around here, he was waiting for a bus. He'll get the area a bad reputation, if he's not careful.'

She laughed again. 'He was shouting something as well, but luckily the army just drove past him. They probably thought that he was just a bloody old fool, another stupid Paddy. I've known him for years. He's no fool, he was just making a point I suppose – fed up with being ignored. It can get to you living here.'

Even for a couple of hours, I thought, but kept this to myself. I needed a breather.

'I'm just off to the off-licence, morrrr, I'll be back in a few minutes.'

Drinksville

I stood outside Crazy Price Drinksville, trying to work out how to get into the place. The lights were on, but the front door was locked. I tried the handle again. It opened this time. 'Security,' said a grey-haired man with a thick grey moustache behind the counter. 'We've had too many hold-ups in here recently. We keep the door locked. You can't be too careful around here. I just saw this figure in the darkness. You could have been one of the Commanches from Ardoyne or the Falls for all I knew.'

I surveyed the shelves of whisky and vodka, all at crazy prices, or so the handwritten cards said. 'Crazy' was spelt 'crazeeee'. I thought they were all very expensive. The off-licence seemed to stock vodka from every country in the world except the Soviet Union. I commented on this. I thought it was an amusing little quip. I thought that it would help break the ice.

The grey-haired man's smile froze on his face. 'Oi, yes, you're very observant. Very good. Take a biscuit. Ten marks out of ten for observation. Go to the top of the class . . . smart baaaaalicks.'

I could feel my temperature rising. Had he just insulted me? Or was he just trying to break the ice himself? To show that despite my years away that I was really home? Could he tell that despite my new accent I was a local lad who had returned at last? A local lad who would know that insults are part of the social environment, with strict rules governing their use. A local lad who would know instinctively all the rules governing ritual insults in this part of Belfast, a local lad who would call him 'old grey baaaaalicks' back. Or 'mouldy baaaaalicks'.

The grey-haired man could sense my discomfort, in fact, he could probably see it.

'Sorry, only kiddin' ye, fella.'

'Well, why is it?' I stammered, having lived for eighteen years in a culture where comments, like questions and compliments, received answers. Not a load of sarcasm and abuse. The grey-haired man looked taken aback.

'It's because Russian vodka is too fuckin' expensive, smart baaalicks. Now, are you here to be served, or are you just here to look down your nose at us, and make comments on our stock?' I returned to scanning the shelves. I noticed that the grey-haired man had shortened the 'a' sound of 'baaalicks'. I suddenly remembered that the natives did this when they

14

were angry or annoyed. The grey-haired man looked straight at me with a stony face. Suddenly his face melted into a great warm smile.

'How's about ye, Ginger? In a bit early tonight? What's the matter with ye, they haven't barred ye from Topcat's by any chance now? They haven't sacked ye, have they?'

My heart stopped. Surely, this wasn't Ginger? God please, no. Not Ginger. Not that Ginger. I hadn't seen Ginger since I had left home. Ginger was one of my mother's old friends from way back. After my father died, he used to sit on the settee just by the electric fire, soaking up all the heat in our front room. Not doing homeworks again, Geoffrey? A boy your age should be out enjoying himself. Not stuck in the house every night.'

He seemed to resent my education. 'He thinks he is something, that boy of yours. Well I think that he's no better than anybody else. Here's one for you – where does electricity come from?'

I was fifteen at the time. I knew all about the basic components of matter, and the flow of electrons. I understood electricity as well as anybody in the highest class for Physics at Belfast Royal Academy. I was even to get an 'A' in A-level Physics. So without sounding condescending or superior, or desperately trying not to, I explained in great detail exactly what electricity was.

Ginger just sat there. 'Baaaalicks,' he eventually replied. 'You see my brother's an electrician and he doesn't know where electricity comes from. So what you've just told me is a complete load of old shite. You've just made it all up to try to get one over on me.

'Sorry to speak so plainly, Eileen. But that son of yours makes things up, to make himself seem better than the rest of us. He's a snob, all right.'

'Now, be fair, Ginger. He's not a real stuck-up ssssnob.'

'He is.'

'He's just got an education. Okay, he may get things wrong occasionally. You'd better check those books, Geoffrey. After all, if Ginger's brother doesn't know what electricity is, and he has to work with it all day, how the hell could your teachers know? Answer me that one.'

I couldn't stand Ginger. I stood there now in Crazy Price Drinksville facing row after row of non-Soviet vodka.

'Hey fella, have you made up your mind yet? We do close at nine o'clock, you know.'

Ginger started fumbling in his pocket for his change.

'You're all right, Ginger, no probs, take your time. It's just that this guy here was a bit sarcastic when he came in.'

'Oh oi?' retorted ginger.

I could tell that Ginger was drunk by the way that he slurred 'oi', my mother does exactly the same thing.

'He was making all sorts of comments about the place. I thought that he might be a hit-man for a few minutes.'

And they both laughed.

'I knew the IRA were hard-up for their hit squads, but I didn't know they were that hard-up,' said the grey-haired man.

'Only kidding ye, lad. You have to have a wee joke around here, or you'd go fuckin' daft. Now what can I get ye?'

I knew that I was going to have to speak. There was no way of avoiding it any longer.

'A bottle of Cossack vodka, please.'

Ginger stopped fumbling for his money momentarily.

'I recognise that voice. I'd recognise that tone anywhere. It's Geoffrey . . . Geoffrey Beattie. It's fuckin' Eileen's son. How's about ye? Long time no see.'

I tried desperately to smile, as Ginger pressed my hand so tightly in a handshake that my knuckles squeaked.

Even the grey man was smiling. 'Why didn't you say who you were? Eileen's one of our best customers. She won't drink that stuff you've just bought. She likes 'The Sound of the Steppes' the best. She doesn't put anything in her vodka, you see. She likes the smooth taste of 'The Sound of the Steppes' better. Your mother is a connoisseur of vodka. Actually, she's a connoisseur of most drinks. She won't just drink rubbish.'

'You'd better get a litre bottle. You don't want to scrimp tonight,' said Ginger. 'I was just on my way up to see your mother. I haven't seen her for ages. It's a bit of a coincidence

16

bumping into you. We can have a party up there tonight, and talk about old times.'

I was quite ashen as Ginger, with his hand on my shoulder, led me out of the security door and onto the wet grey street.

The Party

'Oh, Ginger. Long time, no see. It's lovely to see ye again. I see you managed to find my son out there wandering about.'

'Look what we've got for you, Eileen – a big bottle of "Sound of the Steppes".'

I could feel myself grimacing. Ginger may have spent some time fumbling for change in Crazy Price Drinksville, but he never got any of it out in the end.

'Oh, lovely, Ginger. It'll be like Christmas. We can have a wee party.'

I sat down on the settee, only to jump up immediately. Something spiky had stuck right into me. It was a large, spiky bag of pins and curlers owned by my mother.

'I was just going to put my curlers in, Ginger, before you came. If I'd known you were coming I would have got myself all dolled up.'

'You look a picture anyway, Eileen. I'm sure you'd look just as good with your curlers in.'

'Oh, you do know how to flatter, Ginger. You are a bit of a smooth talker. Go and get the glasses, son. They're in the kitchen.'

I got up and went into the kitchen. Laughter was coming from the front room.

'I've been telling your morrrr that England's full of perverts, Geoffrey. Now, isn't that right? I hope none of that's rubbed off on you.'

'Oh, Ginger, don't be saying that. No son of mine could be bent.'

'Look, Eileen. No offence, but England's full of perverts. You know that. You read the Sunday papers. Did you read that one about the vicar from Coventry? Or what about that singer in the dress and hat? Now if he's not a bloody queer I

17

don't know who is. This vodka's very smooth – it's a lovely, refreshing drink.'

'But his family's Irish,' I interrupted.

'What's he saying?' asked Ginger managing to talk right over me. I noticed that I let my voice trail off as if what I was saying was of no consequence anyway. 'Look, Eileen, your son's been there a long time. Some of it may have rubbed off on him, so to speak.'

Ginger licked his large, swollen wet lips. 'Have you got your leg over any of them little swingers in England in the past week?'

My mother started simpering. 'Oh, Ginger. Not in front of my son,' she said.

'I was only asking. It's a free country you know. You can ask what you like. We're not run by the Free State, yet. We don't have to ask the Pope or a priest for permission to talk about sex in our own houses. At least not yet.

'Well did ye, Geoffrey? Have ye get the auld trouser snake out this week with any of those wee English birds?'

'I was out with the pensioners' club today,' said my mother, changing the subject. 'We stopped off for a beautiful lunch in Newcastle – we had chicken, chips and salad – lettuce, tomatoes, cucumber, the works.'

'Oh, very nice,' said Ginger showing some genuine enthusiasm, in marked contrast to his reaction to anything that I had to say.

'The only problem is that I don't like cucumber,' she continued.

'Oh, you could have asked to have it removed, you know,' said Ginger with great authority.

'Really?'

'Certainly, you could. Just remember, Eileen, in future when you're in a restaurant, and you don't want any cucumber, just remember to say "no cucumber, please".'

'Oh, I must bear that in mind.'

'You have to ask, Eileen, that's my motto. If you don't ask for something, then you don't get it,' continued Ginger waxing philosophical and looking very pleased with himself.

'Or ask for something not to be there. Or not ask for

something that would have been there, but now won't,' I quipped, having already drunk my large glass of vodka.

'I don't know what that son of yours is talking about half the time,' said Ginger.

'Neither do I,' replied my mother.

'Anyway, Geoffrey, I hear that you're going to visit Billy tomorrow. Bonanza Billy, as we call him. That man's a fuckin' hero. He used to ride his black taxi the way that some of the cowboys in the Old West used to ride stage coaches.'

I stared straight ahead trying to comprehend this analogy. I didn't understand the analogy, and it wasn't even Billy that I was going to visit. In fact, I hadn't even heard of Bonanza Billy.

'I saw him once flying up the road,' continued Ginger, 'with all this gear falling out of the boot of the taxi, just like a fuckin' stagecoach.'

'Oh,' I said.

'Tell him that he may be away – well he has been inside for quite a few years now – but he's never forgotten. He's in all our hearts. Tell him too that he's a genius. I read in the papers at the time of his trial that he had masterminded that big raid on the bookies on the Grosvenor Road. He was the genius who planned the whole thing. The bullets were flying that day. It was like the Wild West. I bet they didn't know what hit them in that bookies. Nobody was shot dead though. Nobody was even hit. You have to be a good shot to miss in a confined space like that. Billy used only the top men. He stayed outside in the car when the raid was on, masterminding the whole thing. It was a pity he ran into that roadblock though. Probably the SAS. I know the papers said that it was just a local UDR patrol, but I know that it was the SAS. It had to be. Probably some informer, some stoolpigeon, some Protestant turn-coat set them up. Some fuckin' shirt-lifter, I bet. Not a bit of wonder they put Billy away for life. A genius like that on the streets and the Taigs would really be on the run in this here town.

'We're not ruthless enough, Eileen, that's our problem. We're just not ruthless enough. The IRA are ruthless all right. They shoot informers, we get them to buy a few rounds down in the club. That's the big difference between us and them.'

19

I said I had had quite enough of this conversation. It had been a very long day, I explained.

'I thought you university types living on tax payers' money weren't meant to get tired that easily,' said Ginger. 'Living off the state still. A perpetual student, I know.'

'I'm not a student,' I protested, 'I'm . . .'

'Look, I wish you'd get off your high horse sometime. I'm on the disability and I'm not ashamed of it. But then again I've got enough to do. I've got plenty of wee jobs.' Ginger winked across the room at me. 'If you get my meaning.'

'You mean that you've got some part-time work,' I asked.

'You could say that,' answered Ginger smugly.

'Oh, Geoffrey, don't you understand. I've heard that Ginger's in the Organisation. They say that he's one of the top boys.'

'Only a foot soldier, really, Eileen,' said Ginger. 'Only doing my bit to Save Ulster.'

Only a bloody hanger-on more like, I thought to myself.

'I'm doing security at Topcat's at the moment. Only the trusted few are allowed to do that. You see you never know who anybody is in this town. So you'd better be a bit careful, Geoffrey. You might get up somebody's nose with your stuck-up ways, and you could end up getting rubbed out. Just like that.'

There was a long, meaningful pause designed to terrorise and intimidate.

'Just like that,' repeated Ginger, this time clicking his fingers for effect.

'Just like that,' echoed my mother.

'Baaaalicks,' I said, and made my way wearily to bed.

I knew I was finally home.

2

Lest We Forget

Golden Autumns of the Past

Autumn is a time for nostalgia. A melancholy time, but full of images, sights and smells that draw out old memories. I lay in bed that morning letting those memories flood through. It's a good time for going home. Home to Belfast, home to the park, with the spreading chestnut tree. It still smells the same, despite everything. Old trees, old tunes, but this one tree still has the best 'cheesers', on the very same branches it seems. We discovered that tree and those branches for ourselves, without prompting and without any help. And no doubt our fathers did the same thing before us – when the tree grew in the grounds of some magnificent house or other, rather than in a municipal park. I managed to knock down a 'cheeser' from that tree that lasted nearly two whole seasons. It helped me climb the social hierarchy in my street. I had baked it. I got to the top of the social hierarchy through cheating.

The glen is still there, at the back of the park, smaller than I remember it, but still overgrown and still wild enough to stimulate the imagination. Glenbank dam in the middle of the glen, where we used to have our illicit swims, is gone – drained because it claimed one life too many. We used to swim in it in the golden afternoons of youth and skinny dip at night. It would have freezed ye. One night somebody fired at us with an air pistol as we dived in. We took refuge in its great murky welcoming depths. I could understand how you could have drowned in it. It drew you into its bosom. Or it did then. It looks very shallow now. Shallow and empty. And anyway Glenbank – the bleach mill is closed, along with all the linen mills in Ligoniel: Wolfhill, Ewarts' and Emersons'. But the greasy hill we used to slide down is still there, and the bank, with the eight-foot drop. We had to jump off this to prove – well, that we could jump off it. But it still gives me vertigo when I stand on it looking down, even if I did once hurl myself off it regularly – to be part of the gang.

We were the 'turn-of-the-road' gang. I know it's not a very elegant title, but it has the advantage that it's reasonably accurate. The Upper Crumlin Road, you see, branches about a mile from Ardoyne, with one road going to Silverstream and one going up to Ligoniel. We hung about the turn-of-the-road. There was another gang that hung about outside a sweet shop called the Mayfair, about fifty yards away, on the first major turn in the Upper Crumlin Road. We called them the 'perfume gang'. They were all in the Boys Brigade, and they all attended Ballysillan Presbyterian Church. Quite a few of them were Christians. At least one later became a Presbyterian minister. None of our gang was a Christian. Some of us were in the CLB – the Church Lads Brigade, but that was different. Our area was on the frontline. Silverstream has always been predominantly Protestant, Ligoniel – at least past St Mark's Church – Catholic. I lived in a street just by the first bus stop on the Ligoniel road. It was called Legmore Street. I always thought that it was a very curious name for a street. The turn-of-the-road was fifty yards from my house, I could see it from our window. There wasn't much there. The immediate area was mixed – Bobby Sands' father grew up at the bottom of our street – on Lavens Drive. But the Catholics from my street didn't hang about the corner. I always thought that they'd better things to do. We were nearly all Protestant, except Moke, who was Italian by descent, so he didn't count anyway. And on hot summer nights and freezing winter nights, we'd go and stand outside the chip shop. It wasn't so much a corner we stood at, as a shop front. Don't ask me why we picked the chip shop. We ate chips, but not that often. I always believed that it had something to do with the hot air vent. We just stood there in front of it, shivering, listening to the crack. I'd do my homework and then rush down to the corner 'for an hour' to see what I was missing. It was never a lot. Occasionally the police would move us on, and we'd leave reluctantly but politely. But it was pointless, we'd nowhere else to go. They knew it too.

Now and again, we'd get into a little trouble. There was a tramp who lived in a derelict lorry near the turn-of-the-road, whose shoes used to squeak as he walked. We called him Squeak – not very originally as it turned out. Squeak, like the chestnut tree in the park, had been around for a long time, and the previous generation had called him Squeak as well. We used to follow him around, shouting 'Squeak', and causing him endless torment. One night – much to our surprise – he complained to the police, and we were chased by a policeman on a motorcycle. It was me that he caught, in the grounds of the local Pentecostal church. For some reason, I thought that I'd be safe there. He insisted on escorting me home, as my parents settled down to *Saturday Night at the London Palladium*. I had to tell them that there was somebody at the door who wanted to see them. The most embarrassing aspect of the whole episode was that I knew the daughter of this particular policeman from church and Sunday school. Nevertheless, I was relieved that I'd been warned officially – by the police – to leave Squeak alone, and I made a great point of saying 'Hello Mr Kyle' every time I saw him afterwards. He seemed genuinely pleased, because few of the respectable members of the community showed such respect to him. My friends didn't make peace with him. One night one of them climbed into his derelict cab and shat right in the middle of where he slept.

In summers we'd swim in the dam. It was full of weeds, dead dogs, and pipes. The water was freezing and there was a prominent 'Trespassers wil be Prosecuted' sign on display. But, in our gang, you had to be able to swim to the pipe and back, and climb over the park railings to get there. One night someone slipped and they were impaled on one of the sharp spikes on top of the railings for some time. I can remember the delay as the ambulancemen tried to remove him. Occasionally

23

the police would arrive as we were trying to have a swim. I could never understand why everyone seemed hellbent on stopping us using the dam, because the mill had long since abandoned it. It was our swimming pool, there were no public swimming baths anywhere near. Peter's Hill baths were miles away and, when they closed, Falls' Road baths were nearest – but they were most definitely out of bounds to us, even to Moke.

One summer we took to raiding 'orchies' – apple orchards – in a big way. We had to walk quite a way to get to the sort of houses that had apple orchards. The walk was full of tension, because once you were there all eyes were on you. Everyone noticed who got in first, and who hung back. You could get away with hanging back once, but not more than once. After you'd got the apples you'd usually take one bite out of each of them and chuck them away. Part of the performance was seeing who could toss the apples away in the most arrogant fashion. I always wondered what the people who owned these orchards must have thought when they woke in the morning to find all their prize apples on the ground, with these strange bite marks out of them, as if a plague of dieting locusts had descended upon them. But this wasn't vandalism to us, it was a rite of passage. Who was the fastest, strongest, bravest? Who would be last to snitch? This was always a very pertinent question, because we always seemed to get caught eventually.

One summer we were raiding orchards, the next a few people started expressing an interest in breaking into shops. Shops had a very big advantage over apple orchards – they weren't so far away. And so two of the best orchard raiders broke into a chemist's shop 'for the drugs'. They'd no idea what they were looking for, and if they found anything of interest I'm sure they wouldn't have known what to do with them. I went to the library, to read up about 'dangerous drugs', just in case they managed to get anything. All I can remember about the book was that it said that 'speed' wasn't any more dangerous than an outward bound weekend. We all agreed that this sounded okay, the only problem was that when they inspected the haul, they couldn't work out which item was the speed, if any. I was given a phial of something

24

and told to hide it in my bedroom. My mother had long since given up tidying this room, you see. So I kept the phial there, and whenever anyone enquired as to what it was, I would reply 'drugs', with great reverence, and great authority. This seemed to do the trick, because no one ever asked for clarification – fortunately for me. Unfortunately, the chemist's shop was just a few doors away from the chip shop where we stood, so the finger of suspicion pointed immediately at our gang. They'd been spotted, as well, climbing in and all the neighbours of the shop knew their faces from all the nights that they'd spent standing at the corner. The burglars hadn't bothered with gloves or anything like that (after all they'd never been needed in the orchards), so conclusive proof wasn't difficult. Luckily, they were just fined.

Life continued much as before. Occasionally, we'd go to discos – The Starlite, or Whites. Occasionally, we'd go to the pub or the cinema. But such pursuits required money, and money was always in short supply. So there we'd be – at the corner, again. I can remember a policeman saying one night: 'Are you lads waiting for something? Because if you're not push off.'

We were always waiting, we didn't know what for.

One night a car pulled up, and four mountain men jumped out, looking for somebody or other. People used to be always looking for somebody or other. The mountain men were men from past the bend in the Horse Shoe Road (which is actually only about half a mile away). Men from over the hill. God knows what religion they were. One irregular member of the group nipped into the chip shop and bought two bottles of lemonade, which he emptied into the gutter as the mountain men were shouting their menaces. He went for them with the two empty bottles. This was one of the bravest acts I've ever seen, and it showed such presence of mind. The mountain men scattered, but screamed that they'd be back with a shotgun. We just laughed, until they returned about twenty minutes later with one. I spent most of the rest of that evening hiding below a car in Barginnis Street. I went home covered in oil, but otherwise unscathed.

On other occasions I wasn't so lucky. It was my very first

date with a girl. We'd gone into town and made two milk-shakes last about an hour each, but with some determination I'd kept enough for two hamburgers on the way home. As we walked along Royal Avenue, someone stepped out in front of me. He said 'You're from Silverstream, aren't you?' Now the truth is that strictly speaking I wasn't. I could understand why he thought that I was, since many of the lads who knocked about the turn-of-the-road came from Silverstream. I tried to explain all this to him. He stared at me in disbelief, and asked me if I was trying to be funny. As he did so, someone stepped out from behind me and hit me with some unidentified heavy object (it could even, with some imagination, have been his fist). I fell forward, and stranger number one put the boot in. My girlfriend screamed, as my hamburger rolled across the pavement. They told me to take *that* back to Silverstream with me. I pulled myself up and tried to crack a feeble joke about the whole thing, as I dusted off my hamburger. Some friends went past in a car, they were from Silverstream. We spent hours that night hunting my two assailants, but to no avail. It was 'us' versus 'them'. They were from Ligoniel, there could be no doubt about it – from way past St Mark's Church. I was sure of that even though, to the best of my knowledge, I'd never seen them before – or since. One of the lads in the car advised me to carry a chain, when I went out on my own. 'Give them a nasty surprise,' he said. The Troubles were now raging.

I saw my first handgun close up, soon after this. It was now well known among my friends that my mother never went into my bedroom. Dennis Eccles one night casually suggested if I'd mind looking after a few of his records for him. I said of course not, until I realised that his record collection consisted of about fifty copies of the same album! What's more it was an album by John Lennon, where he and Yoko appeared on the cover without clothes. Where Dennis had managed to acquire this little gem, I wouldn't like to guess. When I saw the records, which Dennis insisted on unpacking in my front room, I declined to have anything more to do with them. I swore to him that my mother now cleaned my bedroom. He insisted on checking. 'It's not very clean,' he said. But I assured him that this was because my mother wasn't very good at cleaning, rather than because of the fact that she didn't clean it in the first place. He wasn't convinced, but he left down Barginnis Street, his big, brown parcel flapping in the wind, giving passers-by periodic flashes of John Lennon's willy.

It was my friend Tampy who raised the matter of the gun. He said that Dennis had told him that I was going to look after some records for him, so was there any chance of me holding on to a little something for him as well. He unwrapped it, in his bedroom. He'd got it off a relative, but was worried that his mother might find it. I told him I couldn't help. I swore on the Bible that my mother cleaned my bedroom every single day, sometimes twice a day. I told him that he could inspect my bedroom any day to see just how clean it was. I told him to dump the gun. 'I'm not going to get rid of it, it might come in handy some day,' he said.

My nights of homework paid off. I went away to university, quietly and unobtrusively. I'd slip back to the corner during vacations, but everyone else was slipping away. Everyone was busy now, there was so much to do. 'There's going to be civil war,' they told me. 'You're all right over there in England, you don't have to worry about it.' I sat in quiet psychology tutorials, discussing 'relative deprivation' theories of the Troubles, and reading about all the gerrymandering and discrimination against Catholics that had gone on. And wondering where any of it had got me and my kind. In our stinking little mill houses with the outside toilets and slugs everywhere. 'They're just water my mother would always say, don't worry about them – put salt on them and they just dissolve.' The slugs that is. 'What relative deprivation?' I'd ask. The houses at the bottom of the Ligoniel Road, and the houses at the top – even way past St Mark's – weren't that different, after all. And the slugs were definitely just the same.

'Who will save Ulster?' was the question on everyone's lips at the time. I always assumed this was rhetorical. It's the same in any war. Who does the responsibility always fall on? Who always pays the ultimate price? The answer is the kind of lads who hung around the corner. Who decides whether it is a war or not? And who makes the strategic decisions? And who makes the profit out of war? The answer is – unknown individuals, but definitely not the lads from the corner.

And so it turned out.

The North Belfast brigade of the UVF has been one of the most active in the Troubles. Jim Watt, Aubrey Tarr and Alex Smith, who spent many a cold night at the turn-of-the-road shivering, waiting, all became UVF members, and are all now serving life sentences for murder. The pub beside the chip shop, owned by a Catholic, was burned to the ground. It's since been rebuilt, it's not owned by a Catholic now. The owner of the fruit shop on the other side of the chip shop, a member of the UVF, was shot dead at work in front of his daughter. Tampy was beaten to death, and Dennis Eccles and Bill Reynolds, both members of the UDA, were assassinated. Bill was murdered at the turn-of-the-road, he was the manager of the Village Pool Hall, built so that there would be something to do there at last. The IRA claimed responsibility for the murder of 'Freddie Reynolds', claiming that he was a UVF member who had been involved in attacks on Republicans. In reality he was a welfare officer in the UDA, a non-combatant, but a very easy target.

Looking back, I can see that the lads from the turn-of-the-road were always an easy target.

Beyond Segregation

I wasn't going to visit Bonanza Billy. I was going to see an old friend whom I hadn't seen for eleven years. I went away to England, he went away too – sort of. He's been in the Maze for the past ten years. He was given an indeterminate life sentence for murder. I visited him as a friend, and travelled with his brother-in-law and his niece. She's nineteen and she's known nothing except the Troubles, her childhood and teen-age years overshadowed by the conflict. There was no period of innocence for her.

I was worried about the visit because I was concerned not to say anything too inappropriate. What do you say to a man who has spent the past ten years in prison?

'Well how are they treating you, Jim?' I knew that Jim had

28

been involved in the blanket protest, so the answer might be not very well in the past. Do you ask him what he's looking forward to? Or do you reminisce about old times? Do you tell him what you've been doing? – 'Well California is beautiful this time of the year. You should see the surf in Malibu. I was there a few weeks ago. You should go there you know . . .' Would I recognise him? Or him me? What would the security be like at the Maze? I'd heard a lot of stories about the intimate body searches – the gloved fingers up the anus. Were they true? I knew that Jim's brother-in-law didn't like visiting Jim in the Maze, and as a consequence he only went once a year. But why? Was it all that waste of young life which he couldn't bear to witness, or was it all just a waste of time? Hardened terrorists in their element? The visit was full of uncertainties, not least because of the gap in my comprehension – how could he have murdered in the way that he did?

'It gives me a knot in my stomach,' said Tommy, the brother-in-law, 'visiting Jim there that is.' But we set off in his Austin 1100 anyway. He's a coalman, his wife – Jim's sister – is a cleaner in a school. He takes home about eighty quid a week. Out delivering coal in all weathers for that kind of money. Some people seem to have the impression that the Protestant paramilitaries are just rich gangster organisations, all their members, big time crooks, grown fat on protection money and drinking clubs, their families well catered for. It's a myth, as far as I can see. It is true that nobody bats an eyelid at protection money from building sites anymore, but the sums are usually quite small and they have to go round a lot of people. The commander of our local UVF battalion may have a few gold chains but that's about it. His predecessor was assassinated by the IRA – it's an extremely high-risk job for little return. Families of convicted terrorists can draw £10 a week from the Organisation, but many don't anyway. The professional criminals that I've met in England wouldn't even entertain the risks for those returns. There are some big boys somewhere, but certainly not where I used to live.

The Maze is a very hard prison to find, because it's not sign posted at all. The UVF and UDA both run regular bus services

29

from the Shankill to the Maze for relatives and friends, similarly the IRA run a bus from the Falls Road. It's just as well, because the prison is so well hidden. It's down the M1 from Belfast, near Lisburn. Through security gates and past barbed wire that wouldn't shame a camp on the Gulag Archipelago, then it's time to enter waiting room number one, but first you show your identification and the warders check that the prisoner has indeed applied for your visit. From this waiting room you go through one by one to be searched, and any personal belongings removed. There are no fingers up the anus. Then it's through to another waiting room, where you're called by the prisoner's number. From here you're led into a minibus with aluminium walls and the windows blacked out. This bus resembles a refrigerated van more than anything else, it's cold and dark and in this you're taken into the prisoners' compound. One man whispers that we're going on a magical mystery tour. Half-way to our destination, a prison officer boards and checks the number. He says 'thank you', but nobody replies. One woman comments, 'They're checking that nobody's slipped off to break in to the joint.'

The minibus stops and you're led into another waiting room. Wives, children, brothers and aged fathers show the first signs of excitement. Many of the visitors know each other – 'How's about ye, Sammie?' The man next to us, who had been in the UVF, is visiting a friend; he himself spent eleven years in the Maze. 'I don't mind coming back,' he says, 'but only for a visit.' In this room, visiting parties are then called by the number and name of the prisoner they're going to see. When you hear the names, with the O'Neills and the O'Hanlons interspersed with the Smiths, and even the Beatties, it really sinks in that parts of this prison, unlike most of the rest of Belfast, aren't segregated at all. On the outside world the inmates may be mortal enemies, here they're all in the same boat. And their relatives too.

It was soon to be our turn – Watt, J. number—. Jim had been given eight life sentences for his part in six murders and two attempted murders, and a further twenty years for a series of thirteen bombings, and possession of explosives, guns and ammunition. Jim made the bombs which were used in a number of terrorist attacks – one was a car bomb which exploded at an IRA funeral in the Ardoyne killing two, another was a bomb packed with industrial nuts which killed two men in the Avenue Bar in Union Street in 1976. I reminded myself of all this as I waited for him. There was a long, greasy slope leading from segregation, tribalism, and loyalty to your friends and neighbours, but I couldn't see how it could have descended this low. I just couldn't understand it. I might have tried to pass the whole thing off as a temporary bit of gross insanity – like what happened in Hungerford – beyond my comprehension, beyond anyone's comprehension. But here the pathology had been sustained. And it wasn't just one of my friends who had coldbloodedly killed, but several. How?

We were led into the next room, and there suddenly was Jim, in the middle of a room where prisoners, all in civilian clothes, intermingled with visitors. He hadn't changed a bit. That was perhaps the most frightening part, it made all that he had done that much more incongruous. The whole scene was one of extraordinary ordinariness. Convicted killers whom you wouldn't glance at twice in the street. IRA men hugged their wives and children and disappointed (or proud) fathers, UVF men did likewise. The tears were the same from both.

On the surface Jim hadn't changed. But it was immediately obvious that inside there was a completely changed man. I remember reading that at the time of his trial the detective inspector in charge of the case had told the Belfast City Commission that Watt 'had suffered from an attack of conscience and had shown remorse'. That sense of remorse has been eating right through him ever since – for ten whole years he had the time to dwell on the suffering he had caused to his victims and their families, not forgetting his own family. It had become unbearable. He had become a Christian and in the Maze he had severed all links with the UVF, his family didn't accept any money from the organisation. This despite the fact that, as a member of the UVF, he had gone through the blanket protest for two years.

A lot has been written about the IRA men 'on the blanket', it's less widely known that the Protestant organisations were engaged on this as well – for exactly the same objective – the

31

granting of political status. David Beresford, in his recent book *Ten Men Dead* about the blanket protest and the hunger strike in the Maze, pays scant attention to the Protestant side to the protest. When he refers to the UVF, as he does when he talks about Gusty Spence, one of the folk heroes of the Shankill, he dismisses them as 'a gang of sectarian killers'. The problem basically is that although the IRA were seen as fighting for something, the UVF weren't seen as fighting *for* anything, except perhaps the destruction of the IRA and for some reason this didn't count. But they clearly believed in their cause as well, hence their blanket protest against the 'criminalisation' of their offences.

The authorities tried to break the blanket protest through harassment and a series of constant petty degradations, as Beresford's book well documents. Before prisoners could receive visitors they had to squat on a mirror and a light shone down to find any concealed items. This procedure didn't discriminate religious affiliation. Jim remembers those days well. He says that it was an unnecessary degradation because it wasn't effective if you'd properly 'bangled' the contraband. He says that life on the blanket made all divisions between prisoners disappear. He says that one INLA man slipped him a note he'd bangled, which he wanted passed on to a senior INLA man in Jim's block. A prison officer saw the note being passed, so Jim had to pop it into his mouth immediately. A rare form of intimacy. 'We're all the same in here,' says Jim, 'you learn to forget your differences. One of my good friends in here was an INLA man. He's out now but he still comes to visit me. The blanket protest and the hunger strikes paid off in the end, we do wear civilian clothes now.'

Jim lives in a mixed H-block – H5, through choice. He says it's easy to get segregated – all you have to do is tip out the contents of your slop bucket in your cell. When you're asked why, you say it's because you want to be segregated. You get three days solitary confinement, before being moved to an IRA wing or a UVF/UDA wing. The segregated wings are run on military lines, and according to some prisoners there's less harassment of inmates by prison staff of whatever sort on those wings. The Maze doesn't just take prisoners who have committed terrorist offences, but anyone serving sentences of four years or more. 'As soon as they're inside,' says Jim, 'they're sworn into the organisation – all sorts – burglars and all.'

The alternative to a segregated wing is a mixed wing, like H5, where Protestants and Catholics find themselves locked up together. 'The problem here is that although we usually get on well,' says Jim, 'you can sometimes cut the air with a knife when there's been a sectarian killing in the outside world. We watch the news on the telly, and read the papers, and not surprisingly it can sometimes get very tense.' Jim was particularly upset about the murder of Bill Reynolds – a boyhood friend of both of us. 'It was just because he was an easy target – nothing more. He was a welfare officer in the UDA, no hit-man. You wouldn't have taken him with you on a message, let alone on a job. He worked as a manager in that snooker hall, day in day out. Just an easy target.'

Two years ago Jim appeared in a supergrass trial. The supergrass had implicated him and others in further terrorist offences. All the other defendants – members of the organisation – dismissed their solicitors. Jim didn't dismiss his Christian solicitor. 'It was hard sticking to this because I felt that I was letting all my mates down. We'd been through a lot together. But I didn't want to be involved any longer with the organisation. The UVF commander at the Maze is very sympathetic, because he realises that my Christian beliefs are very deeply held.'

Jim has had a lot of time to reflect on what went on. 'I've got a better understanding of the situation now. Basically I was attracted to the military side of the life in the UVF. There's a proper military structure and I felt that I was following orders. At the time I thought that we were fighting a war against the IRA. I thought that we were fighting to save Ulster. If I'd killed a load of Argies in the Falklands, I'd probably be considered a hero by some now. The war that we were engaged in, according to some politicians, wasn't a war at all. They were just prepared to let Ulster sink. Somebody had to take responsibility. It annoys me how the media portrays the UVF – as just sectarian killers. When the IRA carry out a sectarian

33

assassination, it's usually attributed to some higher goal. The UVF are seen as carrying out sectarian killings for the sake of them, or worse for financial profit. I, and others like me, weren't in it for the money. We thought that it was our duty to defend the Protestant people. But I've had plenty of time to reflect on all this, and I've come to the conclusion that all killing is senseless. There are always too many innocent victims. What about the families of the Argentinians? Who ever gives them a second thought? In the Falklands war, Britain was fighting for sovereignty, in Ulster we were fighting for sovereignty. In both wars innocent people suffered. It's hard to justify either of them, when you think about it.'

Jim was married shortly before his arrest. His wife stuck by him for nine years but no more. The strain on his whole family shows. 'And when I think about the families of my victims, it breaks my heart.' He works in the prison laundry and is studying accountancy, praying that someday he'll have a future in which to practice it.

'They only ever caught the little guys, anyway,' says Jim, 'the ordinary volunteer on the ground. The guys who were giving the orders are still out – big cars, boats even. What did the ordinary volunteer get? Certainly not money. But I hear that I'm mentioned on a gable mural. John Bingham, the UVF commander at the turn-of-the-road who was assassinated last year, has had Silverstream Road named after him. Unofficially, of course. The truth is that it was funny to come in here and see how much I had in common with the ordinary Republican prisoner. It really shocked me.

'All I can say is that somebody, somewhere must be doing very well out of it all, and that's for certain.'

3

Rough Justice

I had been standing in silence for a few minutes trying to get my bearings. A video-shop, a Chinese take-away, an off-licence, a fruit shop, a Spar grocer's, a chemist's, plenty of graffiti. Nothing out of the ordinary. Urban Britain in the nineties. This could be anywhere in the United Kingdom. Anywhere.

And then I just happened to look up. I had somehow managed to miss it up to that point, but there it was in all its glory – streamer after streamer, fluttering in the wind – defiantly. Red, white and blue bunting hoisted high up into the air – a constant reminder just in case you forgot which side you were on. I averted my eyes. I looked down and noticed that the kerb had been painted red, white and blue. Whichever direction you looked, you got a genuine reminder, or not so gentle reminder. 'UVF', the graffiti said, 'Fuck the Pope'. I was now starting to get my bearings.

You could say that these are the only bearings you need in parts of Belfast. Those and the metal grilles, and the barbed wire, and the general feeling of dereliction. I wanted to feel that atmosphere in perfect silence. The United Kingdom today under threat from within, and this was the response. The grey landscape was daubed with red, white and blue paint. I was lost in my thoughts, or nearly.

Suddenly, a voice rang out of nowhere, the high velocity sound piercing me in my moment of calm. '*Hey, mister*'. It had

that kind of shrill tone only found in certain parts of Belfast –
Protestant North Belfast to be exact. My home. *'Hey, mister'*. It
was louder this time, louder and more insistent. I prepared
myself for the worst. Then I felt the tap on my shoulder. It was
a child of about ten. He was looking puzzled. 'I wouldn't hang
about there if I was you, mister.' 'Why?' I asked somewhat
indignantly. 'Because you might get shot, that's why. They
shot the wee Chinaman who owns the Chinese take-away,
and some others as well. My uncle Harry says that the bullets
were flying everywhere. He says it was like Dodge City. The
wee Chinaman got it in the chest and the legs. But my dad
says that you don't get a punishment shooting for nothing.'
'So what did he think this particular shooting was for?' I
asked. I had already heard about this particular shooting,
when I had been briefed by the RUC Press Office. The shooting
was a little puzzling to say the least. The RUC had not wished
to speculate about possible motive. My ten-year-old informant's dad was obviously not so reticent. But I was still going to
have to wait for an answer. 'I'm going home for my tea. I'll tell
you tomorrow if you're still about.' And on that note he was
off. I was now worrying. What did he mean if I was still about?
I had no intention of going anywhere. Here I was in Belfast,
part of the United Kingdom, a part that has had to put up with
the threat of terrorism for a generation. But is this where all
this threat eventually led – to random violence, where any
outsider puts himself right in the firing line, so to speak?
Chinamen in the take-away, curious onlookers in the street?

But what had actually occurred in the take-away? The owner
of an adjoining shop gave me her account of the shooting. 'It
was just before nine o'clock when I heard the shots. I thought
it was a young lad I know with one of those wee air guns, and
I thought that it was him shooting out the back because
normally when you get out of the car he shoots out the
window at the front of you. But then I heard a lot of commo-
tion. So I ran out to the back and then everything went very
quiet. So I thought it mustn't be anything about here. And
then this wee lad of fourteen who works here ran in and yelled
that 'someone's been shot in the Chinese'. I ran in and asked
if everything was all right, and this girl who works there said,

'The three of them's lying shot in there.' It was a terrible sight – one of them was lying in his dinner. Two of them were strangers, it was their first time in the shop. They'd only been there for about half an hour and they were all just starting their dinner. Two masked gunmen had apparently run into the Chinese and ordered all three Chinese men to lie on the floor. They'd then been all shot in the legs, except for the owner – he also got shot in the chest. It must have been a punishment shooting. The gunmen mustn't have meant to shoot him in the chest – he must have jumped or something. The gunmen must have been local because they made their escape on foot, down one of the streets opposite. The police and the paramedics were on the scene in no time. If I'd gone in about two minutes sooner, I would have run straight into the gunmen on the way out. The take-away opened up two days later. Two brothers came over from across the water and took over while the owner was in hospital. Now it's business as usual. The UVF issued a statement saying that they hadn't intended to kill the owner of the take-away or his friends, and that it was a punishment shooting. Most people around here know why you get a shooting like that.' She threw me a very special kind of look. I was unfortunately none the wiser.

But at this point I was starting to register a mixture of shock and admiration anyway. Shock that people can talk so calmly about a shooting on their doorstep, admiration that despite it all life goes on much as before. Business as usual. My expression must have shown. 'You know, it's not that bad around here,' continued my informant, 'I read in the paper the other day that there are eighteen murders in a month in England, you don't get eighteen murders a month here. In England there are women raped and murdered in their own homes nearly every day. You don't get that here at all. You can still let your wee child play outside your door here and know that a man is not going to drive along and pick it up. England's full of perverts. Here we're brought up differently. We're not as broad-minded as those across the water. Things are changing though a little. I heard about some sex parties that happened up in Kilcoole recently, but they've shocked

37

everybody around here. In Belfast the morality is different. The family is more important here. We help each other out.'

They would need to, I thought. As you pass between Protestant and Catholic areas in Belfast, the graffiti on the gable walls acts as a constant reminder of the sectarian murders in those areas. 'We got Marley' boasts one lot, 'Freddie Reynolds snookered' boasts another (Bill Reynolds was the manager of the local snooker hall – the Village Pool Hall, who had been gunned down by the IRA in broad daylight. The IRA claimed that he was a member of the UVF who had been involved in attacks on Republicans). There is even a mural on one gable wall just opposite the Chinese take-away, which proudly presents the names of those members of the local UVF Company – Ballysillan 'B & D' Company – either currently serving prison sentences for sectarian offences (a substantial proportion serving life sentences) or themselves murdered in the conflict. It is a very large mural. It needs to be. 'Always remembered and never forgotten' says the inscription in the middle of it, just above 'In God Our Trust'.

Perhaps in absolute terms, my informant was right. Perhaps there are more murders in England, but then England is a big place. Belfast isn't. It's a village, and in that village they cope with murder quite literally on their doorstep. Business as usual. Back to renting out the latest video releases: *Force of One*, *American Ninja* or *Next of Kin*, starring Patrick Swayze. 'An eye for an eye, a tooth for a tooth' says the blurb on the cover. One section of the video-shop is reserved for 'Horrors and Thrillers', the next for 'Thrillers and Horrors'.

I left the shop for the thrills and horrors of the street, and the local shebeen. There were little clusters of people gathered around the tables in the bare room, a room devoid of almost any decoration whatsoever. Presbyterianism at work, even in sin. Two pensioners sat side by side staring ahead, not communicating in any way. I guessed that they wouldn't mind being disturbed. I asked about the shootings in North Belfast. The man refused to answer. Indeed he even refused to acknowledge my presence by looking at me. The woman was more forthcoming. She started with the ritual denial. 'I don't

38

know what happened in the take-away, son, don't ask me anything about that.'

It has often been pointed out before by commentators on human behaviour that you can sometimes learn as much from any conversation by what is left unsaid as by what is actually articulated. And here I was – surprised already. I expected her to say 'don't ask me anything about that terrible incident' or 'that terrible shooting', but she didn't. This cold-blooded shooting was brought up without any elaboration or expressed concern. I changed angle. I moved away from the shooting in the take-away. 'What have you heard about other shootings then?' I asked. I wanted the view from the streets – the gossip – the ordinary explanation of the kinds of offences that give rise to punishment shootings, and how shootings can become just 'that' in casual conversation.

The pensioner looked slowly at her companion. There was a long pause. 'I know of one case where this other guy who had this little business was shot, because he was said to be supplying young people with drugs.' It may have been my imagination, but the word 'drugs' caused momentary signs of interest from the adjoining tables. It was like being at a cocktail party, or so they say, and hearing your name whispered in some adjoining conversation. The pensioner sat back. It was as if she had now provided all the necessary and sufficient conditions for the shooting. It was as if nothing more needed to be added. 'He got what was coming to him.'

'But what kind of drugs?' I asked. 'What are we talking about here – Aspirin, Valium, heroin, what?' 'Just drugs – he'd been warned a few times, right? He'd had his car vandalised as a warning.'

'Who by?'

'The UVF.'

'How do you know that?'

'Well, that's who shot him, and . . .'

The 'and' here took on new and strange dimensions. I don't think that I have ever heard any initial syllable of any word in any conversation extended for so long, to build up the atmosphere in the story-telling.

'. . . a . . . n . . . d it was the UVF who did those wee

39

Chinamen as well. The night they went in, the owner was just back from holiday, right, and he had two compadres there with him, and all three of them were shot. The next day on the radio they said that none of the three of them could speak English. After the shooting when they were taken to the hospital they were waiting for an interpreter. But that's all bloody nonsense. The cashier was told to lie on the floor – it was nothing to do with money. But your wee man spoke English, certainly he did. If he didn't what was he doing with a cashier from round here? How the hell did he speak to her? Now that's all I know.'

There was a long very pregnant pause. The pensioner, who was called Betty, looked quite pleased with herself, pleased that she had managed to explain if not justify the whole sordid business of punishment shootings. Even Jimmy her companion looked my way. It was time for other matters to come up and run their course, for the shootings to be embedded in the more mundane affairs of everyday life. 'Jimmy's not my husband, you know, I'm a widow woman. Jimmy's just a friend – he takes me out occasionally. If you're a woman, you can't go out on your own around here.'

'Why? Is it too dangerous?' I asked. 'No, a woman can't sit in a bar or a club on their own or all the men would think that she was trying to be picked up. Isn't that right, Jimmy?' Jimmy still didn't answer, and whilst waiting for a possible reply from him, I had to remind myself that Betty was seventy years old. I returned to the shooting of the alleged drug dealer.

'But how do you know that he was dealing in drugs?' I asked. Betty pulled a face. It showed that she would have one last try at an explanation, but only one. The logic had now changed in Betty's response. The logic now was that it had to be drugs, because it couldn't have been anything else. 'This guy had a little business. But, it was nothing to do with the money he paid – absolutely nothing to do with that. They didn't touch any of the money in the till – they just shot him.'

Again I had to remind myself that this was part of the United Kingdom where protection money and protection rackets were as casually brought up in conversation as ground rent or rates. 'He did pay protection money, of course, everybody pays protection money, but that had got nothing to do with the shooting. It was something else. I can't put it into words. I can't tell you because I forget, but there was a statement from the UVF about that shooting and the way that it was put was that it was either sex or drugs. But I can't tell you the exact words. They must have had him under surveillance, because they're not stupid the UVF you know.'

At that point a somewhat involuntary 'really' issued from my lips. It was out before I could do anything about it. Betty saw this as a direct challenge to the organisation, the custodians of morality in this particular community.

'God, they're not stupid the UVF – anything but. Basically he got a bit of a warning about selling drugs by being shot. It was just a warning. You don't get shot for nothing around here.' She returned to her drink. When I asked her what she knew about drugs, she replied 'damn all'. But then she admitted that she had once seen someone under the influence of drugs. 'They were carrying him round from the park, and he was up to his eyeballs. There was one on each side of him, supporting him. It was like somebody drunk, only it was in the morning before lunchtime.'

Jimmy could sense my scepticism and spread that day's *Belfast Telegraph* out on the table. 'All the organisations are at it over here – even the IRA,' he said pointing to the paper. That day's *Belfast Telegraph* told how 'A Londonderry drugs counsellor has handed over to police cannabis resin worth more than £3000, which he says was given to him by masked men representing the IRA. Mr Denis Bradley, a consultant at the Northlands Centre on Drugs and Alcohol, was given a package containing two blocks of cannabis resin by masked men in the Creggan area of the city yesterday. "They said they were the IRA and that they had busted a drug ring in Derry," said Mr Bradley.' Jimmy gave me time to read the article, before commenting on it, lest I miss its full significance: 'We hate the IRA, you realise that I'm sure, but they're doing some good work in their own areas with the drugs. But our boys will crack down even harder on these drug pushers. Isn't that right, Betty?'

'Look, it's like this,' said Betty, taking up the challenge.

41

'Some people around here agree with punishment shootings. If people break into old people's houses as they do in different parts of Belfast, they get a punishment shooting for that. I agree with it, because the police can't be everywhere. The police aren't supermen, you know. If the UVF find out that these cowboys are doing this and that and torturing old people into the bargain then they should punish them. I don't agree with shooting, I'd prefer other forms of punishment, but if that's the only way that they can do it, then . . . The police have enough on their hands. These Chinese must have deserved it as well. I've no idea why they were shot, but it must have been for something. Look I'll let you into a little secret – I hate the Japanese – my brother-in-law was a prisoner-of-war of the Japs. He was captured in Burma. They were evil pigs, and the Chinese aren't much better. When I was in work, I knew this young girl who was a Roman Catholic who used to go to the dances on a Sunday night. She told me that there were Chinese there, and they were dirty pigs. She used to tell me about them. She was only a young girl and they were feeling her bum. I remember a good lot of years ago on this long weekend we went to this Chinese restaurant where the Alhambra used to be on North Street. This big Chinese guy took a shine to me. You know they're all small, but he was big with a moustache. We couldn't get rid of him. If we'd played our cards right, we would have got our dinner for nothing. The dinners I could have had for free. Isn't that right, James?'

But Jimmy was remembering other past glories. 'We are the people, son. Remember that. Put that down. The UVF are tightening up around here, and not before time, if you ask me. We are the people.'

'True blue,' added Betty. 'If I was a younger man, you know, I'd join the organisation,' said Jimmy. 'True blue,' added Betty again thoughtfully.

The next morning I made my way to the Chinese take-away and wandered down past the alleged drug dealer's little business, for one last look. There stood the ten-year-old boy with the piercing voice, whom I'd met previously, standing talking with some friends. 'You still here, mister?' He seemed quite surprised. I thought that I would try one last time. I wanted to get away from nods and winks and generics.

'Do you have any idea what specific sorts of drugs certain people might sell in this area?' I wasn't really expecting any sensible reply. In a world of black and white morality, the word 'drugs' alone pulled the shutters down and threw any room into complete darkness. A darkness that welcomed the organisation. I expected nothing back, at least nothing of any interest. The young boy looked thoughtful for a second, and then just came right out with it: 'Oh, just Angel Dust, that sort of thing.'

'But it's terrible bad for your health,' he added. 'You wouldn't want to go and get mixed up with that.'

'But why exactly is it so bad for your health?' I enquired, genuinely relieved to find someone, even a ten-year-old, with a more substantive knowledge of the alleged illegal substances that were supposed to be on sale in North Belfast.

'Because you can get your legs blown away for it, that's why,' said a voice emerging from the shadows. The voice, I discovered, belonged to a plumpish twelve-year-old, with a round innocent face, but it really could have been anyone talking.

At least anyone from North Belfast today.

4

The Art of Dying in Mid-Ulster

I met him at the barrier in Aldergrove airport. He looked untidy. His black suit looked formal and crumpled, as if he had been on his way from a wedding or a funeral but had had to sleep rough in it all night. He held up the card with my name on it, as they do at all airports now. But he looked a little embarrassed by the whole thing. This was no way for a working man from Cullybacky or the remote side of Ballymena or wherever to behave. His ruddy, country cheeks were almost red with embarrassment, but it really was hard to tell because nature had made his cheeks flushed already.

I was the wide boy from Belfast – deathly white below my fake tan. I could see it in his face. He had an open, honest face which hid nothing. I had the kind of face which hid a great deal. His told me so. He led me to the limousine that I had been promised, waiting outside. A Ford Granada.

He had driven all his life, but it still took him an age to get going. There is something called pace of life. I was late for my appointment. He checked the gear lever and the brake and readjusted his seat belt. I fidgeted and looked at my watch. I looked out at those green fields for a second and looked at my watch again. He seemed to be checking the ash trays. Then he held up the hat. It went with the suit. Old, black and shiny. Like the Ford Granada it had been around for years. The hat was not from the nostalgic past – it was not pristine and neat. It had not been locked away in some pine chest as its value increased by leaps and bounds. The hat was from the past in Cullybacky. Used every day or every week. Its material worn transparent by use. He asked me if I wanted him to wear it. 'I'm your official driver,' he said in a thick country accent, 'I'll wear the official cap if you like.'

I sat in the front of the Granada feeling a little strange. What would we look like, with him with that black shiny cap? I said that it was okay if he didn't wear the cap. I said that I was sure that he would be much more comfortable without the official cap. He readily agreed because he explained it was a long drive – over an hour to Coleraine, then the trek to Belfast. I wanted to tell him that I was just back from California, and there I'd driven for an hour for a hamburger. But I didn't want him to think that I was some big Yank, back to snort and howl at rural Ulster. 'Why call that a Norman castle? We've got bouncy castles in Mickey's kingdom bigger than that.'

I asked him instead if the cap was part of an undertaker's uniform. It was just a guess on my part. Actually, more a joke than a guess. We only dress that formally when we're dead or with the dead.

His speech was all circumlocution. It wound like the river through Dundrod or the brook out the back of Cullybacky. 'I was an undertaker all my life, my whole life. I was the conductor. I was the man who walked beside the hearse, with the castor hat and the umbrella. I didn't carry the coffin, not at all, I changed the pall bearers over. That was my job. Then when it came to the cemetery, I'd give it the last lift and put it into the hearse. There's always the car man, the hearse man and the conductor. I was the conductor. I got this cap off one of the drivers. Well if you're driving in a hearse you have to wear a cap. Or if you're driving a limousine you have to wear a cap. You know if you're driving . . . if you're driving in a limousine you have to wear a black cap but if you're doing a wedding you have to wear a cap with a white top on it. A white top on the cap.'

His speech was Mid-Ulster. I strained to understand it. It quickened towards the ends of phrases and sentences. He sometimes left the end off anyway. His speech was full of repetition, which made him appear uncertain.

45

'Yes, a white top on the cap.'

'Really?' I said this before I could stop it. I sounded like a bored Yank. Really? It didn't make any difference to him. He was a story-teller without me. An undertaker all his life. He relived death and dying every night in life. He didn't need me or anyone else for this. It occurred to me that he probably knew as much about dying in rural Ulster as anyone.

'I remember it was on the Tuesday,' he started as if I should have known which Tuesday in which month, in which year. 'Yes, it was Tuesday sometime in the afternoon – an auld boy said to me, "There's a man dead in Cork and he's a Coleraine man." I knew who he was when he told me. He owned one of the big garages in Coleraine. "Well, he's dead," says he. He was coming down to Coleraine to a funeral at Jacob's here, and says he "dropped dead himself".'

Even the grammar was different. I twisted my torso to catch a glimpse of part of his face to help me understand.

I did not want to discourage his story-telling. Another 'really' shot out of my lips. This preceded understanding. I realised that what he meant was that the dead man was just about to set off from Cork for a funeral in Coleraine when he dropped dead. He had died before leaving Cork. My driver's speech was not a foreign language, even though I strained to comprehend it, but it was foreign enough. There were lots of alien inferences necessary to bridge the gaps, to allow me to walk right over those hills to Cullybacky. A place I would never visit, although I liked the name. A place he might never visit. Cullybacky just had the right ring to it. I could imagine him saying it, with that hard 'k' sound.

'And he said they want us to go for him and bring him home. I never said too much. He said to me, "you'll take the small hearse." I says if I'm going, who else is going? So says he, "You're going and Q's going" – that's the son.'

It was definitely Hugh who was going, even though it was pronounced as 'Q', like something out of a James Bond film, or 'queue' like something you might do outside the bread shop.

'But says I, "You go yourself or send Norman or someone if you're using the small hearse. The shock absorber's bloody

46

broken on her three weeks ago and you never got her fixed. You couldn't sit on her for a long journey." "But," says he, "I need the other hearse for a funeral. Could you use the wee hearse then? You're not going that far."'

There was a long gap. It was intended for me to appreciate the extraordinary foolishness of the proposition. The driver oriented my way. 'Not far,' he said. 'Not far. Jesus, it's a long run to Cork, it's a long trek there, boy. Cork over the border, Cork in the Free State. All that bloody way with a broken shock absorber. Says I, "I'm not sitting in that bloody thing all the way to Cork." When you get up to fifty miles an hour you couldn't sit in her, neither you could. You couldn't sit in her, with it bumping the hell out of you, with a broken shock absorber in the front of her. I told them for weeks that they had to fix her, but we had to order one an' all. That's what he said. "Well," says I, "that's too bad but I'm not going anyways." I says, "Take somebody else with you." He never said too much. He came back to me at half four and said, "Get that hearse filled up with petrol." "What hearse?" says I. "The big one – get her filled up with petrol and you and Q are leaving tomorrow morning at ten o'clock." So I says "Right." Me and Q left at ten o'clock on the dot.'

My driver turned towards the green fields of Antrim, the green fields of home, as he recalled the green fields of a foreign country. 'Oh Jesus it's a bad road to go down across the border, you know. We need a good road, you know, for our big automatic you know – she's got a 2.3 engine on her. We were going a bit. Sometimes you get on a bad road you know and you have to slow down, but we were going a bit that day. But some of the roads over the border are shocking bad.

'So we stopped and had something to eat. Two pints of Guinness each, and we started off again. We stopped at another place for a drink, and then another. So eventually we landed in Cork. I remember you just went over the bridge into Cork, and the big hotel was on the right, I remember this well. So we just stood there, and this man says, "There's a place here for your hearse." So we got the hearse in all right and then we had a couple of drinks and there was a whole lot of boys who were dying to come up to the funeral. A whole gang

47

of them, about twenty of them. So we had got our meal and right enough we got a lovely meal – lovely meal – great meal. We had a few more drinks, and Jesus we were in all the pubs of the bloody day. It was fucking terrible. It was bloody dark when we left the pub. It was twelve o'clock at night and we didn't know where we were. By Jesus, we didn't know where we were and we asked this and we asked that and what the hell, we didn't know where we were. We knew the name of the hotel all right, we just didn't know where it was. Then we met this auld boy sweeping the streets, and says I, "Jesus, there's a right auld boy there who'll know a thing or two." Q gave him a fiver. Q was full. We must have walked two miles with this auld boy till we got down there, and Q says, "Come on in for a drink." By Jesus we must have given him two or three drinks.'

'Two or three' was a careful understatement. This was Northern Irish hospitality on offer. Country hospitality. Two or three drinks wouldn't have wet the auld boy's whistle.

'The auld boy was out staggering round the fucking whole place. Q says, "We'll never find our place now." So, we drunk till three o'clock in the morning, till we were full. What a bloody carry on. We had to get up at six o'clock the next day. The chapel was at this wee place outside Cork. Jesus, we got the hearse out up to the chapel, and they started the Mass and I says to Q, "Jesus, I wish I could see this Mass over. Jesus," says I, "I'm well dry." I'd a sore head as well from all that drink.

'We got off eventually. We started off for home. I bumped on about sixty. Oh I didn't know where we were. I couldn't tell you where we were. So we went into this big hotel and stopped and had two pints of Guinness each. Jesus we were ready for it. Then we got our dinner. So we started off again, and landed in Coleraine at six o'clock that night. We took the hearse down to the brother's house. We took her back to the chapel in Portstewart, and then we had the Mass next morning. They buried him up at the cemetery. You know this, I wasn't the better of that for weeks, the bloody drink nearly killed me. It was whisky, whisky, whisky, whisky, whisky all the bloody time. It was a bloody wild night. Anyway, we got

48

mixed in with a lot of other boys you know. I think me and him shouldn't have mixed with 'em. We were drinking and by Jesus we didn't know who they were, or what they were. We didn't know anything about them, and we never asked them with just the two of us left. I'll never forget Cork. I don't get down to the Free State that often, but when I do . . . By Jesus, you have a wild time down there. A bloody wild time.

'Then we went to Innis for a man, and we stayed all night again. Q says that "these people want this man to lie in chapel all night so we have to stay." I says, "That's a bloody carry on staying," so it wasn't young Q went with us, it was Andy – his uncle. Innis was a bloody auld hell hole. The drink was bad, the food was bad, the beds was bad. I didn't drink much. I said, "By Jesus I'm not going to drink much." But right enough, Andy himself dropped dead one day at the funeral parlour. They were doing a funeral and he just dropped dead. He just died in the hearse. Sure, you're never sure now, are you. Life's short.'

It was obviously a maxim for undertakers. Probably part of a pair of maxims. Life's short, but business is brisk. I suppose that I should have had something like that prepared. It didn't matter.

'I've had plenty of experience in the undertaking business – that boy Andy see, he was a bus driver all his life and old Q says to me, "Andy's here and I don't want him here." Andy you see and Mrs Quade were brother and sister and Q had to give him a job to get peace there. "I want you to try and learn him the business," says Q to me. "I don't think he'll be any good at it, but try and learn him anyway. Just keep him with you," says he. But he never came with me. I tried my best with Andy, I swear to Jesus. But by Jesus, he hadn't got the hands for it. This day Mrs Wallace rang up Q and said, "My husband's dead. Send Bobby out." You see that was me. So Q says, "You and Andy go out and take your particulars when you're out. I says, "When can the funeral be?" He says Wednesday at two o'clock will do he says, if that suits her. Anyway I shaved the body, I put the shirt on him and then she came in. She says, "Bobby, here's his teeth, they haven't been in for twenty years, but I'd like them in now." So I says to Andy, "Go and put them teeth in, and don't forget to put the bottom row in first." I gave him a little tip, I says this job calls for a lot of cotton wool, as much as you can put in, because we hadn't put the top teeth in yet. We needed a lot of cotton wool to pad it out, and then we needed to tie the whole thing up. The cotton wool holds it nice and tight, you see, then we stitch the mouth up. I told him how to do it. I explained it all to him.

'But wee Andy says, "Oh I can't stitch it up, I can't do that job. That's a terrible job and a half that." Well, I says, "You'll have to learn to stitch it some day, so you might as well start now. You're never going to make an undertaker, if you can't stitch the mouth up. So you'd better get started."'

I was aghast at how the conversation had switched from seven drunken nights in Cork to the stitching up of the mouth of a dead man. Up in the country, life in all its pleasure sits next to death.

'You had to stitch the teeth into the mouth?' I asked in that Belfast sort of way, as if these kind of things happened by themselves without human intervention.

'I had to stitch the mouth up all right. Yeah, to keep it closed nice and tight. You don't want the corpse lying with his mouth all open and the teeth hanging out. See, if a cancer case dies, the mouth won't stay closed, so you have to stitch it up to keep everything right. You're better to stitch everybody's mouth and then the relatives are happy. Then you don't get no complaints.'

'Don't the relatives get a bit upset when they see the mouth?' I asked.

'They don't know it's stitched. Oh no, no, no, no, no. I've seen the old boy carried out of the house, with these Bibles tucked down below their chin, you know – to make the head sit up better and to keep their mouth closed. But it's easier if you just stitch the mouth. Then you don't have to worry about getting Bibles in under their chin. Their mouths just stay closed anyway. If you just stick a Bible under them, you come back two hours later and the mouth will have fallen open. I stitch their mouths up anyway. Auld Q used to say to me that he had never seen a boy for stitching mouths like me in his life.

Auld Q used to ring me up to do his stitching for him. You can't depend on other people to do a good job for it. So I got wee Andy to do some stitching. I left him to it. I let him get stuck in on his own. So he comes back a few minutes later and says he: "the teeth's gone." "What!" says I. "Gone?" "They've gone all right," says wee Andy. "They're down his throat," says he, "they're down his fucking throat, get them out." Andy was sitting with this auld boy at a funeral, and he says to him, "Did you hear the yarn about the teeth?" "No," says he. "Bobby wouldn't tell you anything. That's one thing about Bobby, whatever he does, he goes ahead and does it, and that's it. He never says anything about it." Well, you can't in this job, can you? I was a good man at my job. I didn't have to bum and blow about it. Oh I knew my job, och aye, I knew my job all right.

'The money was pretty good in the undertakers. I got two pounds for dressing a body and two pounds for a funeral. It's far better now. If you lift a body now it's eighteen pound. If you go and lift a body and bring it in it's eighteen quid. You dress it when it's in there. You get an extra tenner for that. If you do a funeral, it's twenty pounds. You can do about three or four a day. The money's great these days. Some of them boys have two hundred pounds a week. You also get ten pounds for a wedding, and you can do three weddings on a Saturday. That's thirty pounds. Of course, you walk to the cemetery so it takes a wee while to do the funeral. But the money's still good. But you have to know the job. When you lift a body, you would know by yourself whether this man needs to be embalmed or not. But some people don't want you to embalm them. Some people say, "No I don't want my da embalmed." I don't want this and I don't want that, they say, but if he's a big heavy man in warm weather, you have to embalm him because he'll start giving you a lot of trouble – leaking and all that carry on.

'You have to screw him down to finish him. Put the lid on, and screw him down. If you don't, he'll start leaking all over you. If you balm a person and take them home, then you've got no worries, no worries at all, no worries myself. There's nothing left to come out. It's all out, you see. I took a lot of

51

pride in embalming. They make a terrible job of it over in England. I went over to England to see one of the wife's sisters. The wife has three sisters. She was a good friend, and I knew her very well. When she was over here, me and her had a drink together and a wee yarn and a dance an' all. She was only forty-something and the wife said she wanted to see her after she'd passed away. "So," says I, "I can't see any reason why you can't see her." That's what I told her. So I asked them to open the coffin. They'd got the coffin screwed down and everything. We had to unscrew it. I said that I wasn't leaving the undertaker's until they unscrewed it. They said that they couldn't do that. So I just sat there. Jesus, she was a terrible colour. I told them that they hadn't done the job right. I told them to get her drained properly, and I'd be back. Eventually, they got it done right. They gave her a bit of colour. The wife was happy to see her like that. When we got to the graveside they didn't want to fill the grave in. They just wanted to throw one shovel full over her, and send us home. I said, "Give us that fucking shovel and I'll do the job myself. I'm not leaving until you've filled the grave in. I want to see her properly buried." They've got no fucking idea across the water.'

The headlights picked up some frightened animal just making the verge at the side of the road. 'They've no idea over there,' he said again.

'I remember me and Q on a Sunday evening having to go to Portrush to lift this woman. The police an' all was there. She was lying halfway on the bed and halfway out the bed. She must have been twenty bloody stone and I said to the police, "We'll never get that woman down the stairs, unless you give us a hand." "Well we're not going up there," says this policeman. "Well," I says, "I'll tell you something else, she can fucking stay up there, because," says I, "I'll tell you something, me and him couldn't carry her down." So the two boys had to go up and give you a hand, because she was some weight of a woman. Fuck me, I've never seen anything like it. She must have been twenty-two stone. She'd taken an overdose of a tablets. Well, we took her down the mortuary, and they had a postmortem on her on the Monday. They had a postmortem

52

and everything on her. I remember auld Q saying to me, I remember this very well, "I wish I could see it in the grave."'

My pale city looks were starting to shine right through my fake suntan. I was starting to register shock that cars on the run down to Cork or wherever are referred to as 'her', whilst women, even overweight, dead women who have died at their own hand are 'it'. Auld Q may have been used to dealing with dead bodies on a daily basis, so that it all became routine, but this last statement seemed heartless in the extreme.

'Why did he want to see her in the grave?' I asked cautiously.

'Och, because she was that big and heavy a woman, she was a rare weight. They never embalmed her or nothing. They just opened her up in the postmortem. You know the way a postmortem is. Auld Q was frightened of having a leak or something, you know. The coffin was well lined, but still something could have happened. Auld Q was just glad when she was safely in her grave before there was a mishap.'

I was relieved that it was professional concerns that had occasioned the remark and not something else. Somebody has to dispose of bodies. Somebody has to see what nature does to us, or what we do to ourselves, or to others, before nature gets a chance to do its bidding. Perhaps more so in Ulster. The Troubles were about to be mentioned. I could feel it, and I couldn't help noticing that the darkness of Mid-Ulster was settling in around that narrow road.

'I've picked a lot of bodies up in my time. There was four boys blew up in Coleraine. Their father was a sergeant in the police in Ballymoney. I knew every one of them. They were nice chaps too. They were priming this bomb – I don't really know what it means – but that's what they were doing. They were getting the bomb ready for a pub just outside Coleraine. They were UVF or UDA, I don't know what the hell they were. They were priming this bomb and the bloody thing went off on this wee back road they were on. It blew them to bloody bits. The army lifted the bits into bags. They were still picking up bits the next day. The first two funerals was in Coleraine on a Sunday. I was driving the front hearse. There was nothing but black taxis at the funeral – black taxis all over the fucking place. You wanted to see the black taxis at Coleraine cemetery.

53

Holy Jesus, I've never seen so many black taxis in my life – all UVF in uniform, and they all walked beside the two hearses. The streets of Coleraine was lined with people, and there was not a policeman in sight. Not one. And whenever the funeral was over, the UVF disappeared just like that. They took their uniforms off, and they just disappeared. There was bus loads from Belfast at the funeral, bus loads from here and bus loads from there. I've never seen a funeral in Coleraine like it in my life.

'It didn't upset me picking up the bits. You get used to it. The only thing that did upset me was three youngsters burned in their house. The father and mother got out, but the young-sters didn't. That was the worst thing that me and auld Q had ever to do. It was hard to get over that. I can tell you. They were seven, eight and ten years old. But there was nothing but the bones left. It's a very hard thing to do that. I can tell you. It's sore on you, when it's a youngster, you know. A big person's not half as bad.'

For the first time on the whole drive, there was silence.

'It's not half as bad, when it's a big person.'

'Och, I don't think that I'd go back to undertaking now. I'm too old for that game. It's a heavy job, you know.'

But it was not the heavy carrying that had got to him in the end. That was clear.

'The undertakers from Belfast must see some sceneries with all them boys getting blew up and all that. Them boys have seen the lot in Belfast. The lot. All them young boys blew to bits by their own bombs, or somebody else's. But I think that these young lads have auld hands behind them, guiding them, telling them what to do. One of those four young lads' father was picked up after that. He was in the UDA. He had a long time in jail, but he got out after that. They started a flute band in Coleraine named after the lads. I wouldn't go back to the undertaking if you paid me.

'The auld fella who owned the undertaker's died anyway. I did him myself after he'd gone. I dressed him and shaved him. You have to shave them very carefully, because you see if you cut a body, it's a hell of a job trying to get the bleeding stopped. The only thing that works is a piece of newspaper.

54

You have to wet it and stick it on the cut. I've never cut a body in my life, but there are a lot of boys who do nothing else. I know one boy who was cutting somebody every bloody day. If you cut the body, you can't put the white shirt on him. You have to wait until the blood stops. I found that a bit of wet newspaper was the only way. But you can shave them without cutting them. The secrct is that you have to rub the soap right into them. Some boys think that you just have to put a bit of soap on for a good shave. But that's not right, you have to rub the soap right in. But I gave the auld fella a good shave. He had his coffin already picked out. He always told me, "See that oak coffin on that wall, never you touch that coffin. There's nobody taking that coffin. That's my coffin." It was real oak. Jesus, it was as heavy as he was. So we took him down the stairs on a stretcher. Jesus, he was a big man. He had some funeral, I can tell you.

'We did Protestants and Catholics alike in Coleraine. The local priest was a gentleman. He cried like a wee 'un when the auld fella was buried. But the priest got a right kicking one night. It was in all the papers. I went to see him in hospital. He was a decent man. He said, "Robert, you'll be fit to take Mass yet." We got full together a number of times.

'This auld place has seen some terrible things over the past wee while, and I don't see any end in sight. It's fucking terrible, but that's life isn't it. Fucking terrible, the whole bloody thing. But what can you do?'

There was a long dark silence as the Granada heaved itself around the Horseshoe Bend and into North Belfast. The chippings on the road shot up against the rusty railings and the rust speckled sides of some derelict buildings. 'UVF' said the graffiti on the side of an old barn as we left the quiet countryside for urban life. 'But what can you do?' he repeated.

I had still no answer. I shook my head slowly in that big, slow car. I think that I said 'indeed'. Pace of life slowed immeasurably. It was him who broke the silence.

'Do you take a drink, by the way?' It was the first time that he had asked.

'I'm sure you Belfast boys need one from time to time.'

5

The Torment of Hell
and More

In Belfast, it is sometimes difficult to avoid hearing the word of the Lord. In Corn Market on a Saturday, there they stand telling you all about the hellfire and brimstone. You can spot them a mile off. I always wondered when I was a child whether the boils on the neck came before or after the religious conversion. Skinheads stand and jeer, and yes Belfast even today does sport skinheads – it's always been a fashion with a particular appeal in that city. But watch over the weeks and you will see the occasional skinhead giving his testimony. That is how powerful it is.

The Elim Pentecostal Church was our local evangelical meeting place. That is where people went to to be saved. When I was ten, I went for the free lollipops. We sat at the back chuckling. I could put up with some hellfire for a few free lollipops. Or so I thought. We slipped out half way through. 'Boring, eh?' my friend Bill said. 'Yeah, boring' as the brimstone engulfed another city. Sodom, Gomorrah and . . . Ligoniel. 'There will be nowhere to hide in Ligoniel. It'll be no good hiding below those wee beds when the brimstone pours through your open windows. It'll be no good hiding behind those paper thin walls when the trumpets sound. If the walls of Jericho fell down, then the yard walls of Ligoniel don't stand a chance.' I already recited eight prayers every night before I went to bed. That night it was nine for good measure.

But then they were acting on an impressionable young mind.

56

I'm older now. Stronger. So one bright sunny night in September I went up to Springvale to meet the pastor of the Elim. I thought that I would try not to laugh if the boil was too noticeable. Jack McKee greeted me. In Belfast, it seems that class and position are inexorably stamped right on you through basic physiognomy, and Jack's build said it all – he was a wee Shankill Road man. He comes from Brown's Square at the bottom of the Shankill. He used to be a dispatch worker in a brush factory, and then a shoe packer in Queens Street before he went to Bible college.

When I looked at him closely, I could see that he was not the sort of person to develop boils on the neck. 'I don't talk down to my flock,' he said. 'They know that at heart I'm no different from them.' He has been the pastor at Ballysillan for ten years. He was saved in 1967 when he was fifteen and a half. He had just gone to his local Elim church 'for a bit of a carry on'. He was, he explained, ejected several times for messing about in the church, before eventually being saved. 'That night, I just thought that God was speaking to me, and there was something that I had to do. I haven't looked back since. Six of my mates came in with me that night, and they all fell by the wayside. A couple of those guys are alcoholics now. Virtually all of them have been in prison. One's dead, killed during the Troubles. That was a guy called Kellsie. The IRA kidnapped him and kept him prisoner for a few days. He had some loyalist tattoos on his arm, so the IRA cut those off and sent them to his mother through the post. They squashed his private parts and cut his penis off and shoved it down his throat with an iron bar. They broke every bone in his body. They did terrible things to him. Terrible things. Sinful things.'

I found myself slightly quivering. I could remember Kellsie from way back. He was full of life, full of joy. Another lad that I had sometimes wondered about. So this was where he had gone. Sodom, Gomorrah and some backroom in Belfast. Hell and brimstone had returned. Vengeance is mine, sayeth the Lord. One day perhaps, but not yet. Now just terrible deeds to frighten us to embrace something. Anything. The Old Testament had returned. We were back before the God of love, back to the God of justice. And injustice. Back to suffering and punishment and pain and eternal damnation for the fall from grace. So this is where Kellsie had gone.

Jack's friends had indeed fallen by the wayside. 'There's been a couple of divorces as well. I know that if I hadn't changed that night there in the wee Elim hall, that I would have ended up down the same road, and I just don't know where I'd be today. But here I am sitting in a house like this, and not in the wee kitchen house that I lived in.'

He looked around at his semi-detached, red-brick house, with its small square garden out the front. The very height of respectability in that part of Belfast.

He continued: 'I'm not unemployed, I've got a good car on the road. Financially, I'm pretty much okay today. I mean everything's good, and that's only because God changed my life and gave me something worth living for.'

I asked how his family had reacted to him being saved. 'My family were great about it. Protestants in the North of Ireland have close links with the Church. Virtually every Protestant in Northern Ireland has a member of their family who is a saved, born-again Christian. Just as every Protestant in Northern Ireland has a member of their family who is involved with the Troubles. So there was no problems there at all with the family. I got into the church with both feet. I went to everything I could. I just jumped straight in – feet first. I knew within six months that I was going to be a pastor. I remember standing up in church and testifying – giving my testimony that is – telling the congregation that I believed that God was calling me to be a pastor. But that took another ten years before I left for Bible college. I've never looked back since. For me it was the right decision.'

I turned now from his personal history to the Church of which he was now a part. I asked him about the origins of the Elim Pentecostal Church. He let out a great sigh. 'You're talking about seventy-five years. I think it was 1916, when it actually started. Hold on to I see if I've got that right. It started in Monaghan – over the border, through an evangelist called George Jeffreys.'

Jack had a soothing kind of voice, rather than the booming sort normally associated with evangelists from Belfast. 'I think that Jeffreys is spelt E–Y–S.' He was almost hesitant. Then suddenly.

'KATHLEEN!'

I nearly jumped from my seat.

'I'll just check up on one or two things while we're talking because I do have a book on it. Kathleen, do you know where the big thick book is? The old book that Neville give me from the Elim?'

Kathleen, his wife, went off in search of the big thick book. 'George Jeffreys was from Wales. He was a Welshman. He was invited along to speak at a small gathering of believers down in Monaghan. From that he decided to stay on and get the Church going. Our Church is different from others in a number of respects. We believe in the foursquare gospel: number one – Jesus is saviour, number two – that he is healer, number three – that he is baptised with the Holy Spirit, and number four – that he is the coming king. We find that virtually all the other Churches believe just that he is saviour and that he is coming king – just one and four, but we believe in all four. We pray for the sick, and witness the Lord healing. A lot of other Churches have a problem with the fact that Jesus is healer. We also believe in baptism of the Holy Spirit. It means speaking in tongues, but it means a lot more than that as well, you know. Speaking in tongues is just the evidence that the person is filled with the Holy Spirit. But there is a lot more to it than that. We pray for the sick and we have the laying on of hands.

'The Elim denomination, as such, is associated with the Evangelical Alliance. We have on the mainland over 400 churches. In Ireland we've got fifty. In Northern Ireland we would have a membership of just short of 10,000 people in those fifty churches. We're talking about committed members here, not just people whose names are on the church roll book. The Church of Ireland and so on can claim to have so many members, but very, very few of them ever darken the church door. We're talking about Christians. Our largest church in the UK is in London – Kensington Temple. They've got a membership of 5000. So half of the members who go to the Elim in Northern Ireland go to KT. We've got ECI churches – Elim Church Incorporated, and then we've got Elim Alliance

Churches, which are fully aligned with Elim. The properties of Elim Alliance Churches belong to Elim as a movement, whereas the properties of the ECI churches belong to the local fellowship. The largest Elim church in Northern Ireland could be an ECI church, that's Whitewell Metropolitan Church. It came into Elim about four years ago. They have a membership at present of something like 1800. My church Ballysillan would have a membership of approximately 120, with 150 or 160 attending on a Sunday night. Again that's committee Christians, otherwise they wouldn't be members of the Church. I would say that we have about 250 people connected to the Church. At some stage they would come along to the church, but they're not there all the time. If we have a special Sunday night meeting, we could have 180 or 190 people along.

'Elim is a very active church. It's not just a Sunday church. We have a youth meeting on a Monday night with about forty young people coming along. Quite a few of them would be committed Christians. We have Bible study on a Tuesday night, and a coffee morning for ladies every Wednesday afternoon. Every Wednesday night we have a ladies' fellowship with forty or fifty ladies coming out to that. We have an outreach on a Thursday at Glencairn community centre. We would knock on the doors of Glencairn and invite people along to the hall, and then we put the minibus up in Glencairn on a Sunday to bring people along to the church. So we reach out to the community a bit by doing this.

'At the moment we're also putting a double-decker coach on the road that's been converted. In the bottom section all of the seats have been ripped out, and it's going to have charts on the walls, charts which will have something to say about drugs and alcohol abuse and the violence in Northern Ireland, so that we can talk to young people about different issues. Upstairs on the double-decker, there will be wee tables and chairs, a television and video and so on, and we'll give them a cup of tea or coffee, soft drinks and so on. We'll take the bus up the Shankill and up this area, going to some of the places where young people hide out and where they sit drinking and glue sniffing, and we'll have a chat with them. I get young people coming here at one o'clock or two o'clock in the morning just looking for somewhere to sleep. I just bring them in and put them down here on the floor. I give them their breakfast and send them off in the morning again.

'Gone are the days, at least for me anyway, when the Church just sat behind closed doors and talked about the nice things, and talked about the bad things in the world but never did anything about them. We'll never change the world by sitting in our churches talking about it every Sunday night. You've got to get out there and try to do something about it all.

'I personally through my own life and ministry have tried to break up the mould that the Church has got itself into over the years. One reason why people don't want to go to church is because of the mould that the Church is fixed in. I think that the Church ought to have a lot more to offer people other than just preaching at them. We believe in ministering to the whole person. We believe in ministering to the physical needs of the person as well as to the spiritual needs. We also believe in ministering to the mental needs and the financial needs of the person. If we are able to help financially, we do. We have rallied around people in financial need and helped a fair bit. We've helped to house people, and to furnish a home at Christmas time. We also took up an offering in the Church to help a family in need buy Christmas presents. I was able to hand them two hundred pounds.

'We also have an ACE scheme which is "Action for Community Employment". Through it we employ 167 people. They are funded by the government. They would do things like visiting old people in their homes, just sitting with them and chatting with them and making them a cup of tea and so on. They would do painting and decorating. They would also do people's gardens. So there's all that work going on. We have also bought ourselves a large youth centre on the Shankill Road – the Stadium Centre. We've been running that for the past two years – we've got a programme on for pensioners, and a playgroup in the morning. So the Elim isn't just sitting back and doing nothing.'

I asked about the effects of the Troubles on Protestant church-going and the holding of Christian views in the Province.

61

'In some ways, it's had a beneficial effect. In that what's going on in Northern Ireland has made people examine their spiritual needs rather than ignore them. I think that in a very strange sense the situation that has prevailed in Northern Ireland the past twenty years has helped the church. It's made people aware of their needs, because they are constantly thinking of death. There's so much hurt and so much pain in the nation that the Church has an opportunity to minister to the people. Because of the fact that people are hurting, they are open to receive some kind of ministering. Whereas the situation in England is that people are so well off, they don't have too much to worry about, so they can manage okay without the Church. In England they can manage okay without God. The fact that there is so much trouble here – unemployment as well as the Troubles means that people are open for help, and very often the Church is there at the door. So instead of hindering the growth of the Church, in some ways the Troubles have actually helped.

'I myself visit some prisoners in the Maze and Maghaberry. What I have found is that when a man is locked up, and his freedom is removed, he has a lot of time to think. There's a lot of guys in prison who, when they start thinking about what they've done, turn to God. It's all that's available to them. They have plenty of time to think, so they make a commitment to God within the prison. Not because it's any easier, because in many ways it's very difficult in the prison. Unfortunately, some of them when they get out fail to follow it through. So this filters back into the prison: "So and so was a Christian as long as he was in here, but as soon as he got outside he gave it all up – he jacked it in." But you get a lot of people in Church life who commit themselves and after a wee while they back off. That happens no matter whether people are inside or outside. But I believe that there a lot of genuine people who have turned to Christ in prison, and ten years down the road they're still going strong. But they aren't the ones that you hear about. The ones that you hear about are the ones that kind of blew it, when they got out. They're the ones that people inside like to talk about as well: "You're only doing that, so that somebody can write you a letter, and try to get you out of jail." Christians inside get flak that way, as well.

'Of course, you have to be able to weigh up the prisoners who profess to be Christians. You can weigh them up quite easily at times. You can tell by the way that person talks, whether they're genuine or not. For example, if you want to talk to a prisoner who claims to be a Christian about the Bible, and they say that they would rather you didn't, then you know that something's up. You can just tell that they're not comfortable with it. Whereas you get other guys inside and they're quite sound on the Bible. You can also tell by the letters that they write. There's one chap from the Shankill who I've known since he was a child. He's been inside for ten years for murder. This same guy was ruthless, ruthless when he was at large. He showed no mercy. About four years ago, he committed himself to Christ, and I know without a doubt that the person who went into that prison is dead. He doesn't exist anymore. I know by the letters that he writes. I know by the things that he has said to me. One thing that struck me was that about two months after he was saved, he said to me, "Look, I don't want anybody writing letters to anybody about me being saved. I will serve my time here without people intervening on my behalf." I was impressed by that. It struck me that his whole attitude had changed. He has wept for the person that he killed. He never did that before. You just know that the change is genuine with this particular man.

'Of course, turning to Christ can create problems for them in prison. Their whole status in the prison paramilitary hierarchy depends upon their former self. So when they give up their ruthless ways, their whole identity in prison is threatened. You get other prisoners seeing how far they can push them. That puts added pressure on them. The other prisoners know that the reformed hard man can't hit out anymore. But sometimes they do hit back, sometimes they have to. Sometimes they've got to forget about the decision that they've made and the wee prayer that they've said and just go, "Right, I'll just give that a miss for a few minutes here," and maybe deck the person that's been needling them. Once they've done this, the

63

other prisoner knows that they've tested him, and they know how far to push him. That certainly does happen. But a lot of the conversions among the long-term prisoners are genuine, in my experience.

'The conversion of some of these hard men of the past augurs well for the future of the Province. There are other things that are happening which are positive as well. I get the impression that the ordinary Protestant feels that while Catholics have brought things on themselves because they didn't do anything about the Provies way back at the beginning of the Troubles, nevertheless they sympathise with them now because they know that the ordinary Catholic is suffering more at the hands of the IRA than the Protestants are. The IRA are doing more damage to the people that they say that they represent than to the Protestants. The Protestants therefore sympathise with the ordinary Catholics. Protestants are also having the same problems in their own areas with the paramilitaries, because their own paramilitaries are doing more damage in the communities that they are supposed to represent than the IRA are. There are young people getting shot virtually every night by their so-called own people. There are pensioners who have been beaten up around this area by their so-called own people. There are times when lights in the streets have been put out by the paramilitaries just to show who rules the district. The paramilitaries just want to show who's boss, they want to prove that the police and the army aren't in control of the area. The UDA and the UVF want to demonstrate that they are in control. Pensioners come out to complain about the street lights because they can't see to get into their houses, and then they're beaten up. There was one man who had both his legs broken because he dared to complain.

'We also had one family who was threatened because the young fella turned to Christ. The Organisation threatened to burn them out because of this. The young son had been one of their members, but he turned to Christ and recognised the error of his ways. The Organisation decided that they weren't going to have it, that they wanted him back in again. Their threat was genuine enough – they were going to burn out

64

the family. We enquired about it and we got it from the top – as it were – that they were going to burn them out. I intervened and I actually went to the home of the Commander of the UDA in the area. Him and I had a few words. It certainly was quite tense. We had a few words to say to each other – I think that our looks at each other said it all. I think that I was probably more scared than he was. I knew that he could do more harm to me than I could do to him. He was the kind of guy who sits watching television while it's all happening, so that he can't get arrested. These godfathers will give the orders to their troops all right, but they will make sure that they're maybe at work when it's happening so it's not going to be traced back to them. They're quite shrewd, so they are. But that's the kind of thing that we have faced over the years. In Northern Ireland, you can't hide behind the doors of your church, you have to go forth and face the community – head on. You have to be able to talk to these people, and hope one day that Christ's message gets through.'

But that night I kept thinking that God's message was not getting through. Pastor McKee could sense it as well. He was thinking about Kellsie as well. 'Poor auld Kellsie. They were passing round photographs of his mutilated body. That was a terrible way to go.'

I walked back out of Pastor McKee's house on a cold autumn evening, leaving the comfortable but modest red brick houses behind. I thought about Kellsie's terror that fateful night, Kellsie's hell in those last few days of his life. What went through his head? At what point did he eventually lose consciousness? What in his childhood would have prepared him for that, except maybe some half-eaten lollipops hastily gathered, before being ejected from some meeting hall on a cold autumn, smoky night. Like this one.

A smile of realisation half-formed on my lower face. It had seemed like a long way from Brown's Square on the Shankill to the pulpit of Ballysillan Elim Pentecostal Church, but as the pastor had talked, I realised that it was no distance at all. The suffering was everywhere the same. And there would be some judgment. Somewhere. For all of this.

6

Hard Graft in Hard Times

There had been a bomb at Shorts that day. Someone had smuggled it in. Or that's what they were saying. 'You don't need too much intelligence to guess who that might be, or what foot they kick with.' He was wearing a yellow golf jumper, and sipping malt whisky from a large, cut glass tumbler. An Asian girl in repose looked down from the wall. I sat talking in a neat, modern three-bedroomed house, with a great view over Belfast Lough. The garden was well maintained, the house spotless. He had levelled the garden and built a wall right across it. Hours had evidently gone into it. This was where the Protestant Work Ethic could bring you – all the way up the hill away from the graffiti below, indeed so far up the hill that you could see Scotland on a clear day. 'Our ancestors rowed across that stretch of water,' he explained proudly.

'They need to tighten up security at Shorts. You need to keep an eye on some of the Catholic workers. It's as simple as that. When it comes down to it in the end, there are those you can trust and those that you can't trust. The shipyard is too important to the future of Ulster to be put at risk. The IRA have got us where they want us – on the run. But we have to stand our ground. It's time we stood and fought. Fire with fire.' His wife nodded passionately, 'Fire with fire.' It was like an echo. 'It only stands to reason.'

These were traditional values. I wanted to ask about the very heart of Protestantism, about the Protestant Work Ethic, which I had heard one academic compare to the Holy Roman Empire, because its name too was meant to be a misnomer, in that it was neither Holy nor Roman. So what had the Protestant Work Ethic got to do with Protestantism?

I began by asking whether in his opinion there was such a thing as the Protestant Work Ethic. It was a difficult question for him. 'I'm not sure whether it's . . . you know it's hard, it's hard to . . .' This was clearly not something he expounded on every day. 'The government have changed the whole thing. They've made it so easy for the Protestants to get handouts. For instance these unmarried, I mean single-parent, families, it's made quite easy for them to get a house *each*. They get all the perks that's going. So what used to be the Protestant Work Ethic has been weakened, by government policy. You see the Protestants always had a different attitude to work than the Catholics. The Protestants were always workaholics. They took pride in their work. The Catholics didn't. At least not always. The Catholics may say that it was because the opportunities weren't there for them, but now they are beginning to grasp the opportunities.'

I was interested in the way that apparent contradictions were starting to build up already. I was also interested in the use of an apparently negative word like 'workaholic' to describe one's own reference group. 'Is there such a thing as working too hard?' I asked. There was no reply, as if this question was so outside the bounds of sense that it needed no comment. I changed tack. 'Workaholic suggests something like addicted to work, do you think that this is true?'

'Protestants enjoy their work. It's an important part of their lives. Catholics seem to have a different attitude. Now don't get me wrong. I've worked with some Catholics who are very good workers. Catholics and Protestants often do different kinds of work. Put it this way . . . for instance Catholic bars employ nothing but Catholics, and I suppose that they were able to pay them whatever they liked. They weren't going to get Protestant workers anyway for those wages, and in such a menial job. The same thing applied to the catering trade. Protestants were working in the shipyard where the wages were good. And these other jobs were left to the Catholics to fill. In particular, the bar trade and the hotel trade and the food trade. A lot of them would also be labourers in the building trade. You know, there could have been a wee bit of victimisation in it. The Protestants were being offered the better jobs. Of course, you worked beside Catholics and there was never any animosity. I always worked with Catholics, and I must say that in the old days they worked just as hard as Protestants.'

His wife chipped in: 'I haven't much experience of working with them. But work is very important to certain sections of the Protestant community. Only certain sections mind. The younger generation unfortunately have different attitudes. I think their attitude is that if the other ones can get it why can't we?'

I was starting to register mild shock at linguistic usage here. Catholics were either 'them' or 'the other ones'. Never explicit.

She continued: 'I never signed on in my life. When I got married and had to go down and change my name, I was asked at that point whether I was looking for work. And I said, "No, I had left work to get married." And they said, "Well, that's it then, you needn't come back here." And I never did,' she said proudly. 'But I know people who did sign on and got the bureau for quite a while, by pretending that they were looking for work. But I, being honest, said that I was not looking for work at that moment in time, and I was told "that was it". So that was it. I never signed on.'

This clearly was a badge of respect. It was almost like a slogan. 'I never signed on,' she repeated.

Her husband had not been so lucky. 'I left one job in the 1940s, when jobs were plentiful at this particular time. I had about two pounds saved up so I didn't go near the bureau. I thought that I'd take a week or two off. A wee holiday. I then went to look for a job, and I discovered that they were harder to get than I had realised. So I went down to the bureau to sign on, knowing that they would have jobs to offer. What they did do in those days was that when you went to sign on, if they offered you a job, you had to take it. So I went down anyway, and this clerk asked me whether I was paid off from my previous job or whether I left. He cut a strip of me for not

68

coming down right away. I said to him that that surely was my business. I told him that I thought that I'd be all right for a week or two with my savings. So he was very nasty with me. He made me sign all the forms and told me to come back on the Friday. But in the meantime I got word to go back down to the bureau. They were offering jobs in Manchester as bus conductors. There was a flu epidemic on in Manchester and so they were looking for people from Belfast to go over as bus conductors. So they said to this group of us, "Anybody who is interested, stay behind." I said that I for one was not going to go across the water, because there was a flu epidemic on in Manchester, so I says, "When the English boys are able to start work again, you'll be out on your ear, and you'll have to find your own way home from England again."

'We all turned it down flat, and he got no takers. There was maybe twenty of us there. So this clerk said to us, "You all realise that your bureau will be stopped for six weeks." Up to this moment I hadn't got any anyway. I'd signed on right enough, but I hadn't got any money. So there it was, it was stopped for six weeks. So the next day, I went back to the bureau. This same clerk was there, so I said to him, "By the way, could I see Mr McMaster, the supervisor?" I played football for him, you see, he ran Albert Street football team at the time. But the clerk didn't know this. So the clerk says to me, "Why do you want to see him? Do you have an appointment with him?" So I says no, but if you tell him who wants to see him, I'm sure that he'll see me. It's personal. So he went off to have a word with the supervisor, and when he came back, he was suddenly calling me Mr Smith. He said to me, "Go on up now Mr Smith, Mr McMaster will see you now." So I heads up to wee Johnny, as I knew him, and he sat me down and asked what he could do for me. I explained my position to him. So he got up from the desk and he went over to the filing cabinet, and he brought over maybe a dozen letters. He threw them down in front of me and said, "Here, have a look through these and see if there's anything suits ye." So I picked this one out, and went to work within two days. That's the only time that ever I was out of work in my puff. I left school the day

69

that I was fourteen, and started work the very next week. That was fifty-seven years ago, and I'm still working.'

'I left school on a Friday and started work on the Monday at fourteen,' echoed his wife of forty years. Here there was a certain dedication to work, and a certain allegiance to something remarkably close to the Protestant Work Ethic.

'My first wages,' continued Mr Smith, 'were so bad that my mother had to put money to it to get me from my home in Dunadry to Belfast and then to Rough Fort. I wasn't even making enough money to pay my bus fare. Five bob a week. My first job was with a wee mobile grocer who worked from the house. He used to ride his bicycle from Rough Fort to Knock War Memorial twice a week to do deliveries.'

'But I never got any money from the bureau in my whole life. I knew that there was work there for anybody who wanted it. Wee Johnny had the authority to show me maybe something better. But if you refused any work through the clerk, then your bureau was automatically stopped. You were suspended for six weeks. They didn't treat you very well either down at the bureau.'

I had found this account very informative. Why hadn't this experience of signing on made him much more sympathetic to any group – even Catholics – who had to go through this indignity more often? I tried to put this as delicately as possible. 'I'm just trying to pull out the moral of the tale. Your experience at the bureau wasn't very nice, because they treat you like shit. In fact, I think that they're trained to treat you like shit. Now, isn't that true?'

He readily agreed. 'I've never felt as small in my whole life.'

'Does that mean therefore that you would have a lot of sympathy for, say, Catholics who are having to sign on on a regular basis?'

Mrs Smith obviously didn't like this direction of questioning and she snatched the floor. 'Sure they don't have to go now. It's posted out to them, as far as I know. It comes in the post once every two weeks. You don't have to go near the place. It's all done by post now.'

Mr Smith had a different rationalisation of the whole thing. 'The only people who felt embarrassed about going to the

70

bureau were people who were keen on work. The other people weren't embarrassed at all. They give as much shit as they get. There's only the like of myself, who felt embarrassed about it. I mean you felt embarrassed even going into the bloody place, even before anybody even spoke to you. You didn't want to be seen going into it.'

'There was a slight on you having to go,' echoed Mrs Smith.

'But some people wouldn't feel embarrassed about having to go there. It would have no effect on them whatsoever. There's people who would give as much back as they got.'

Mrs Smith had rationalisations to cover almost everything. 'Maybe that's why the bureau clerks were a wee bit tense and on edge because they got so much stick from some people. I've heard about some people hitting them and all sorts of things. That's why there's usually a wire cage around them – to protect them from the public. I would be sympathetic to anybody who has to help the public. I've had to deal with the public all my working life, and I can tell you what it's like. And when you think about the stick that the poor police get all the time, and are taking at the moment. They get a terrible amount of harassment from the public, and they're just trying to do their job in very difficult times. I said to my husband that it was going to happen more and more in England, and there were those riots in North Shields the very next night. I was right yet again. There are these yahoos all over the place, who are just waiting to take over. It's yahoos in Northern Ireland egged on by the IRA that are causing all the problems over here.'

Mr Smith had obviously still been reflecting on his experiences with the Social Security system. 'I think the Catholics knew the ins and outs of the system more than the Protestants. I've heard it said often enough that the Church keeps them informed of all the perks that they're entitled to. The Church will tell them how to go about getting any perks that are going. The Protestant Church doesn't get involved in that side of things.'

'But how much of this is true or false, we wouldn't know,' said his wife. 'You just hear certain things about what the Catholic church gets up to, in helping its own. We Protestants are just left to ourselves – to just get on with it, as best we can. We're left to fend for ourselves.'

'But the point is,' said Mr Smith, 'that I would rather have taken any work than to have signed on. I haven't had it so easy. I went from a senior managerial position in a food factory to sweeping the floors in a joinery firm. This was a terrible step down in the world for me. But I was prepared to brush up rather than sign on. If anybody had passed any remark when I was sweeping the floors, I would just have said to them, "Well, I hope you never have to do it." I was prepared to do it, because my pride wouldn't let me not work. My managerial job went when the firm was taken over in 1975. There was a buy-out by one of the big concerns. They got a young fella of twenty-one with a degree, who knew so much about the business that it just wasn't ordinary, to take over my job. He didn't last six months in the firm. I could have told them that he was never going to be able to do it. But he was a Mister Wonderful at twenty-one. I was out of work, but I didn't sit about the house all day. I went out and found another job, using whatever contacts I had. I got another managerial job and retired out of it at sixty-five.

'But we still weren't financially all right, so I had to work in my retirement. I couldn't afford not to. So, I retired for a short time and then I got a job as a handyman in a joinery firm, putting in window frames and fitted kitchens. After that I got a job as a delivery man. But I lost my licence for drink-driving and couldn't drive anymore. I had a few too many coming from the golf club one day. I then applied for a job at sixty-nine years of age, and got it. But I still hadn't got my licence back, so I went on the bus every day to work. I worked from 3 p.m. to 7 p.m. I was sweeping up. With the bomb scares in Belfast city centre, some days I didn't get home to all hours. The firm that I was working for made window frames and patio doors. I brushed up the chippings. So I went all the way from a manager with a good salary to £32 per week as a sweeper-up.'

He leaned back on his dark green settee and gazed up at the Asian maiden. He took a long sip from his chunky whisky glass. 'But I'll tell you something – it was better than not

72

working. I could have got £26 per week on the bureau, if they'd given it to me.'

'If they'd given it to you,' echoed his wife. 'But you have to know the ins and outs of the system before you get anything.'

I visualised priests in long black cassocks holding the key. Hurrying hither and thither on cold windy nights across the grounds of the chapel, reading inscriptions in Latin, which explained how to get money from the DHSS. These images did not seem that far fetched when plugged into certain world views.

'But I'll tell you something. Working even for those rotten wages was preferable to not working. For peace of mind, it was worth working as far as I was concerned.'

'It keeps you from going bananas in the house,' chipped in Mrs Smith. 'I've worked for the past twenty-three years in a shop, after bringing up my children. I only went to work to buy some curtains and blinds, and I ended up staying for twenty-three years. I enjoyed my working life dealing with the public. But they can be very difficult. I have a lot of sympathy for the staff from the bureau or for the police. I know the kinds of things that they have to face. But it's always better to be working, no matter what stresses you have to put up with. Sure, you're far better off when you're busy. But you have to be reared in the right way to appreciate this. For example, when we were young, you had to be really ill to get off school. Children nowadays don't even attend school the same. Now some families do make their children go to school – even today, don't get me wrong. But there are children who wander into the shop, and say to them, "Are you not at school today?" And they say, "No, I'm sick." And I say to them, "You don't look sick. Why are you out shopping, if you're sick?" They just grunt back at you. In my view, if the children of today don't attend school, they'll not be good time-keepers at work. It rubs off on them. Any excuse at all these days, and you can have a day off work.'

Mr Smith took another large sip of his whisky, obviously reflecting on his last day off work.

His wife was in full flow. 'People will tell you that there are fellas and girls working who never do a full week. Never. They have a day off nearly every week in the year. I was never off sick from work, except when I was in hospital. My husband was only off work when he was hospitalised. He also went back to work sooner than he should have. The doctors were amazed that he went back so quickly. They told him that he could have a few extra weeks off on the sick, but he explained to them that he would be happier at work.'

'I never got any unemployment benefit of any description,' reiterated Mr Smith.

'You may have got two or three weeks at £26,' corrected Mrs Smith, 'Before the job in that second food plant turned up, before you got that wee job. I think you got a couple of weeks' unemployment benefit.'

This seemed like a remarkable about face. After all that he had said, suddenly it had been remembered that they too had managed to connect with that system that weakens and corrupts. That system only properly understood by men in long, black flowing robes. That system that one day may erode the very basis of Protestantism.

'But I never had any trouble in finding work,' continued Mr Smith unabashed. 'I always went looking for work and got it. If you're genuinely looking for work, you can get it. My attitude is that I will always take a job, but look for something better. It's always easier to get a job when you're in a job. You can turn jobs down any day of the week, if you are that way inclined. I would rather have fifteen pounds a week working than the equivalent not. My pride wouldn't allow me to do it. If I heard about a Catholic up the Falls Road, who had been out of work for six months, I would assume that he hadn't been trying to get work. Some Catholics wouldn't work for low wages, and it gets to the stage where they don't bother their arse looking for work. They just throw up their hands and say, "Och, there is no work." When I was sweeping up I was getting £2.24 an hour. There's no way a Catholic would entertain that job. I was happy working for that. I would have liked more. I looked at the paper every night – to see if there was anything better. I never gave up. But I was still happy. In this last firm, the workforce generally was Catholic, but the three men who did the sweeping up were all Protestant. There was plenty who came down when they saw the job advertised, but when they heard the wages, they didn't want to know. I, on the other hand, swallowed my pride and did the job. To the best of my ability. Despite the fact that for me, it represented a considerable step down in my social standing.'

'You know,' said his wife thoughtfully, 'there are some people who would consider my husband a mug for working for those wages. There are those who would sneer at him for his dedication. They would argue that he would have been better off claiming the bureau, but we hold traditional values on these things. It was this attitude to work of ours which made this country what it was.'

It was now my turn to lean back and draw on my whisky glass. To look around at all that hard work had got them. It wasn't much. Big bills and heartache and membership of a golf club, which they could barely afford. I had accepted their hospitality and sneered out of the side of my mouth at the same time, at least at all those critical moments. And yet as I walked back down from the house on the hill to those little houses way below, those cramped little houses often paid for by the bureau, those cramped little houses with which I was always more familiar, I couldn't help feeling some admiration for a person who was prepared to swallow his pride and sweep up rather than sign on. This took some courage.

There were many easier ways, but he never took them. Why should I therefore be that appalled at his attitudes to those who did take the easier options – be they Catholics, young unmarried Protestant mums or Protestant backsliders? He himself had been the victim of economic factors outside his control. What right did I have to sneer at his simplified attempts to make sense of his social world, when few can even hope to compehend any of it? Perhaps he just needed firm explanations to support his firm course of action. It's easier to be agnostic or liberal or broad-minded when you've not committed yourself. When you're not under pressure.

7

Heaven and Hell

Hell?

It was a Sunday evening – wet and misty. The kind of weather
that you can't easily see through, with car headlights emerging
towards you at the last minute. It was typical Belfast autumn
weather. The gunfire had, however, stopped. The previous
evening I had stayed up to try to count the soft bangs in the
distance. I lost count as sleep closed in. I couldn't tell how far
away the bangs were – probably not far in real, objective
distance but in terms of how they measure distance in Belfast,
they were very far away. 'Not about "the turn-of-the-road",'
said my mother. 'Not around here – possibly Ardoyne.'
Ardoyne is less than a mile away, but it's not here, not in our
territory. Our territory had seen enough trouble recently – four
local UDA men were sentenced to life imprisonment a few
days earlier for a series of sectarian murders in the area. Most
of those convicted were twenty years old, the same age as the
Troubles. Our territory was resting.

I ordered the taxi to take me from my old home in North
Belfast to The Martyrs Memorial Free Presbyterian Church on
the Ravenhill Road. 'To where?' said the taxi operator. 'Paisley's church,' I said. 'Oh why didn't you say so,' he replied.
'How far up Ligoniel Road do you live by the way,' then
enquired the taxi operator. I reassured him that it wasn't that
far up. Past St Mark's Church and we would be in a different

76

territory – Catholic Ligoniel, a no-go area for this particular taxi firm. The taxi duly arrived.

The driver scrutinised me as I got in. I was wearing a leather jacket, not because I was trying to make a statement of any kind, but because that was all that I had with me to protect me from that kind of weather. 'You're not one of Paisley's mob, then,' he said immediately. I said that I wasn't. He then asked why I was going to hear the 'Big Man'. I said out of interest. He asked had I seen his antics at the European Parliament when he demonstrated against the Pope – 'the Antichrist', he called him. I said that I had. The taxi driver thought that this was a little over the top, but then added that Paisley has a lot of followers in Northern Ireland 'who would agree with *anything* he did. There's nobody who could ever pull him, you know, his information's always right.' There was a bit of a gap in the conversation, then he asked: 'Are you sure you're not one of his followers – well, okay, here's a wee joke for you. The Pope, the Queen and Paisley were in a plane over Northern Ireland, and the Pope says, "I'll throw out something for my people", and he throws out some holy water. The Queen says, "I'll throw out something for my people", and she throws out a few knighthoods. Paisley then stands up and booms, "I'll throw out something for my people", and he throws out the Pope. A cracker, eh?' And the taxi roared down the Crumlin Road past Crumlin Road jail and the Law Courts, and the big chapel at the bottom.

The Ravenhill Road seemed in the mist to be full of busy, bright churches. But Paisley's is the biggest and the brightest of them all. It was opened in October 1969, and I had already learned that it is the largest Protestant church to have been erected in the United Kingdom since the war with a seating capacity of 3,000. It is said to attract the largest Sunday evening congregation in the United Kingdom. The first thing you notice about it is the message above the clock on the front of the church: 'TIME IS SHORT'. The bells chimed out the tune from 'Are you washed in the blood of the lamb'. It was easy to see how the taxi driver told me apart – all the men were in suits, all the women in hats. I was greeted several times on the way in, one man shook my hand so hard that I thought that he was

77

trying to see if it came off. There was no security personnel, however. I don't know why this surprised me – you don't expect to have security at churches, even in Belfast, but then again Ian Paisley is no ordinary vicar. Perhaps the Elders that greet you provide an effective security cover. I was asked to sign the visitors' book several times. I was glad because it made a good read. Paisley's word has spread far and wide. Visitors arrive from all over the world to this church in East Belfast to hear the man that is prepared to stand up and call the Pope 'the Antichrist', and prepared to stand up and shout 'No surrender' at his followers. Religion and politics reconciled. A Union Jack stands at one side of the pulpit and The Red Hand of Ulster at the other. 'Salvation to the Uttermost' says the banner to its right.

I sat downstairs. Here sat the old and infirm – pensioners in walking frames, widows preparing as best they could for the hereafter helping each other into the pews. Widowers sitting alone, often dressed in suits that have seen better days. Up on the balcony things were different. Many young people dressed more for Ascot than Armageddon – trendy suits, fashionable frocks and hats. Paisley's appeal clearly extends across the economic, if not the political spectrum.

And then suddenly the organ music started and there was the man in black – the 'Big Man', 'Big Ian', 'the Reverend', I'd even been told earlier that day that Catholics in Belfast had started to call Paisley 'the Antichrist'. He conducted the congregation with great expansive staccato hand movements to 'Come to the Saviour'. He stopped the hymn after the first verse. 'Hands up all those who weren't singing their very best,' he boomed. There was an embarrassed laughter, but no one raised their hand. 'Come on BETTER!' We were singing the hymns from a hymnbook printed by the Puritan Printing Company (71 Ravenhill Road), 22,000 copies in the first printing 1973, printed for the Free Presbyterian Church. Paisley is the Moderator of this church, which he co-founded in 1951. It is the most rapidly growing Protestant Church in Northern Ireland.

Now I've been to Charismatic Christian services in England, and I can understand the attraction of this movement which has revitalised the Protestant church there. It's easy to understand – the services are so joyful. But it's not joy that fuels the Free Presbyterian Church, it's fear and hell and eternal damnation. You don't get away from hell in here. And don't reassure yourself with the thought that all your friends will be down there with you. The American cartoon book I found on my pew in the church had one character, a Christian, say to another character, a patient in hospital dying of cancer: 'You won't be able to see them [your friends]. It's a place of thick darkness. Sulfur has a dark flame. You'll have all your desires but they will never be satisfied. It will be horrible! You'll see no one.' To which the unfortunate cancer victim replies: 'You go to Hell.' To which the Christian adds, rather smugly I thought, 'I can't'. Up on the Ravenhill Road the talk is all about hell, you're bombarded with it.

From the pulpit the Reverend Paisley told the story of how he was asked for his views about God and the hereafter for a book to be published this week. He got a laugh by mentioning that Archbishop Runcie and Ken Livingstone were also in it. 'I was the only person to talk about HELL in the book. The only one.' There were gasps from the congregation at the stupidity of all the others. He followed this with the story of Lazarus and his master. He dwelt on the 'torment in the flame' of the master. I must confess that he is a very effective orator, because I felt myself getting very hot at this point as the flames of Hell were mentioned over and over again. But, on the other hand, I might have been feeling so hot because I was trying to write notes during the service, and this was definitely attracting attention. Paisley followed the story of Lazarus with the news that he was leaving for Georgia in the morning to preach and to give a number of seminars at various theological classes in the States on the subject of preaching, and presumably on how to put the fear of God into people. He also told us that he had just had some X-rays taken after a recent demonstration, where he sustained some damage to the base of his spine. 'But the reformers suffered with their lives for their faith, so what's a few knocks?' He was constantly putting himself into a historical and geographical context. We're not alone, he was saying to his flock. Why, here's a letter from Barcelona I got only this week, congratulating me on confronting the Evil One at the European Parliament. And here's a letter from an ex-Roman Catholic from Malta congratulating me on seeing through the Pope's mask. He then told us that he had made a ninety minute tape about the protest at Strasbourg, which included last week's sermon and the demonstration itself, which we could experience in the recording studio at the church, after the service. He had also written a book called *Anti-Christ*, which he said needed to be well circulated.

Then it was time for the part of the service 'that everybody can take part in' – the offering. Details of that morning's offering were given. The offering was substantial. The sermon followed on its heels: 'there is a hell', 'there is a hell of torment and fire'. There wasn't much about love anywhere in the service. I watched the faces of the pensioners twist and contort as the pains of hell were spelt out in loving detail. He wanted all 'back sliders' to repent, all 'Christ-rejectors' to repent. He wanted them to raise their hand, as we sang 'The Old Rugged Cross', at the end of the sermon. Nobody did, presumably because nobody wanted to be identified as a back slider. We sang three whole verses, but still nobody came forward. Perhaps there were no back sliders in the congregation that night, although there were a lot of very worried faces about the place.

After the service, the Reverend Paisley sees any members of the congregation in his room. The small anteroom felt exactly like a dentist's waiting room. You could just hear the booming voice of the Reverend praying for a cure for some youth's bad leg. Suddenly, it was my turn. I just said that I thought he had considerable skill at oratory, and that his sermon was very . . . very forceful. Coincidentally, I had noticed that his whole sermon was delivered in a series of three-part lists, structures discovered by the Oxford sociologist Max Atkinson to be very effective rhetorical devices with a particular air of unity (The father, the son and the holy spirit' or the more popular 'A Mars a day helps you work, rest and play'). Paisley gave me a hard look: 'It's not the oratory, it's the message, my friend.'

And the message, as they say, was loud and clear. I told the taxi-driver on the way back to take me back to that hell-hole in

North Belfast, where I'd grown up. For some reason it was the only joke that I cracked that whole evening.

Heaven?

The air smelt heavily of smoke, as it always does in Belfast. A thick fragrant smell that makes your nostrils tingle – and your brain cells. A very distinctive smell that stimulates old memories. You can remember how things were, which is all the more sad when you see things as they are.

We walked past the snooker hall where the manager was gunned down by the IRA last year. Then the local bar where a year ago someone having a quiet drink stepped into an argument that was none of his making, and stuck up for one of the two protagonists to try to make peace. The other protagonist stepped outside and returned with a concrete block which he smashed over the peace-maker's head. In court the accused was acquitted, because the witnesses to the horrific murder were too frightened to testify. Then we passed the dry-cleaners' where last week the owner's son was found on a rubbish dump. His head was found elsewhere. 'They identified him by his finger prints,' said my mother, 'nothing else. I don't think it was sectarian. Some other reason – money I think, but you can't be sure.'

Some people think things are getting a little out of hand in parts of Belfast today. 'And we have to live here and try to live a normal life,' said my mother, 'and try to enjoy ourselves,' as we made our way out for a drink, a normal Friday night drink past the chamber of horrors that makes up that part of Belfast today.

We were going to the club at the local Orange Hall. There is a choice these days, if you want a drink. For most of the Troubles there wasn't – after the local bar was burned down in a riot. One of the leaders of that riot is now in the Maze for something quite different – murder, or rather a series of murders. Burning down the local bar was hardly worth a mention. But the choice in where to go for a drink is becoming restricted again – the local bar, now rebuilt, is often dead, and the only other alternative, the Pigeon Club, is trying somewhat desperately to restrict its doors to members only. So it was the Orange Hall or nothing. The building used by the Orange Lodge once belonged to an affluent local family, but the Orange Lodge bought the premises after it was forced to move from Ligoniel village. The Orange Lodge felt that it had to move from Ligoniel after several of its members were machine-gunned coming out of a lodge meeting one night. One died, several still walk about with the bullets inside them, a permanent remainder you might say of being caught on enemy territory. One of the victims with several bullets inside him has been nicknamed 'The Golden Shot'. Now Ligoniel past St Mark's church is out of bounds for Protestants. As one UDA member explained if he has to go to the local doctor, which is situated just past St Mark's, he rings him up and insists that the doctor comes to him. 'St Mark's is the frontline,' he said. So the Orange Hall is now on the Horseshoe Road, with all the lamp-posts on that road daubed in red, white and blue, and the club is somewhere out the back.

'Somewhere' being the operative word here. You try to find the door out past the metal grille fences, with the spotlights and the videocameras. We knocked at a wooden door, which was tight shut. There was no answer, or indeed no sound. We stood as the rain started, knocking impotently. 'There's been so many shootings around here that they probably won't open the doors to strangers,' said my mother, even though she is no stranger. The rain started in earnest quite suddenly, and you could get a good idea of how heavy the rain was falling by looking into the spotlights that surround the building. It was torrential. We made one final effort to get in, and tried even further round the back. Finally, we came across a metal bomb-proof door. 'This looks more like it,' said my mother. There was a bell to ring, and an intercom that didn't work. But we pressed the bell, and the door swung open. There was no one on the door to search you on the way in. The door opened onto a long narrow room with a small bar at one end. It was sparsely decorated, with a single picture of the Queen on one wall. It was evidently an old photograph, because she looked around twenty-five years old in it. Age had also discoloured the photograph, and the Queen looked as if she might just be wearing black lipstick in it. I assume that she wasn't at the time.

The club was surprisingly empty for a Friday night. I counted nineteen people in it. 'Where is everyone?' I asked. 'People just stay at home,' said my mother, 'they don't want to risk going out. Off-licences round here do a roaring trade. You should see the queues for the discount drink. You just sit in your wee house and you get full, and that's your life around here. That's your lot.'

The jukebox was playing old hits from the sixties, and earlier, 'I got you babe' by Sonny and Cher, 'Little Old Wine Drinker Me'. The kinds of songs that after twenty or thirty years people can sing along to, and that's what they were doing. One more recent song had them all stumped. Then came a more traditional song. 'That's a bloody rebel song, and they're too stupid to realise,' said one pensioner beside us. He raised his voice, because he thought that nobody had heard him. 'That's a bloody rebel song, and you're too stupid to realise.' He kept repeating this until the song ended thus spoiling it for everyone. I think that this was his intention. 'It's a bloody good tune though,' said the barman eventually. 'Never mind the tune, it's a Fenian song, there's no two ways about it,' continued the now irate pensioner. 'I had a pal who tried to sing "The Sash" here and you asked him to be quiet, and he had been marching all day with the Black, not the Orangemen, but the Black – the élite. But you can sit here and sing rebel songs all day if you like, just as long as they're on that bloody jukebox. I think that the committee should have a close look at the tunes on that jukebox sometime, and find out who selected them in the first place.'

Everyone winced as he mentioned the committee. When the auditors were called in last year to inspect the club's accounts, it is said that the club was found to have made a profit of just over four pounds for the whole year. The committee was a bit red-faced at the time and was forced to make a few sackings. No one ever mentions the committee now.

The argument continued, nevertheless, about whether the songs on the jukebox should or should not be censored until another Frank Sinatra song came on. Miraculously, this succeeded in shutting the pensioner up. A middle-aged woman dressed in something resembling a net curtain then got up and started to dance. She was swaying very unsteadily on her feet. Her husband eventually joined her. It wasn't that he was too embarrassed to get up and dance with her immediately, rather he'd had so much to drink that it took him all that time to get to his feet. The Sinatra song was nearly over by the time he joined her. Luckily it was followed by something else they both liked. They both swayed unsteadily, almost together, not in time with the music.

The other couple that they had been sitting with, just sat staring ahead of them the whole time. They didn't speak to each other, or anyone else for that matter. Suddenly – and without any warning whatsoever – some pink vomit jetted out of the man's mouth all over the floor and all over his shoes. Nobody said anything, not even the culprit. He just stared down at the vomit, as if he was trying to work out where such an enormous volume of liquid could possibly have originated from. Nobody made any attempt to mop it up. The watery substance just started to seep into the cracks in the floor. By the time his friends had returned from the dance floor, most of it had just trickled away. A few minutes later, the man who had been sick picked up his pint of lager, and took a good mouthful, presumably to wash the taste away. You could hear his wife say to him that it was just as well that they weren't at the Pigeon Club that particular night, because they've started barring people for being sick there. It was nice to think that this was one of the reasons for choosing one club rather than another in sectarian Belfast today.

The metal grille came down over the bar at 10.45 p.m. exactly. The barman in the black Guinness T-shirt and the huge beer gut shouted: 'Is everybody happy?' All nineteen people shouted back as one: 'No!' It was the first time that evening that some of them had shown any life. It was evidently time to go home. The rain had slackened off and you could smell the smoke again. You could also hear these very soft bangs, not loud cracks, but very soft noises, somewhere in the distance. They weren't at all like how you would imagine gunfire to sound from the movies.

'It's okay, it's not at the turn-of-the-road,' said my mother reassuringly, 'probably Ardoyne.' The other customers filtered out slowly. The pensioner who had been complaining about the rebel song on the jukebox all evening seemed to perk up when he heard the bangs. 'I see they're at it again,' he said as he made his way out past us, whistling. The tune seemed familiar enough, in fact it was the one that he had been complaining about all that night.

8

A Very Natural Ambition

A hard man to follow

When I was young, I always wanted to be a hard man, but I had few of the natural attributes. I could talk, though, and I came to realise early on that this was really rather important, perhaps the most important attribute of them all. I used to practice feverishly, and, it seems, I reached a certain level of proficiency because as my brother used to say to me, 'If I didn't know you, I'd be frightened of you.'

Others didn't know me and, if not frightened, I'm sure they were at least a little wary of me. I thought I sounded really hard, although in reality I suppose, I sounded for all the world like some crazed teenager with Tourette's syndrome; the words came whirling out and spinning round and round: 'I'll kick the clinkers off you', 'I'll knock the fucking bollocks off you', 'I'll kick six colours of shite out of you.' My imagination worked overtime on these constructions. But the amazing thing was that it worked – it did actually put people off – most of the time. But perhaps it was because they thought I was disturbed.

Being a hard man was always a very natural ambition for me. I had lots of role models in my street in Belfast. Up my street there was a real hard man. He not only looked hard and sounded hard, he was hard. The whole family watched him in action. My mother looked admiringly on. But I'd seen enough – the tough talk, the ease with which it's possible to put people away, the admiring glances from adults who should have known better. I wanted to be like him.

Others weren't so impressed by this particular character, however. My Uncle Terence was a hard man of the old school. He believed in two men stepping outside to settle their differences with rolled up sleeves, and without any fuss. He didn't believe in all that swearing, and bottles and things. In the Belfast that I was growing up in, that just wasn't how it was done. Being hard was all about talk and the various props. With any luck it was *only* about them. Terence had a different sort of background – he used to be an amateur boxer of some repute. He didn't even agree with men using their feet in fights!

My Uncle Terence valued traditional hard-men-type values. He said that my father was too soft. My father was a gentle man. One Christmas Eve my brother, then aged seventeen, went out carol-singing. At five minutes to twelve there was a knock on the door. An RUC man stood there and asked my father if he had a son called Bill. My father quietly nodded. 'Is this him?' said the RUC man as two others dragged Bill's lifeless body towards the door. A nearly empty bottle of vodka stuck out of his pocket. His new mod pink buttoned-down shirt was stained with vomit. There was silence in the house as my father and my mother and my aunt stared at each other, wondering what to do. My mother started crying, my aunt started swearing. Only my Uncle Terence knew what to do. He dragged him upstairs. For the next few hours and right into Christmas morning you could hear the sounds of Bill retching as my uncle poured vodka down his throat and over his shirt. 'That'll teach him a lesson.' My uncle wouldn't let my father into the room. 'You're too soft, Billy, go away.' I was only worried because I had to sleep with Bill in the back bedroom. 'Don't worry,' said my aunt, 'your uncle will be holding Bill's head into a bucket. Your uncle wouldn't let him throw up all over the bed.'

My uncle did let me into the room because he always thought I could take that sort of thing. I was the one that wanted to learn how to box, Bill had no interest. I was the one that had given my uncle a black eye, Bill hadn't even scratched him. I was the one who admired the local hard men – Bill thought they were all idiots.

When I did get the opportunity to see Bill's face, when his head was eventually dragged out of the bucket, I discovered that he was as white as the ghost of Christmas past. 'This will put him off drink all right,' said my uncle. It didn't, but it did put him off Smirnoff vodka. It was the quietest Christmas we ever had. Bill was deathly pale, my father was deathly pale. 'Only your uncle knew how to deal with the situation,' said my mother admiringly. My father died soon after that. There was a valuable lesson here for any schoolboy – only hard men can deal with emergency situations.

There was one particular Catholic family I used to go on about. 'Why do you talk about them so much – they're all losers,' said Bill. 'They'd knock your pan in, any day,' I said, 'even Jimmy.' Bill told me not to be daft, so I told Jimmy. Jimmy just laughed – he could recognise an easy fight. 'Round the park – six o'clock.' I passed the message on to Bill. I'd only seen him that pale once before. A crowd gathered to escort the two pugilists round to the park. There was no turning back now, not even for Bill. I couldn't bear to watch, even though Jimmy insisted that I'd enjoy it. He knew I didn't think much of my brother at the time. I was feeling distinctly uneasy – after all I'd engineered the whole thing. Isaac the barber turned up to cut our hair; my mother asked where Bill was. I said he'd gone round the park to fight Jimmy. My mother raced after him and got there just before the fight started – much to my brother's relief.

'If I caught the little bastard that told on me I'd kill him,' said Bill. 'Who was it, morrrr, tell me?' And he looked at me and I looked at him and it was obvious to everyone that his hard look masked the most enormous smile of relief. But he hadn't lost face – at least in the street. And that was most important. Even people who didn't aspire to be hard men couldn't afford to lose that much face in my street.

But being hard was all about not losing any face in *any* situation. I learned that very early on. I also reasoned that most people, unless they were very unlucky, weren't actually called on to do anything that often. You just had to have a good reason for not doing it. So one afternoon when I was thirteen, when some rather large schoolboy started jumping on top of me on the back seat of a Belfast Corporation bus, I wasn't that worried. It was just play fighting after all. Some rather large child just wanted to wrestle, unfortunately with me. But after about twenty minutes pinned to the back seat by some immutable mass, I decided that enough was enough. 'Get up you big fat bastard,' I shouted. The boy was stunned. 'What did you call me?' he replied. 'Look I know you pinned me down but that's because you weigh thirteen stone you fat shite. In a real fight you'd be flat on your back.' I most definitely sounded hard, but that wasn't enough here. I had after all been pinned to the seat for twenty minutes.

'Well okay, then, if you want to sort things out, I'll see you at the plots at nine o'clock.'

'Okay but don't be surprised if I turn up with a baseball bat or a bottle. That's how they fight in Legmore Street, fat chops,' and I was off.

I didn't turn up, and I'm sure he didn't either. But when we bumped into each other again, we both asked why the other one hadn't come. I'm pretty sure that we were both equally relieved. For all he knew I was a psychopath who fought with milk bottles – full of milk. And that of course is the essential problem with challenging anyone in the street. You never know for sure who or what you're dealing with. They might be quite normal but, on the other hand, they might not. This makes fighting in the street potentially very dangerous indeed. But, of course, there is another side to all this, because if you're clever you can exploit this to your own advantage. All you have to do is send out the right signs to create some uncertainty in your opponent, and not allow any contradictory evidence to get in the way (like being pinned to the back seat of a bus for twenty minutes). I was getting it about right – the way I talked seemed to leave them guessing most of the time.

And this was even more true of the hard men dotted around the place. Now, I always knew that the hard men in my street were not psychopathic or disturbed in any way, but with some of the others you couldn't be that sure. When our local hard man moved away, Sammy graduated to be the hardest man at the turn-of-the-road. He was as broad as he was tall, although, come to think of it, he wasn't that tall. He didn't need to sound like a Tourette's patient – his walk said it all. He was the kind of person that walks in a straight line on a crowded pavement, without adjusting his speed. He just sent out certain signals.

But one night the word went out that someone even harder was coming to the turn-of-the-road – straight out of prison. His name was Hawkeye. I assumed it was something to do with the fact that he had a friend who was an Indian – a Red Indian, as in the last of the Mohicans (this was after all pre-*Mash* days). 'Yes, he has been to America,' said my friend Mousey confidently (and it turned out inaccurately. We later found out that the *Ponderosa* drinking club on the Shankill was as close as Hawkeye had ever come to the Wild West). We awaited Hawkeye's arrival with some trepidation. It was said that he was coming to take over the turn-of-the-road. Hard men were always taking over somewhere or other. Now some of the hard men we knew used knives, chains, hatchets in fights – this we all knew – even though we hadn't necessarily seen them all in use with our own eyes. Hawkeye used 'saws' I was reliably informed. 'Electric saws?' I asked nervously. 'Don't be daft – he'd have to find a plug,' said my friend Mousey. 'Hacksaws,' he whispered. 'Hacksaws?' 'Yes, *hacksaws*' As if I shouldn't have been that surprised. A distinct shiver went down my spine, as I imagined the rusty hacksaw we kept at home. 'Old or new hacksaws?' I enquired even more nervously.

And there on that first night in the Rendezvous Café at the turn-of-the-road sat Hawkeye. It was immediately obvious where he had got his nickname from – he had the most terrible squint. When he called me over to fetch him some chips ('just tell Greasy Jim that the chips are for Hawkeye, son, you won't have to pay'), I couldn't be sure that it was me that was being summoned. 'But, look,' said Mousey, 'he's carrying something in those rolled up newspapers.' And sure enough, some small metallic object could be seen protruding from the newspapers under his arm. I looked out for signs of rust. I thought that I was going to be the first to get it – whatever it was. And when Sammy came to pay his respects, Hawkeye's fame was guaranteed. The rumours were rife. There was no part of a man's anatomy that he hadn't sawn off with that thing. I kept saying that I just couldn't imagine it but Mousey told me that was because I hadn't been in enough fights. My apparent Tourette's syndrome seemed to be working, you see, except one night at a party when I was too drunk to get the lines exactly right and one of my friends spent a very long Friday night picking broken glass out of my neck with a pair of tweezers.

But that was kid's stuff compared to Hawkeye and his saw. But Hawkeye disappeared as quickly as he had arrived on the scene. He's probably in the Maze today – the star pupil of the woodwork class.

My brother left the hard men to it. He never got involved and went away to climb instead and when he came back from the Alps, the Hindu Kush or the Himalayas, I'd try to impress him with the stories about Hawkeye's saw, or how Sammy stopped ten men dead in their tracks with just three swear words. But Bill wasn't impressed. I always assumed that there was something lacking in him.

After he died in the Himalayas, I was talking to Mousey about him. We were remembering Bill sleeping in the snow in December outside my aunt's house rather than wake her in the middle of the night. And Mousey admitted for the very first time that Bill was really quite hard but in a different sort of way, an odd sort of way, which is really quite a compliment coming from someone in the Organisation.

'But,' he added after a short pause, 'I just can't understand why your Bill never wanted to get involved in fighting.'

'Or all the rest,' I said, 'or all the rest.'

Whatever happened to the heroes?

So whatever happened to the hard men? The Shankill Road Heroes, the men who ruled the turn-of-the-road, the men with the improbable walks that everybody noticed, the men with the improbable local respect?

Our generation of heroes had moved on – I wasn't sure where. I met up with my old friend Mousey, still surviving somehow, in the local bar. I was told to meet him before

2 p.m., 'he'll be full anytime after that,' I was warned. I hardly recognised him. We sat in the gloom with metal bars on the windows, to frustrate the bombers. Little groups sat huddled in each corner of the bar, shouting across to each other, 'just a bit of banter,' said Mousey. Mousey was already on his third pint. It was a chance to work our way through our past – it was almost therapeutic. I dredged up the names from the past, and Mousey filled in the details. 'Den Eccles? Long dead – shot in a chippy. Tampy? Beaten up and killed by his own side. Tragic really. Hawkeye? The moonman with the saw who used to hang about the chippy? How to hell do you remember him? I think he's in Purdysburn. Or jail, one or the other.'

We both laughed as we worked our way through our childhood and our adolescence – through our heroes and through our hopes and ambitions. Were we that naive to look up to those people? It made me laugh just to think about them all – a gallery of no-hopers, who conned their way into my imagination and dreams with their cheap talk and their cheap antics. And to think that I once thought that there was something seriously wrong with my older brother because he wasn't like them. It was all so sad in the gloom of that Belfast bar at midday.

Suddenly, an ashtray went flying across the bar. 'Hey, Mousey, it's your round,' shouted some spotty teenager in the corner, with the first faint hairs of a moustache beginning to show just under his nose. 'That miserable bastard never buys a drink, you know,' he continued. He was obviously trying to impress me with his cheek. 'Shut it,' ordered Mousey, and the bar fell silent. 'Okay, Mousey, don't get excited, just a bit of banter.' One large fat man in the corner, who up to then had been engrossed in the day's racing form, started to laugh uproariously at the way the young upstart had been silenced. 'That's Andy Tyrie's brother there,' explained Mousey. 'Andy has just resigned as head of the UDA, but you probably know about that already.'

I asked Mousey if he always drank there. He said that he did, ever since he was barred from one of the local drinking clubs for being sick on the floor. 'I knew I was going to be sick and I tried to get to the toilet, but I couldn't get out in time. I just put my head between my legs and let rip. I got a three-month ban for that. A pal of mine fell asleep, and he got banned for life. If you get into a fight, nobody bothers, but fall asleep or throw up and you're out. The drinking club at the local Orange Hall ended up banning so many members that they had to have an amnesty to get customers back into the place.' We all laughed. 'I hate drinking in town though, you're always looking over your shoulder to see who's behind you. At least here, you can relax, even if it is a dive. Bill Reynolds, as you know, was gunned down across the road in the snooker hall, but still you feel safe here. After Bill was shot they wrote on the wall down in Ardoyne: "Reynolds snookered". They caught the bastards that did it, but they got off, because the key witness was too scared to testify.'

More rounds arrived on the table. I was drinking halves of lager. 'Geoffrey's been away in England,' Mousey explained to the assembled company.

And then I noticed a couple of other adolescents arrive in the corner of the bar glancing our way. The same denim jackets and the same Wrangler jeans that we used to wear, now without turn-ups. They nodded: one shouted, 'How's about ye, Mousey.' Mousey nodded back in recognition.

When I lived in Belfast, I used to count the number of people that used to nod to me when I walked through the city centre on a Saturday afternoon, as a measure of the respect I commanded at any one time. It was never many. But recognition is important in a small community like Belfast. It's important to see who's prepared to declare that they know you. Mousey seemed to be very well known.

'Put it this way,' said the barman, when Mousey went to the toilet, 'he doesn't work, but he can afford to drink here every day, if you get my drift. The money has to come from somewhere, now, doesn't it? If you know what I mean.'

And then it dawned on me – slowly but very surely – that time does not stand still, even in Belfast. Once the hard men were the hard talkers. Sure there was some action, but not a lot. Hard men once had reputations, names, they took over areas – with their very presence. There was little tangible benefit, little reward to being a hard man once. One of the few benefits was that kids looked up to you and would therefore do things for you, so that maybe one day the hard man might nod back at them. In those days if you were a hard man, you could summon some kid to go and fetch your chips for you, on your way home from work. But little else. But now, now things were different. Hard men didn't work for a start.

I scrutinised Mousey's face trying desperately to imagine him as a role model, anybody's role model. His paunch hung over his trousers, he wore glasses, which he occasionally removed and put in his pocket. 'I got so full last night I sat on them. My pal Chuck says they'll last me a week.' Was this one of the hard men of today? Things were certainly different – everything seemed to be the other way round. The hard men now weren't the guys with the swinging shoulders, they were the ones in the shadows who didn't attract attention to themselves. But you knew who they were. They were the ones who said very little. But when they did speak you had to take notice. Kids were now growing up trying to emulate these men – men like this, men in shadows, men with paunches and glasses. Men who didn't have to work, men who didn't say much. 'Whatever you say, say nothing' was always Mousey's motto, it seems, and it was working. It was all nods and winks now.

At least I'd learned how to talk in my youth like a hard man to put people off. Now, the kids were learning nothing of any use. Except that Easy Street's just around the corner – somewhere among all those dark shadows, and somewhere among the screams in dark, dark corners.

Mousey asked me if I'd heard the news that day. I said that I had. You couldn't avoid it that particular day. The day I arrived in Belfast, another four members of the UDA from the turn-of-the-road were jailed for life at Belfast Crown Court for a series of 'vicious and depraved' sectarian murders. The victims were Edward Campbell, a forty-year-old Catholic, shot in the head and back in a disused quarry on the outskirts of Belfast after his taxi was hijacked on 3 July last year, and twenty-two-year-old James Meighan shot dead as he kissed his fiancée goodnight outside her home in Ballysillan on 20 December last year. Campbell was murdered because he overheard

94

the group discussing the killing of another man as he was imprisoned in the boot of a taxi. 'He might have survived had he been a Protestant,' added the judge. The member of the UDA killer squad who actually pulled the trigger – Alfred Hoycroft – was twenty years old. The oldest of this group was twenty-three.

Freddie Hoycroft and his accomplices had heroes all right, and presumably they were just trying to please these heroes – up in that quarry where we, and presumably they, played as children, or outside that girl's house as she kissed her boyfriend goodnight. But Hoycroft and his friends – Robert Molyneaux, Darren Larmour and Joseph Morrison – all fell for it. All fell for trying to impress the men in the shadows. They had to, they couldn't imagine any alternative. None of them were more than three years old when the present Troubles started all those years ago. None of them knew anything different.

And what about today's heroes, these godfathers they were looking up to. What do they do? Well, I'd grown up learning to talk and that's what these new heroes seemed still to be doing. Talking – giving orders, commands, instructions – but they all just came out as a series of nods and winks in the dark, dark, shadows. Whatever you say, say nothing. A nod's as good as a wink to a teenager keen to make a name for himself, keen to impress the men in the shadows.

Mousey got some more drinks in. As the detective sergeant said at the trial at Belfast Crown Court, a number of ringleaders of this particular UDA group were interviewed during the course of the investigation but they had been released for lack of evidence. And in bars all over North Belfast, and West Belfast, and East Belfast, there the godfathers sit still waiting for some other kids to come in and nod in that peculiar and comforting Belfast manner.

But now the kids know that they'll be expected to do more than fetch the chips.

A Night Out in No-Man's-Land

The Troubles in Northern Ireland have claimed several thousand lives. The Troubles also killed Belfast night-life, that is, all night-life except the frantic activity of men with hoods and soldiers with their faces camouflaged. Bombs in city-centre bars drove the clientele to the comparative safety of more local public houses and, quite often, bombs in these establishments drove the customers to even more local drinking clubs. The drinking clubs had very tight security and were often associated with the paramilitary organisations, of one denomination or another. Many were anything but plush, some were downright basic: spit and sawdust bars without the sawdust. But the drinks were cheap and you were with your own kind, and the drink and the talk and the old sectarian hate flowed. Belfast city centre would virtually close when the shops closed. The shopgirls and the bank clerks and the insurance office workers would hastily board the buses or black taxis (cheaper than buses and again run by the paramilitaries) and make their way back to Andersonstown, Ligoniel or Silverstream, and stay there. Bars in the city centre closed at six-thirty p.m. Since the centre was the most mixed area of Belfast this seemed like a great shame. The paramilitaries with their clubs and taxis were undoubtedly delighted.

But by the mid-1980s things seemed to be changing. The security fences around Belfast city centre had gone. There were tit-for-tat killings in Belfast, and intimidation on a large scale, but the bombs in pubs had decreased. Belfast didn't now close with the shops, night-life returned and you could almost detect the envy on the squaddies' faces, through their camouflage, as they drove through the city's mean streets.

The centre of this new activity wasn't really the traditional centre of Belfast at all, which is Royal Avenue. The new activity was based around Dublin Road and Great Victoria Street. It was nicknamed 'The Golden Mile'. The reason why the centre of night-life had been translated perhaps a mile across Belfast was explained to me by one club manager. 'Royal Avenue is too close to where the Falls and Shankill enter Belfast. The bottoms of these roads are the personal territory of one side or another. Open a club there and you'll get taken over. You'll be paying protection money – the lot. Dublin Road is no-man's-land. Nobody's got a foothold here. It's mixed and we intend to make sure it stays that way.'

Many people would wish to take credit for bringing night-life back to Belfast, and take credit for the normalisation of this city. Undoubtedly Barney Eastwood, the boxing promoter, played a big role in all of this by arranging fights at the Ulster Hall, involving Wee Barry McGuigan, and getting large numbers of punters from both sides into the centre after the pubs were shut – punters who needed to be both fed and watered afterwards. Wee Barry was going to span the sectarian divide, or so they said. Then Barry and his manager, Barney, fell out. They never forgave Barney for this. 'What do you call a cowboy with not enough money?' they asked. 'Skint Eastwood,' they replied. 'What do you call a cowboy with too much money?' 'Barney Eastwood.'

But the entrepreneur who probably contributed more to the success of the Golden Mile than any other was Bryan West. Bryan West was a country boy from Fermanagh in Northern Ireland who took the traditional route for self-improvement in Ireland. He emigrated. He first went to Canada for two years to work on an oil rig in Northern Alberta, then emigrated to Australia in 1968, to Sydney. Irishmen, he said, are very well accepted there. Australians, like the Irish, are very down to earth. In Australia, he was a builder, buying up land to develop. He was also involved in a small casino. Casinos were illegal in Australia, but the police generally speaking turned a blind eye, he said. Northern Ireland could be a very parochial place, set in its habits. Sydney was anything but. 'It was young and thriving, there was a lot of money about. It was just what I needed at the time,' explained Bryan.

The work-hard, play-hard philosophy gave Sydney an exciting night-life. Bryan said that he learned a lot during his time there. He stored in his head many new ideas from Sydney, to be retrieved at some future date, on his return to the old country.

The move back to Ireland was occasioned by his father's death. His father visited him in Australia on his seventieth birthday and died there. Bryan came back home to comfort his mother and to try his luck in Northern Ireland. He took over the Helmsman in Bangor in 1977. He aimed to make a go of it for two years in Northern Ireland before returning to Australia. Bangor is a small sea-side resort about fifteen miles from Belfast, and while night-life had died in Belfast it had sprung up in a few places outside Belfast like holiday resorts on the coast and in some bars and restaurants in the country. The Helmsman did a roaring trade, with a thousand eighteen- to twenty-one-year-olds packed into the club on Monday, Friday and Saturday nights. Unfortunately, there was also quite a lot of trouble. Bryan employed twenty-four doormen and the Royal Ulster Constabulary were called 'quite a few times'. Bryan wanted to go up-market and he wanted to cater for the slightly older age-group because, he says, 'the older you get the more you want to enjoy life, or what's left of it, and the less you want to fight about religion all the time.' He hit upon the Dublin Road end of the town: 'the better end of town, away from the Shankill and Falls. It was a good area,' he said, 'because it was close to the city centre and it was a very big business area with lots of insurance offices, and the BBC on the corner. There were also lots of English reps about. Office workers make good lunchtime customers. The original premises were part of a terrace I bought for £18,000. I've now turned it into a million-pound complex with a nightclub and restaurant – Pip's International and five bars. One of the bars is called the Elbow Room.' On my first visit there, I remember thinking that it was an apt name, because there wasn't any. Pip's International had a barbecue right in the middle of the nightclub area and two French chefs. 'This is an idea Bryan brought back from Australia,' said Michael Gibson, the restaurant manager, 'and the name Pip's, too, was borrowed from Sydney. The Irish are very conservative in their eating habits – it's all fillet and sirloin steak and mixed grill. I'm trying to educate them with our French chefs.'

The whole complex did indeed look as if the ideas had been borrowed somewhat willy-nilly from elsewhere. The bars were very much in the mould of the traditional English pub – all horse brasses and wooden beams – and, said Bryan proudly, 'English people feel very at home in them.' I had always found English pubs on the Costa Del Sol amusing enough, but right in the centre of Belfast – well, it seemed a bit odd. And yet they were comfortable and inviting. However, the bars were traditional for Northern Ireland in that customers were seated, where possible, and there was a waitress service. 'I call them sales ladies,' said Bryan, 'they're here to promote the place. In Australia it's common to use waitresses in this way.'

The toilets were also quite distinctive. 'I got the idea of pinning the front page of local papers on to the toilet walls from London, from Fleet Street actually – it's to give people something to occupy them when they do the business. It's another first for Belfast.' But I couldn't help wondering how many front pages of local newspapers pinned up in toilets in the rest of the UK have 'A man found murdered in the Clonard area of West Belfast early today is believed to have been the victim of a punishment shooting' as the lead story. This story was from the *Belfast Telegraph* for 15 August. But then again August is always a bad month in Ulster.

'I've gone up-market,' said Bryan. 'I've got a exclusive cocktail bar, and to be honest my bars are the most expensive in Belfast. To keep it up-market I want to charge that little bit extra – it puts some people off. If they can get a pint elsewhere in the town for a little less some people will happily leave us alone. If the drink is a bit pricy for a customer, we'll in fact direct him to a bar down the road. The truth is that we have no trouble here. I only employ four door stewards on the whole complex. We keep trouble out – on the street where it belongs.'

I talked to Millar Beresford, one of the door stewards, who's been working on the door in clubs in Northern Ireland for close on twenty years. 'Of course, I've seen trouble in my day. I've been chased down a street in Portrush by about forty yahoos – they wanted blood – it was going to be a proper gang-bang. But Pip's is the quietest place I've ever worked. Very up-market, very up-town. We don't get the common man in here, to be honest. To stop troublemakers getting in I look for their dress and their manner – these two things. With some people, no matter how much money they had to spend on dress, it wouldn't change their manner. I just say, "Regulars only, tonight, sir." We want people who are respectable and know how to respect. Pip's has really taken off in a very big way.'

I was to go on a Saturday. I had been in town all afternoon, thinking about what the doorman had said. A proper gang-bang. That was one way of putting it. It was time to go home in a 'black' taxi. This was going to be a long way from my big night out at Pip's International. There were three women in their thirties, two drunk men in their sixties and myself all crammed into the back of the taxi. The two drunk men were coming from a loyalist club on the Shankill, and they were practically sitting on each other's lap. We all knew that one of them was going to speak – sooner or later. 'I bet nobody in here has grandchildren, except me and him,' said the one sitting on the other one's knee. 'What about you big girl? I'm right, amn't I.' He gazed expectantly at this large blonde woman, who was so cramped that her short polyester dress was pulled right back. She had great wads of thigh squashed down on the torn black vinyl seat. 'Go on, big girl. I bet I'm right.' She didn't answer. She just smiled in that kind of indulgent way, which says that here we have a drunk man who fancies me, and who can blame him. But I've no need to answer.

His friend kept nudging him. 'Go on, Ernie, show them all what you've got in your big brown bag.' The grandfather was indeed clutching a big brown bag full of God knows what. For some reason, I assumed that it was going to turn out to be a gun. It had to be something of significance or why would his friend want us all to see it. It took the grandfather a while to get into the bag, because he was so drunk. We all craned our necks for a better view, even the big blonde – you could see her big thighs lifting off the black seat. You could even see the big red welts on the underside of her dimpled flesh. Eventually the grandfather got the brown bag open.

'It's twelve Aero bars for my twelve grandchildren,' he said, 'for when we watch the Sunday film on the telly tomorrow.' He held the bag open for us all to see. My mind was reeling. Why in God's name would he want us to see this? And then it occurred to me. He wanted to chat up the big blonde but he didn't want to be rejected. Surely she wouldn't reject some harmless old grandfather, who could even prove that he had reached that particular station in life, by producing twelve Aero bars?

'They're for my wee grandchildren,' he repeated. 'We'll all sit in front of the fire and eat them. It'll be smashin'.' He was painting a picture for us all, and for the big blonde in particular, of domestic bliss in front of the telly. Romantic bliss even. As he got out at Woodvale, he stumbled and the Aero bars all ended up on the wet street. Both he and his friend were on their hands and knees picking them all up, as we drove off.

It was time to get ready to go out. I went to my nearest drinking club first – the Pigeon Club – for an aperitif. A friend from Sheffield once asked me why it was called the Pigeon Club: 'Is it from stool-pigeon, as in informer?' he asked. 'No it's from pigeon as in pigeon fancier,' I had to tell him. One customer thanked me for sending his brother a Christmas card. His brother is serving life in the Maze for murder. The prisoner who gets the most Christmas cards in the Maze gets a prize on Christmas day – a Mars bar. The man in the club wasn't sure whether his brother had qualified for the prize or not. 'But I'm keeping my fingers crossed. A wee prize would cheer him up.'

I got a taxi from the Pigeon Club to Pip's. 'It's a different world down here, boss,' said my taxi driver. 'It's full of fucking jet-setters.'

'Have you ever been in?' I asked.

'No way. No fucking way. Fuck's sake, I'd be out of my depth. It's full of fuckin' gold diggers anyway. They're more interested in the size of your wallet than the size of your dick. It's full of the jet set.'

I thanked him for his advice, and went to the toilet to catch up on the news pinned up in the urinal. I read about the terrorist killings in Belfast that weekend, with all the other jet-setters. Then it was quickly back to the restaurant. There was a candle on my table floating in a dish of pink-coloured water. The wax was dripping into the water. 'It's champagne, you know,' said a fellow jet-setter who had just engaged me in conversation. 'Pardon,' I said. 'In the dish, it's champagne, you know, watch this.' And on that note he picked up the dish of coloured water, which was by now full of candle wax, and knocked it back. 'Gorgeous,' he said as he licked his lips. 'Only the best in here you know,' he added. I said that I could see that.

People from Belfast certainly know how to enjoy themselves, and that night it was no exception. Nights in Belfast drain me. But that night of non-sectarian pleasure had to end sooner or later.

I called a taxi, and stood outside with the hordes heaving towards any taxi that should so much as slow on the way past Pip's. A scuffle broke out to my right and in the distance I heard some faint gunshots. It was only I who strained to listen. My taxi eventually arrived and I beat my way out towards it. Close up, the vehicle looked a wreck. The driver knew my mother, so he insisted on telling me the whole story of how it had happened. 'I got stoned on the Oldpark the night before last. They could tell it was a Protestant taxi, you see. They look out for our number. Just the way the boys from Silverstream would stone the "Park" taxis up here. I carry blind people though, just imagine if it had been stoned with them in it. They wouldn't have known which way to duck.'

I remember thinking that this was a peculiarly Belfast thing to say.

The taxi driver turned out to be a qualified electronics engineer who had served three years in Crumlin Road jail at the start of the Troubles for terrorist offences. He also turned

102

out to be one of the operators of Golliwog Radio, a pirate radio station broadcast by the UDA in the early seventies, designed to send messages 'up the Falls'. 'We'd send messages to irritate them, and the IRA would send messages back on their pirate station to irritate us. We used to interview this wee dog on the radio, and we used to say to it, "What do you think of Protestants?" It used to bark, you know, "yap, yap". Then we'd say to it what do you think of Taigs, and it would go fucking mad. We lost all our equipment in the end though. It was all confiscated. It was a great wee hobby though at the time. And when I was in Crumlin road I used to help all their maintenance staff out by fixing dud wires and so on. You have to keep busy after all.'

He asked me how long I'd been 'across the water', then he asked whether I'd heard about the death of one of the UDA leaders John McMichael over Christmas. I said that I had. 'They blew his legs right off . . . They came right off,' he said again for effect. 'I know his minder, but he'll never be the same again, you know. He escaped with minor bruises. But he's never going to get over that. I can tell ye.'

Recounting the story was making him pensive and depressed. 'You just have to be that bit extra careful all the time in this here town. You're always out checking under your motor for bombs. I check mine first thing every morning. You also have to be careful about who you pick up at nights. You could pick up a few yahoos and it would be "Goodnight, Josephine". But the clients of Pip's are alright. Fucking jet-setters every one, and gold diggers.'

I nodded. 'I know, more interested in the size of your wallet than . . .' as I wiped the candle wax from my lips and trudged wearily back into my mother's house.

10

Remembering the Past, Trying One's Hardest to Understand the Present

Figuring out the rackets

Every now and again, when some particularly awful tragedy hits our screens, there is a demand from politicians and other social commentators on the Mainland that the ordinary people of Northern Ireland must stand up and be counted, that the ordinary man and woman in the street in Northern Ireland must come forward and name the guilty men. Someone must be shielding the terrorist, a much larger group must know who they are, or so the logic goes. It is about time that these ordinary decent people came forward, they say.

This all assumes that the ordinary decent people of Northern Ireland actually know something, as opposed to thinking that they know something or suspecting that they might know something, whilst believing that they might be wrong. It all assumes that you can believe what people tell you and that even when you see something with your own eyes that you have the total picture. It all assumes that gossips and rumours and whispers have some basis in fact and that even when you see the gun in front of you it is *the* gun, *the* gun that shot Marley, or Lenny Murphy, or whatever big name it was supposed to have been used on. Beliefs, suspicions, knowledge and certainty are often mixed up in a very tangled web anywhere in the world, and Belfast is no exception. It is certainly no exception and sometimes it needs more than mere

104

exhortation to pull apart all of these complicated components of what people know.

Rosemary and Jean are both in their late sixties and have lived in this one particular part of Protestant Belfast all their lives. If anyone knows what's going on, surely it must be locals like them. They told me immediately that they knew nothing. 'But all I do know is that I'd be shot if I did know anything and I told you,' said Rosemary. 'That's all I know.'

This was, of course, sound knowledge, and in some senses all she needed to know – to stay alive in this particular district.

They were both mill girls, before the mills closed. Later, Rosemary worked for Ulster Plastics. 'We had loads of wee plastic tea caddies, plastic tops for the bottles, even plastic calendars in the house. You name it and you could get it from Ulster Plastics. There were loads of perks from that job.' Now they're both past retirement age, and past worrying about work.

'There is none in Belfast anyway,' said Jean, 'it's just as well. We worked all our working lives.' Rosemary is a widow, her husband died after an operation. 'He would have been a vegetable, if he had recovered consciousness, and he wouldn't have liked that,' she said, trying to make herself feel better about all the wasted years.

Her husband died when she was in her mid-forties.

Rosemary and Jean remember that part of Belfast before the Troubles, when the area was still mixed, that is when Catholics were still their neighbours. 'We always had Catholics in our street, and there was never any trouble. We all got on well.' The Troubles changed all that. 'Somebody took a shot at one of the men at the bottom of the street and escaped through the house of one of the Catholic families. They just ran in through the front door and jumped over the yard wall. After that some-one fired into their house. So this family had to move away.'

So Rosemary and Jean have learned to adapt to the Troubles, to live normal lives trying to understand what is going on around them. Although as they pointed out repeatedly they knew nothing about what was going on.

'Nobody does,' Rosemary said.

105

Rosemary sat in her kitchen in her dressing gown and curlers. 'We don't stand on formality here,' she said by way of explanation. 'You can get very depressed about what's going on in this town. It's all about money. The whole thing these days is money, money, money. It's not religion. It hasn't been for years. Everybody in this town is paying. On building sites they pay four hundred pounds a week. The contractor has to pay. One of the workmen pointed out to me the man who came to collect.' There was a long non-committal pause.

I had to ask if she recognised the man.

'Mm . . . Put it this way it was somebody from the locality. I was very surprised. I can't tell you who it was. You wouldn't know him anyway. I never knew he was in any organisation. It just goes to show, Jean, you can't be too certain about anybody around here.'

But there were certain things I wanted to know. How does all this racketeering operate? How do you prove who you are for a start? How do you prove that you're the official collector from the UDA or UVF, or whoever. I put this to them: 'You could be anybody, right? Say I went down to the building site around the corner, and said "I'm from the UDA" what kind of proof would they ask for, do you know? I'd have no ID on me presumably?'

It was Jean who took up the challenge. 'You could stick a gun in their ribs, that might help. Or put your finger in your pocket. I'd hand over my money, if somebody did that to me. Do that and you'd probably be accepted that you're part of them. But it's all such a racket. The shops all pay protection money. I know the guy who walked into the sweet shop down there one night for his money.'

'So how much would a shop like that have to pay?' I asked.

'Oh well I wouldn't know that, that's none of my business,' replied Jean. It was Rosemary's turn to help out: 'I saw two of them in the butchers, and they collected a hundred pounds. I don't know if a sweet shop would have to pay the same as a butcher's though.'

Jean had seen them in the butcher's too. 'I saw them in the butcher's one other night collecting their money. Do you know who else is paying protection money? Wee Billy had a hundred

106

pounds a week to pay. He wasn't gonna pay up and they went round to him. Bill is a – what do you call 'em? He lends out them big JCBs and all.'

But I still wanted some details of how the whole thing operated. 'What about the logistics of the whole thing? If you pay to one organisation does that mean you don't have to pay to the other one or do you have to pay to both? Rosemary thought that you would only have to pay to one.

'Surely to God, they've got some way of checking this out. They're not mugs, you know,' she said.

Jean didn't want me to lose sight of the fact that the IRA were at it as well. 'They started it, you know. We were just taking a leaf from their book. It keeps you from getting blew up or your place burned down. It's your money or your life, you know, around here at the moment.'

Was the situation hopeless then?

Jean said that she thought that it was. 'The British Government's always bringing out all these checks. They say that they're gonna clamp down on this and they say that they're gonna do this and they're gonna do that. But they never do anything. You're left on your own around here.'

I wanted to return to specifics. The butcher's seemed the best bet. 'You said that you saw somebody in the butcher's? Who exactly did you see in there?'

Rosemary said, 'I didn't know them personally, I was in with Ann, and she says to me "look at your two men, they're in for their money" and we saw Barry give them it. We didn't see how much, and they wouldn't tell you, for they'd be shot if they opened their mouth.'

This was a day-by-day transaction, perhaps shrouded a little in mystery like your husband's pay packet. Like a pay packet was it put in an envelope? It was Rosemary who answered, 'No, it was in notes, but they didn't count it out or anything like that. He just handed it to them. But they wouldn't tell you how much they handed over, or God they'd be shot.'

'And every single place pays do they?'

It was now Jean's turn: 'Well I couldn't tell you that now, I heard this UVF guy's wife hates your man in the greengrocer's. This lady I'm talking about, her husband's UVF, and she hates

107

– what do they call him – Tommy. Well this other person's told me, "You know why she hates him don't you? Because he wouldn't pay up". I don't know if that's right or not but shortly after that he was . . . wasn't he robbed a couple of times?'

Rosemary backed her up on this.

Jean continued, 'Remember they broke his window and took the cash. Well then shortly after that, did you notice that he has no big shop window left, he filled that up with breeze blocks or something. You know the way a store has a big window? Well he has no window there. But as I say that's why he got robbed, because he wouldn't pay up.'

Rosemary just shook her head: 'Awful isn't it? They're just gangsters.'

I wanted to know about the people who collect the money. How were they distinctive, if at all? Jean said, 'Well they're running about and all the jewellery's tripping them. Isn't that right? They're running about in their leather coats, and they hadn't an ass in their trousers before that many a time. They're doing well out of it all right. They've all plenty of money and they're not working. Very few of them actually work, you know. When you see them down in the local drinking club, obviously they're all having a drink and they can afford to buy it. Everybody has to pay for their drink down there. We're not mean here like the bloody English, who sit in a bar and wait for somebody else to buy their drink. There's a whole lot of them, who were in the Organisation, who have taken off to Spain, by the way. They're able to buy pubs over there. There's Andy, I knew his mother well. They're from Ardoyne originally. Well he took off to Spain, I think, that the UVF were watching him you see and he has a pub now hasn't he?'

Rosemary knew all about Andy. 'He's done very well out of it. He's got more than one pub in Spain, his sister told me. So there you are. He's done very well for himself, but he can't come back here, or the Organisation would get him.'

I wanted to change tack. 'But, aren't there some of these people living in great anxiety as a consequence of their membership of one of the organisations?'

Rosemary said she didn't think so. 'They don't look as if they have. No they just strut about here as if they own the flippin' place. Have you ever seen the big fella? Do you think he has any anxiety – the big godfather? Sure he parades up and down – he wouldn't speak to anybody. He wouldn't even speak to his father-in-law. I've heard more times that he's a marked man – that he's going to get it. But the IRA never bother with him. They haven't tried. He would be an easy target after all. Certainly he's coming up here at the same time every night. He's walking down there at eleven o'clock every day – no, he gets up at eleven and at about twelve he's walking down there. He goes to his mother's and feeds the pigeons and then – I don't know whether he goes over to the drinking club or not now.'

'He doesn't drink anyway. He drinks Coca Cola. He doesn't drink, he smokes a lot, but he doesn't drink. He sits and he buys his round, but he doesn't drink. He has got a bit of a belly on him but that's because he doesn't work. He hasn't worked from before he was married. He's a spark, by trade. But his mother warned his wife before she was married, she said to her, "Now he'll not work for you because he wouldn't work for me," but she said she loved him anyway. So now he spends his days in the club. He goes and he sits about, and if he's sitting with men drinking he buys his round, just like everybody else – even though he doesn't drink. He's got plenty of money. But his whole world revolves around his pigeons and the wee club. That's how he gets his day in. He's a lazy big so-and-so.'

Now, I had heard quite a lot about this particular Godfather – one of the shadowy bosses of the Organisation. I had met a taxi driver the previous night, who spoke of him with great reverence. Why was everyone so frightened of him? What had he done to impress everyone so much – apart from buying his round with the rest of the men, despite only drinking Coca Cola? I put this question to them.

Rosemary answered, 'But you see the taxi driver was maybe in the Organisation too and you see they probably think that he's a great guy. He's the Godfather, he's the boss. You see the other boss was shot. As far as I hear Big Davy stepped into his shoes. It was the IRA who shot the other big boss. They went up into his house, and he was in his bed at the time, and they shot him dead where he was lying.'

But what exactly does this Godfather do?

Rosemary said she had no idea.

Jean thought, 'He's a colonel or something like that. They have all these ranks in the Organisation. I think it's run just like the army.'

Rosemary corrected her. 'I think the Godfather is the general, or lieutenant or whatever . . .'

Jean suggested, 'The Commander.'

Rosemary settled for 'the Commander-in-Chief'.

It was Rosemary who came clean: I don't frankly know what he would be. They just call him 'The Godfather'. The big boss. You wouldn't know what he does. The Organisation doesn't come out and tell people about it. They don't tell you anything, you just have to put two and two together. You see he started wearing all this gold jewellery – these gold rings and all these big gold bracelets an' all like that. He has all this expensive tackle. He even has a big gold horseshoe around his neck. Only the best. And the next thing is that his wife went and took driving lessons which aren't cheap and then the next thing is she got a car. He can't drive. Anyway, he'd be afraid to drive around here, and she only works in a wee shop. The wages is not awful good in a shop like that. Now how could she do all that on her wages? Tell me that. And they go away on these big fancy holidays – her and him goes off somewhere swanky every year. You have to be in something to be able to afford holidays like that. You have to be in one of the Organisations to afford all that.'

So what was the house of this Godfather like? Was it like in the movies? My mind flitted to Marlon Brando, and then it flitted just as easily to the severed horse's head lying in the bed.

Jean said, 'I couldn't tell you what his house is like – there's nobody ever in it. You aren't allowed in it. His wife used to stand outside and knock for ages and then you'd hear her shout "Davy, it's me" and then sometimes she'd walk around the side. I saw her. She'd go round the side because there's a wee window there. "Davy, it's me." When his mother goes

110

she goes round and raps three times on the window. He got that door on and I'll tell you better than that, there's no letter box on it. He wouldn't get a letter box on it. You'd get a bomb through the letter box, if you had one. His sister-in-law told me that he'd never get a letter box installed. She also told me that the outside door is supposed to be steel – now it doesn't look like steel but maybe on the other side it is solid steel. I don't know – it could be camouflaged you see as an ordinary door. And then there's a wee hall like Rosemary's and then the stairs and he's a door on the stairs too. He's got it all protected with doors everywhere, but like I mean that wouldn't save him if the IRA wanted to get him. If they were anxious to get him that would be it. Nothing would save him.'

Rosemary suddenly and without warning announced that she had a very bad cold.

'Have ye?'

'Oh my throat's terrible and then my ribs are sore coughing, you know that auld tickly cough, just like that wee thing in your throat, last night it was awful.'

'Tunes are good, Rosemary.'

'Aye Tunes are great. And then when I cough, see my ribs – oh my God.'

I was becoming slightly alarmed at how the conversation had suddenly switched from a description of the movements of one of the Godfathers of the Organisation to Tunes. The shift in topic was not helping me breathe any easier at this point. I had to pull the conversation back again.

'So what about the local drinking club? Who owns that?'

Jean said she had heard that the UVF was running it. 'I heard long ago that the UVF were running that. But you don't know whether that's true or not, because it's all UVF that go into it. The Organisation walked in one day and says, "From this day on, we're taking this over." I know one regular who said he wouldn't go back. And to be honest, I suppose there was a whole lot wouldn't go back. But there's a whole lot more who would like the Organisation being involved. Well they must, because it's packed every night.'

'When I say that they run the club, I don't mean that they would order the drinks and that sort of stuff. They wouldn't be interested in that sort of thing. But they'd be interested in the profits naturally. It's the takings that they would run. Maybe give them back so much you see, but they would take the bulk of it.'

I wanted to ask if there was anything that either the UVF or the UDA didn't have some hand in in the locality? Both said 'the church', more or less simultaneously.

'No profit in that, otherwise they would be.'

I was now wondering aloud how many people locally would be in the UVF.

Rosemary was aghast at the question. 'You wouldn't know that. They don't come out and broadcast it. It's not a thing that people's in and come and tell you "I'm in the UDA or I'm in the UVF." They're afraid of anybody knowing. God aye, they'd get shot. You maybe get the odd one – maybe a big slabber, who mouths whenever he gets a few drinks in him. But normally they don't go about telling you about it. Some people like to talk when they've had a drink, but that can be very dangerous around here. There was one case near where my sister lives on the Newtownards Road where this guy's wife was murdered, because he was slabbering all over the place about the Organisation. They didn't mean to shoot her mind, they thought it was him. You see there was a glass door in her wee house and she was a big tall girl and she'd got short hair like him. She had dark trousers on as well, and she was just in from her work, and so was he. They must have been watching out for him, and they went and knocked at the door and when she came to answer the door, what with her height and the pants an' all . . . they just let it rip through the door. They riddled her dead.'

'They had a machine gun too because the woman next door, who was out cleaning her windows, saw it all happen. She saw two guys run away down the street. Terrible. My sister saw a friend of his in a shop one day after it happened and said to him, "Yer man had better watch himself now, if it was him that they were after" and this fella said to her, "No the debt's paid. He's been punished enough with his wife getting it." Yer man was in the know, you see. The Organisation can sometimes just make a mistake and shoot somebody else. It can be very dangerous living around here – even for the innocent. But I wouldn't think that fella would be in anything now. I'm sure he's left the Organisation. My sister says he's got awful old looking. She told me she saw him in the bakery only yesterday, and he was talking to her, and she told me – honest to God – she was sick with his breath, with the smell of the drink on him. She didn't know what he was saying either. He was full yesterday, and she says to her friend, "Come on, let's slip past him." She didn't want to have to talk to him, you see. But he's been through a lot. That man's seen a lot of suffering. He's had more than his fair share.'

'There have been some big funerals around this place,' said Rosemary, changing the subject but only slightly. 'You should have been here the time Den was shot, that was the first UDA funeral around here. Den was a character all right. He had a place in the auld blocks of flats on the road. One of the flats was empty and he went in and I hear you wouldn't believe the style he had in the place. I heard his bed had two steps up to it, two steps. His bed was sitting on this big platform. I don't know whether that was right or not like. But he had great style in the flat. He had a great funeral as well. UDA I think. Minnie was in it. There was a whole lot of women in the UDA in them days, and they wore uniforms and all. They used to parade and everything. The place was black with people. I saw the gun and all, firing shots in the air outside the house, but I wasn't near them. I didn't know who was firing the guns but I saw the guns. The UDA had on all their gear – they wore arm bands then. The only one I recognised was Minnie.'

'Terry was in it as well, and his mother was in it, she's a Catholic. Terry lived down below the Campbells', a couple of doors, isn't that right? You remember Terry, everybody knew Terry. Och, I mind our Mary talking about Terry. Terry done this, or Terry done that. But I think he went to the Catholic school. Well, when the Troubles started all the Catholics were either ordered out or moved out of the area. But Terry, his mother was – what would you call her? A good thing. Anybody's, you know, all rouge and all. When she had a couple of drinks, you were all right and she was a terrible-looking thing.

113

She was anybody's. And the father was an Englishman; he never was out of the house, he done all the cleaning and all, while the auld lady was out boozing. I saw her myself with young fellas coming home and she couldn't walk, but anyway all this trouble started and they sat their ground. And the next thing they changed their religion and – what do you call her – Rosie, Rosie joined the UDA, the ladies' section. She's dead now. She joined the UDA and Terry was in the UDA.'

'I mind our Jackie telling me that they were having a bit of a sing song in the 41 Club, that was one of the flats – that was the 41 Club. It was a *drinking club* – a shebeen. They just called it the 41 Club because of the way like it sounded awful swanky. I was in it one night. There was just wee wooden tables and chairs all round and well the bathroom was the toilet an' all. We only went in there one night just to see it. It was clean an' all. Kenny used to say that Terry used to sing there – "I'm the only Fenian in the UDA". There was a whole song about him – he was daft you know. And one night they had a bet on that he wouldn't do a streak. So Terry done a streak up the road one night. Betty saw him – she was putting her milk bottles out, and she saw the bare body come running up the road. He was wired up.'

'And then they went in one night to beat him up. Now I don't know who done that. He was beat up and he was nearly dead. Och, he got an awful hammering. But nobody seems to know who done it. But it must have been somebody. They don't tell on each other, you know. Aye, they don't, they don't let you know anything. But Terry was beat up, and they nearly killed him. They beat him with a hatchet, didn't they? And then he went away to England, and then he came back again. He's back now like.'

'But you don't see so many UDA funerals now, not like Den's, anyway. There were hundreds at that funeral and loads of women, all in their uniforms and Minnie was walking up, smiling like a queen at everybody that she knew. I don't think there's any women in now. This was the time they used to do parades. You don't see them now on the streets the way you used to, but they do still have bands. There's a UDA band. Oh

114

aye, it says so on the drum and all. There's also a Ulster Volunteer Force band, but then you see there always was an Ulster Volunteer Force. My grandfather was an Ulster Volunteer.'

'So was my father,' added Rosemary proudly. 'He was always in the UVF, before they let all the cowboys in. Was the UVF an army or was that a regiment? I can't remember. Yes, when my grandfather was ill he didn't go into an ordinary hospital, he went into the UVF hospital and there's still a UVF to this day.'

'We just call it the Organisation now,' added Jean. 'The UVF hospital is still standing. It's way about Stormont or somewhere. I remember going to it when I was wee. It's way out on the old Holywood Road, out that way.'

Rosemary was recalling her own glorious past. 'My Uncle Tom and my father were in the UVF in the old days and they were connected with the gunrunning. And one night they come for my father and my mother didn't waken him, because he was drunk. I don't know whether there were any Catholics in the UVF, or not. Was the Ulster Volunteer Force not something to do with . . .? Maybe I'm wrong, I'm only surmising, but was the UVF not connected with the uprising, you know? Yeah and then war broke out, and they all went to war.'

Jean remembered her forebears with equal pride: 'Well my Uncle Sammy and all was at the Somme, I'm sure he was.'

Rosemary: 'Mine wasn't. No my father was at the war before that – that was the war in the Himalayas, I think.'

'Why wasn't he at the Somme, Rosemary?'

'Because he wasn't well.'

Jean's family had served well in the British army. 'My grandfather and my uncle Sammy were in the Old Contemptibles after the war was over. Did you ever hear of them? Well that was some battle they fought against . . . I don't know whether it was the Kaiser or whoever, and he said that they would soon defeat Britain's contemptible little army. So that's how they got their name, you see. I don't think there's any Old Contemptible left now, there's only the ones that was in that army that could join it. I mind when I was young, getting taken to the dinners an' all. We thought that was great, when

115

they had dinners, they had these get-togethers for the old Contemptibles like that. They had to address each other as "chum". And if you didn't you were fined. It was always "chum this" and "chum that", even when they were writing in the papers about them. But all the Old Contemptibles are dying out – a dying breed. But they were our forefathers. The forefathers of the Protestant people.'

We had sat there for most of the morning. They had been very generous with their time, but now Rosemary was signalling that she had other things to do. 'I must get my fire lit.'

Jean started to put her coat back on. 'We had a good auld yarn this morning.'

They both looked my way. 'Do you have any more questions, or is that enough for you? Didn't we tell you that we didn't know nothing? Nobody knows anything around here. We're all in the bloody dark. If you find anything out, let us know. You can come back then and explain it all to us.'

Trying to forget the Somme

He had a funny little walk. Everybody just called him 'Isaac the barber'. His shop used to be on the left hand side of the Ligoniel Road, but that had gone years ago. He was still doing regular house calls at fifty pence a time. He was a dapper little man, and proud. Proud of Belfast – 'and why shouldn't I be? We had one of the greatest shipyards in the world, and some of the finest people in the world.'

He remembered going down with his best friend, Edward McMurray, to see one of the shipyard's more famous ships being launched – the *Titanic*.

'It was an awful big ship, with four massive funnels, they said it was unsinkable, but I remember that I wasn't surprised when it went down. There was a lot of talk about it in the barber's shop for days afterwards. That big ship with all those people aboard.' His voice trailed off.

Isaac was ninety-two years old, and he had been working as a barber for the past seventy-seven years. 'Why stop now?' he said with a shrug. 'I've always liked barbering. Sure it's wonderful right enough, and I'm still able. Pensioners are my

116

main customers these days, it saves them having to go all the way into town, you see. I've always done the same style – short back-and-sides for men, and the shingle and semi-shingle cut for women. Barbering hasn't changed that much. I've got a pair of those modern electric clippers, but there was a time you couldn't depend on a house having electricity, so I've always preferred my hand clippers. I don't do much shaving though these days, and, in fact, I haven't really done a lot since the safety razor came in.'

Isaac could remember most of his customers, who are pensioners, when they were still children and didn't need a razor – safety or otherwise.

Isaac outlived them all. 'The funny thing is,' said Isaac 'that good health doesn't run in my family. My son even died when he was fifty-two. But I've got a sister who's ninety-nine years old, she's in a home now – she can't speak, she can't see, in fact she can't anything. She went to Canada for years, but said she wouldn't die there. So she came back to Belfast, and she's been clinging on to dear life for years now. I put my good health down to my fondness for the open air, and the fact that I don't drink or smoke. There are few men my age who are one hundred per cent fit, but I'm still going strong. But you notice the difference as you get older. You get a little bit absent-minded. Only last week when I went to cut a client's hair I let myself into the wrong house by mistake. The owner came in and found me waiting patiently by the fire with my scissors in my hand.'

Isaac has lived all his life in Ligoniel, and in fact he's rarely been away: 'I've never been across the water to England or America, but I went to the Isle of Man once on a paddle steamer. I've only ever been to the Free State the once as well. We went down to Dublin – it was a lovely city, but I never seemed to have the money or the time to do much travelling. I've seen more of life with the people passing through my barber's shop anyway,' he added.

Isaac was nearly as old as Ligoniel village itself. The village grew up around the flax mills built in the 1860s. It started out as a few rows of white-washed houses for the mill workers. Isaac was born in one of these in Bismarck Street in 1896. He left school at twelve to work half-time, with one day in work, one day in school, in the flax mill as a machine boy. 'The machine boy,' said Isaac 'was in between the "rougher" and the spinner. The "rougher" pulled the flax through the pins and passed it onto the machine room. We got it ready for the spinning room. It was awful heavy work though, and I knew it wasn't for me. The mills were lit by candle light in those days, and the machinery powered by water wheels. The hours of work were from six o'clock in the morning to six o'clock at night Monday to Friday, and from six o'clock to one o'clock on a Saturday. In 1911, I just took a fancy to barbering and got taken on by an Arthur Pollock in Ligoniel as an apprentice. I got six shillings a week in them days, a haircut, by the way, was three pence, and a shave cost a penny. The hours of opening of the barber's shop weren't that better than those in the mill, the barber's shop opened at seven o'clock in the morning and didn't close until nine o'clock at night Monday to Saturday. We had Sundays off though. These hours weren't unusual in them days, the public houses opened at seven o'clock in the morning as well. Our customers were just ordinary local men, good men who were never idle. There was a lot of work about in them days, a lot of hard work.'

In 1914 Isaac and his best friend Edward McMurray, from whom it seems he was inseparable, decided to enlist. Edward was passed as medically fit, but they wouldn't accept Isaac because he had got a weakness in one leg. 'I damaged it playing football. I argued with them about it, I begged them to let me join up. I told them that you don't pull a trigger with your leg. But it was no good. I had to stay at home while Edward went off to war. He was a runner – he carried the messages in the 15th Battalion of the Ulster Volunteer Force. Nearly all the Ligoniel men, both Protestant and Catholic, joined the 15th Battalion. Edward fought at the Somme. He came back without one of his legs and with half a hand missing. He was in a sorry state, I can tell you. He talked about the war a lot, but the funny thing was he never talked about the Somme. He never seemed to want to discuss the Somme itself. He used to sit in his front room, picking bits of shrapnel and bits of dirt out of his good leg when he was reminiscing.

The problem with his good leg was that because there were so many little wounds in it, all the dirt of the day seemed to get caught in it. I used to look after it for him. We were still only young lads at the time, don't forget.'

'After the war Arthur Pollock put the barber's shop up for sale. He was moving on to the shipyard, that's how good the work was in those days in the shipyard. Men would leave a business to go to work in it. I took the shop over. It was right in the midle of Ligoniel village, just opposite the Police Barracks and Ewart's mill, just up the road from Emerson's, and not far from Wolfhill mill, which were all doing great business. The rent was three shillings and nine pence a week, and I had a lot of very steady customers – Protestant and Catholic. When the Troubles broke out in 1922, they didn't really affect Ligoniel at all. Ligoniel was a village, and just like a big family, everybody knew everybody else. On the Twelfth of July, sure the Catholics would help the Protestants put the Arches up for the Orange marches to pass under. For the bonfires on the Eleventh night, the Catholic lads would be out collecting the wood, same as anybody else.'

The start of the Second World War saw Isaac's little business doing well, and the flax industry in Ligoniel still going strong. 'When the Second World War started, it was like the Great War all over again. All the young men queuing up to enlist, again Protestant and Catholic alike. I was a bit too old this time to be bothered, but this Hitler fella was a worse enemy than the old Kaiser ever was. Even though I knew now what could happen to the young lads out there, through looking after Edward, you had to cheer them on. It had to be done. But it was a sad time. I used to get me old fiddle down. No I didn't have any favourite tunes, I'd just get it down and let the sparks fly. The fiddle was one of my great loves, the other was boxing. I've always been a boxing fan, and my shop had photos of all the great boxers plastered all over it. When I eventually sold up at the start of the present Troubles, I loaned them all to the publican from the Terminus Bar in Ligoniel. But not long after that the pub was burned to the ground in the Troubles, along with most of the other pubs in Ligoniel. Everything went up in smoke. But I've still got my memories of all those great

119

fighters, and all the local amateurs, including your Uncle Terence. Nobody up in St Vincent's club was able for him, he was too tough for any of them. But what talent there is today. I sit up all night to watch that Tyson fella. What a fighter, better than anybody I remember.'

But what about the present Troubles, had they surprised the man who wasn't surprised by the sinking of the *Titanic* and who had seen more of this century than most?

'I wasn't surprised that it all came to a head again because it was never properly settled in the first place, but I was surprised and saddened that Ligoniel went the way of everywhere else, and that it got caught up in the Troubles. It wasn't a village anymore, you see, a lot of outsiders were housed up in Ligoniel from all over the town, with all this redevelopment that has been going on. The village has now gone, and all the old white-washed cottages. My old shop has gone now as well. Ligoniel isn't the same anymore. The new houses are lovely, but they broke up the village. You see when you're reared together, it becomes like a big family, you have your arguments but you can settle them in the end without fighting, or without fighting too seriously. But now, you wouldn't know where the end is, or how it's all going to end.'

And as he got up slowly to leave, he presented me with a shiny penny in a little tin can. He had obviously been keeping the penny for years, and polishing it frequently. He had brought it with him that Sunday afternoon as a gift. It was beautifully preserved, if a little worn down from all the polishing. It had Queen Victoria, Queen of England, Defender of the Faith, Empress of India on it, and it had been minted in 1900. Isaac was already four at the time. He saw me looking at the date, and the majestic and regal stare of the great Queen Victoria. The great queen from across the water. He had never set eyes on Queen Victoria, or any other monarch of the past century for that matter. But he didn't need to. They'd been to Northern Ireland, but only briefly, and Isaac doesn't like crowds. But you could see that he was still proud to carry that penny around with him, with her majesty on the front.

The shiny penny that his friend Edward had kept with him at the Somme – for good luck.

11

A Class Apart?

The Protestants of Ulster have always been very keen on education. It is part of their Scottish heritage. They value hard work and diligent effort. In education that can take you a long way. There's nothing morally better to see on a school report than 'diligent effort'. The province has always boasted many excellent schools, and I was fortunate enough to attend one of the best of them. This was my escape route, and I always knew it. It was an effective way out in the end, but occasionally a little painful. The working-class Protestant at a posh school in Belfast, then the Ulsterman at the English university. Not quaintly Irish, just a funny Belfast accent, and a funny attitude to work to go with it. Like generations of Ulstermen and women before me, and no doubt like generations of Ulstermen and women after me.

The happiest days of your life

When I was eleven my world fell apart. I passed the Eleven Plus. It was a Saturday morning, and the thick brown envelope tumbled through the letter box. 'Is it thick or thin?' my older brother shouted down the stairs – from bed. 'Thick.' I shouted back, fumbling to open it. 'Oh shite, he's passed.' My brother, you see, hadn't but he did know enough to appreciate the significance of the relative thickness of the envelope. We were no longer in the same boat – I had been pushed out and I now had to swim away to strange and foreign shores.

I had chosen the poshest-sounding school on the list the Local Education Authority had sent out – Belfast Royal Academy. There were a few other schools with 'Royal' in the name as well but this one sounded the poshest of them all. I didn't know where it was, but then again I didn't know where any of them were. After I passed the exam, and not before, the school asked to have a look at me, probably quite sensibly because nobody had passed the Eleven Plus from St Mark's Primary School in Ligoniel in living memory. The Eleven Plus, by the way, turned me into a kind of local celebrity, people would stop me in the street and press sixpences into my hand. It wasn't that Ligoniel necessarily produced children of below average intelligence, incapable of passing this particular examination, it's just that there was no special preparation for the Eleven Plus at St Mark's. Whilst other schools were running special courses on how to perform in 'culture-fair' intelligence tests, St Mark's just didn't bother. One morning, they simply informed us that the Eleven Plus was to take place the next day. Albert thought that it was a medical examination: 'to see if you're well developed enough to go to Everton Secondary School.' Albert didn't even bring a pencil the next morning, but he was wearing clean underpants. I had six new pencils, and two new rubbers. I wasn't taking any chances. Many of the boys from St Mark's went on to university, eventually, but they all had to go to the local secondary school first. Albert never made it very far in the end, and he became a bin-man, although as my mother says, if you're not frightened of a bit of dirt, it's a very good job – 'good pay, short hours, and plenty of little perks' (I think she means what you can retrieve from the bins).

Anyway, I was being given my big chance – a chance of an education, with a job almost certainly to follow, where the perks wouldn't depend on what you could scavenge from bins. But first I had to get through the interview. My mother took the day off work from Ewart's mill, in Ligoniel, to go with me to the interview. She worked in the 'carding room', where the flax dust tends to give you a very pronounced and very distinctive cough. My father gave us directions to what he always insisted on calling the Royal Academy School. I wasn't sure whether it was the same place as Belfast Royal Academy or a completely different insitution. 'Don't let me down,' my mother whispered as we got off the bus. The bus driver wished me well. He could see that I was apprehensive, as well I might be. He knew my father, who worked as a mechanic on the buses at the Falls Road depot. It was us versus them – 'show them what you're made of, sonny', he said as I got off. I thought this was the last thing I wanted to show them. This more than any other day I knew that I could not afford to be myself.

The headmaster interviewed me personally, apparently this was quite significant – he normally didn't bother. I'm not sure that he knew where Ligoniel was, even though he did look very learned. He wore a gown. He asked a few simple questions and I provided a few simple and truthful answers. Until, that is, he asked me about the last novel I'd read. Now let me get one thing clear – mine wasn't a deprived home. There were some books in the house – invariably obtained as prizes from St Mark's church or Sunday school for excellent attendance. But they were just that – prizes. Nobody really read books in my house, although we did read a lot of comics and magazines. *I* did, however, take encyclopaedias to bed with me every night – encyclopaedias of science, encyclopaedias of art, encyclopaedias of sport, encyclopaedias of pets, encyclopaedias of fish, encyclopaedias of famous men, the *Everyday Encyclopaedia*, *The Encyclopaedia for the Younger Generation*, *The Living World of Science*, the *Wonder World of Nature*. As long as it was an encyclopaedia, I'd read it, but I wasn't really interested in novels at the time. My knowledge of literature was somewhat restricted but I did have an encyclopaedia of famous authors. So when he asked me about the last novel I'd read, my heart sank. Luckily I'd been to the King George V Memorial Hall the previous Sunday to see the film *Gulliver's Travels*. From my *Encyclopaedia of Famous Authors* I knew it had been written by Swift, J. (1667–1745). The only problem was my friends and I had been ejected shortly after the interval for throwing marbles at each other. (We always took bags of marbles to the cinema, by the way, it was part of going to the cinema. The only exception was when we went to see the

123

midnight movie at the Park Cinema, on the Oldpark Road, where we'd take old rags to first soak, then throw, during the horror movies). But that day in the interview, it was *Gulliver's Travels* or nothing: I was short on plot – I had missed a lot of it after all because of all the excitement with the marbles but I was very good on visual description. I got to the point where I'd been ejected and said, 'Would you like me to continue?' The headmaster said he'd heard enough. He was already impressed by my visual imagery – by my ability to conjure up complex images and scenes from the written word. I was in.

I went to the official school outfitter to be kitted out – white shirt, grey flannels, cap, rugby shirt, cricket flannels. Cap! It was a brave new world I was entering and it scared the life out of me. It took two buses to get to the school, all the friends from my street could walk to theirs.

I have always felt that there is a lot to be said for school uniform. On the surface at BRA, or great BRA, as we all sang in the school song, we all looked very much the same. Below the surface, everything was different. I could never understand how anyone could be so unworldly as to write a school song praising a great bra. I used to snigger at the worlds, my fellow pupils told me not to be such a 'pleb'. I didn't know what a 'pleb' was. 'Plebeian, Beattie,' they would explain, 'you're just a plebeian.' I, fortunately, was none the wiser. But great BRA did broaden my horizons, I met children who had been to America for their holidays, I met a girl who had been to Saudi Arabia! I'd never even been across the water, as they say in Ireland. And when I opened my mouth, I stuck out a mile. My accent was as thick as buttermilk. But it wasn't just my accent, it was my whole style of speaking. I wasn't linguistically deprived or anything like that, but I was still surprised to hear eleven-year-olds say, 'He's such a sarcastic and ostentatious person.' I used to look the words up at night in my *Little Oxford Dictionary*, and practice them the next day. 'Don't be so sarcastic E. J. Henshaw,' I'd say. 'Why, Beattie?'

'Because I'll stick my toe up your arse that's why, I'd say. 'Ass' instead of "arse" came much later.

My linguistic habits were deeply ingrained – my accent, my

vocabulary and my whole style of speaking – even at eleven. Now one marked feature of the Belfast dialect is the regular occurrence of the expression 'you know'. At times it almost seems to act as a universal punctuation mark. 'I have to get the bus here in the morning, you know, sir, that's why I'm a bit late you know. Sorry sir, it won't happen again, you know.' Both pupils and staff tormented me. One day, during a history lesson and in front of the whole class, the deputy headmaster decided to rid me of this irritating, nasty little working-class linguistic habit. 'I know that I know, Beattie. Would you kindly stop saying you know? It's you who doesn't know what you're talking about.' The more he insisted, the more I kept saying it. My anxiety was going right through the roof. He told me to get a grip on myself, and I tried, you know, I really tried. I learned to hate the sound of my own voice.

My speech set me apart – I could never be part of the BRA crowd, one of the BRA boys, as long as I continued to speak like that. It was visible for all to see – fellow pupil, teacher, headmaster – there was no hiding it. It wasn't a passive blemish either, which could be covered up with suitable cosmetics. It was active, moving, dynamic, it drew attention to itself. I just had to open my mouth and there it would be – out of its cage, circulating the room, with everyone staring up at it. I would be asked to give an oral account of Gladstone's contribution to British politics, and even the stupidest and least imaginative boy in the class could snigger at my attempt, because of how I spoke.

When we had to write essays at school, about what we did on our holidays, and other pupils wrote adventurous, and true, stories about meeting members of the Saudi Royal Family *in Saudi Arabia*; I wrote about hitch-hiking to a seaside resort about sixty miles from Belfast, because that's all I did. This was a real adventure, as it turned out – since my friend and I were picked up by a man, coincidentally a retired teacher, with quite an exceptional interest in what we had down our trousers. He kept suggesting to us that we should stop for a 'wee wee'. We assured him that we didn't need a 'wee wee' or anything else for that matter. But to children grown accustomed to tales of Saudi Arabia, trips to Portrush, even when they involved lifts from strange men, were hardly big news (I would never have dared to mention what the stranger had suggested to us anyway). The other pupils asked me if trips to Portrush was really the best I could do.

So I started using my imagination, and I started making things up, trying to forget who I was and what I was. One year I went to Egypt for my holidays – or so one of my third form essays says. I was quite good at the description of the place, because after all there were photographs of the Sphinx, and the bazaars of Cairo, in my *Boys' World* atlas, but I wasn't so good at what the 'natives' were like. (The *Boys' World* atlas was always a bit thin on its description of actual people.) So I had to bluff it again; 'We didn't meet many of the natives,' I said imperious in my essay, 'so it is not possible for me to surmise what they were actually like.' I was starting to sound like *them*, at least in essays, even if I didn't care much for the content of the essays or the sentiments I was expressing. The funny thing was that I could only use words like 'surmise', when I was quite self-consciously playing the part of the boy from BRA. It never generalised to my other world: 'I surmise by this slimy trail that we have slugs in our kitchen, mammy . . . I mean mother.' Or, 'I surmise that Albert Cowley is going to be a bin-man when he leaves school.' It just didn't sound right somehow.

One year I went to Egypt for my holidays, the next was – Hollywood. I used to read my mum's *Titbits*, and tried to imagine the place from a thirteen-year-old's point of view. 'We saw Frank Sinatra, but only in the distance, unfortunately, he was driving off in his limousine.' I had to add this for good measure – in case anyone should ask me a detailed question about him, beyond the scope of a *Titbits* exposé. One boy from my English class had genuinely been to Hollywood. His father was, I believe, a top executive in Emerald Records, a record label which seemed to be devoted almost exclusively to Irish showbands, but enough Irish showbands to pay for a trip to Hollywood. One photograph in *Titbits* showed Frank Sinatra leaving San Francisco, the next showed him in Hollywood. I naturally assumed that they were very close together, and said so in very prosaic language in my essay. There weren't many photographs in *Titbits* of the countryside in California either, just shots of Mr Sinatra, at various premières, galas and shows. You could see the odd patch of grass in the background of some of these photographs, but were these patches of grass lawns or fields? I had nobody to check the details with, so I made the best guess possible, under the circumstances: 'As you drive through the elegant canyons of Southern California linking the neighbouring towns of San Francisco and Hollywood, where the climate keeps the grass green, but where it does not rain enough to stimulate growth . . .' My best descriptions were of Mr Sinatra himself, the *Titbits* photographer had after all got him in close-up. 'Uneven in quality,' said my English teacher. 'A load of cobblers,' said Solomon, the boy who had actually been there. 'Green grass my eye – are you sure it wasn't Holywood outside Bangor you were talking about.' (For those unfamiliar with Northern Ireland, it should be pointed out that "Holywood" is actually pronounced "Hollywood" locally, and Solomon was quite right, it was about as close as I would ever get to the real thing.)

My essays were second rate, or worse, third rate, because it wasn't at all clear whether the journalists who wrote these magazine articles had been there in the first place. I decided enough was enough. So in the end I forced myself to stop writing essays about my favourite uncle who was a big game hunter, just back from Africa and concentrated instead on describing my real favourite uncle, who went down to the pub with my father every Saturday night, and was mauled not by any lion, but by our fox terrier, Spot, when he came home later reeking of drink. I tried to describe what a fight was like, because on many a Saturday night when I was waiting for my father and my uncle coming from the bar, I had witnessed the 'B-Specials', truncheons drawn, lay into some drunks outside Paddy's. This was real violence, quite unlike the *Titbits* version, and I found that I was good as describing it because I'd been there. I was even good at describing the behaviour of the 'natives', because they and I spoke the same language. I understood them, and they me. I didn't even have to use the word 'surmise' once. The teacher liked my essays a lot, and I stopped trying to describe or explain them to Solomon, and the like. They went their way, I went mine. Not inferior anymore, just different. This became my motto.

There has to be some convergence somewhere though, and I realised that when it came to A levels, we'd all have to race through the same dark tunnel. I was determined that I was going to be prepared, and that I wasn't going to turn up for A levels without a pencil. I was no Albert Cowley. I had to be self-motivated though – my mother told me that if I kept reading all those books that I'd need glasses before I was twenty, and eveyone would call me 'speccy four eyes'. I worked on a low table in our front room, with the television on permanently, and with my mother's friends dropping in for a chat. It wasn't so bad – there were only three in my family (my father had died). The Rock family, two doors up in Legmore Street, had eleven in an identical two up/two down. There was nowhere for them to sleep, let alone do homework. I got three As at A level in Maths, Physics and Chemistry (and a D in Russian, which I studied in my spare time). I was aiming for grade As because my family could readily understand what they meant – top. I never did fancy trying to explain the significance of grade Bs in terms of percentiles or whatever to them. But A levels were more importantly my passport, my passport to university – away from Legmore Street, away from a Belfast caught up in the Troubles, away from great BRA. I always reasoned that I could never find student digs as cold or damp as my home, and I was right.

Things could only get better.

A chump at Cambridge

There are those who think that the Protestants of Ulster are simply displaced Englishmen or Scotsmen, planted in that foreign land with the seeds of privilege. Protestants support the monarchy, the Church, the State, they benefit from all that privilege and power. All that privilege and power! I came across privilege and power, just the once, at Trinity Cambridge – me and Prince Charles both. We shared a tutor, and more besides. I saw the Archbishop of Canterbury at dinner. I dined with Rab Butler – 'every post in the Conservative Cabinet

128

except Prime Minister, and he should have had that as well, if he hadn't been robbed,' my tutor cautioned me. I saw Prince Charles' helicopter – in the distance.

The University of Cambridge, you see, had been under a lot of pressure in these egalitarian times to open its door to people from different social backgrounds. To people from the lower classes, the working classes, the unemployed classes. To people, well, like me. People who think that Asti Spumante is real champagne. ('It's dear enough,' my mother would always say.) People who not only have not been educated at Marlborough or Eton, or who have never visited Henley, but people who have rarely been to the South of England.

Cambridge was traditionally the home of privilege, but along came the sixties and with it came social mobility on a new scale. By the time we got to the seventies, Cambridge had flung open its majestic gates to all sorts and people like myself dashed in – before they could change their minds and shut them again.

Cambridge is a formidable university, Trinity is perhaps the most formidable of its colleges. Home of kings (Edward VII, George VI), princes (Charles most recently), Prime Ministers (Earl Balfour, Nehru), poets (Byron, Tennyson), philosophers (Francis Bacon, Wittgenstein, Bertrand Russell), men of science (Isaac Newton, Lord Rutherford), and me. It was proud of its history, aware of its reputation, jealous of its position. 'Six of the translators of King James' Authorised Version of the Bible were resident fellows of the College,' the official guide says. 'Watch out squirt,' I got the message all right.

People told me I should be proud to go there: 'Imagine, someone from your background,' they would say, and I would stare back at them, trying to work out exactly what they were referring to. My mother had some reservations. 'I hope it doesn't turn you into a snob,' and she would drawl longingly on the first letter of that last word. She didn't want a snob in the family, but she did want a nob with social grace and education, she wanted me transformed, but not too much. It was always going to be a difficult balance to maintain: 'And don't show yourself up,' she warned. 'I'll try not to,' I said.

Trinity was all I expected and more – magnificent courts,

129

young men in gowns with unfamiliar accents, eccentrics, bells, port, cheap beer. I would walk around the perimeter of Great Court and through the hallowed cloisters of Neville's Court, thinking. Often aloud. Bryon had kept his bear in Neville's Court (and issues of the college magazine were devoted to trying to ascertain exactly which room he had lived in). Wittgenstein had eaten his pork pies (apparently he liked them) in these same cloisters. And here was I. Great ontological questions would rear up in front of me. 'What is existence?' 'Why are we here?' Or more specifically, 'What is an ordinary lad from Ligoniel in Belfast doing walking through the cloisters of Neville's Court at midnight with a half-eaten pork pie in his pocket?'

The social side of college life was problematic. But I didn't feel out of my depth mixing with the cream of English society because I didn't mix with them. They dominated the senior combination room sherry scene. I dominated the Baron of Beef pub. My best friend at Trinity was a working-class lad from Glasgow, and I went all that way to meet him. Great socialist ideals could have pulled me through; even middle-class aspirations would have helped, but I had none of these – just good exam results and my own natural embarrassment.

My idea of a revolutionary act was to go to dinner in hall dressed in a gown and afterwards go to the Midland Tavern (a reggae club off Mill Road full of West Indians), wearing a T-shirt and dancing with the best of them. I didn't hate the old Etonians or the titled students or resent them. I just felt that I'd nothing to say to them. They would sit in clumps over dinner and laugh and joke and guffaw, and I would sit, often alone, staring at that portrait of Henry VIII which dominates Trinity dining room. Henry had a large and fat face but I knew every part of it. I knew it better than my own.

Those privileged students had been reared on polite conversation. I came from a different social background. In the art of conversation I was still at the talking-by-numbers stage. And anyway, I didn't share their sense of humour – I could never laugh like that at those things. I envied them only because they had so much in common with each other. Becoming a

130

Trinity man didn't pull our past or our present together, Belfast and Belgravia were never further apart.

But I tried. Cambridge was renowned for scholarship and sport, so I did both. It thrives on competition, so I competed. I got a PhD. I played for the university against Oxford (in badminton of all things), and became college captain in that sport. All the things that the successful student is supposed to do, in fact. But they were hollow accomplishments – I never did become either a snob or a nob. Any changes were really just cosmetic, and when I had a few pints, the make-up would start to run.

I had been reared with a certain prototype of how a man should behave, and this prototype seemed often to be clearest and to clash more forcefully with that of the old Etonians when I, and they, had been drinking. Alcohol made them tease each other and play pranks and develop self-important poses, and in some cases even surrender to the amorous feelings that they had about each other. It did no such things to me; it made me macho. I had a image of how men behaved with drink, and I stuck to it. Education wasn't going to change that.

One incident in particular sticks in my mind. It was the first year I attended the College Badminton Club formal dinner. I had just won the college singles tournament and was to be presented with a trophy. I was also captain elect. It should have been a great evening. The dinner started well enough, the alcohol flowed. I had to make a speech – it went quite well and the alcohol continued to flow. I was presented with the trophy, the alcohol didn't dry up all night. The dinner finished late and, thanks to Trinity's hospitality, I – and everyone else – was inebriated.

Now a famous tradition at Trinity is the Great Court run (depicted, if inaccurately, in *Chariots of Fire*) in which young men attempt to run around the perimeter of Great Court whilst the college clock strikes midnight (in *Chariots of Fire*, the run seems to take place at midday). It is a very difficult feat because the path is cobbled in parts, and its turns are very sharp. It is an impossible feat if you've been drinking.

But that night alcohol had made me invulnerable, or at least less vulnerable, so I stripped off my dinner jacket and rolled up my sleeves. Gut determination and singlemindedness honed and narrowed by alcohol would pull me through, I was sure. Part of this great Trinity tradition, however, also seems to be that those with rooms overlooking the route should throw water on to the contestants. This makes both the contestants and the cobbles slippery.

That night we lined up – the Badminton Club minus their dinner jackets and a few keen souls in proper running gear. We waited in silence. I kept thinking of William Wilson from the Hornet, barefooted centenarian who appeared from nowhere to beat all the modern, high-fibre, supercarbed, high-tech athletes in the Olympics. I was going to show the nobs. The clock chimed; we sprinted off.

I got to the first bend and then my head struck the head of the person immediately to my right. It wasn't anybody's fault. We were both drunk, and unfortunately alcohol was pulling our bodies in different but converging directions. There were two loud cracks, one as our heads collided and one as my head hit the cobbles. I got up very confused.

I was, however, aware that: (1) I had just been hit on the head with something; (2) my head was sticky; (3) some wet substance was trickling down my new dress shirt; (4) that substance was red; and (5) William Wilson probably didn't drink anyway.

I staggered back to the bar to pick up the badminton trophy which I'd deposited on a window sill for the duration of the race. But, surprise, surprise, it had gone. A typical public school prank. But I was having none of it. One person obviously of upper-class background was smirking. I grasped him by the lapels. 'Where's my fucking cup?' I whispered in his face.

Now I had seen this done a thousand times in Belfast, but I had never tried it myself before. The secret, I understand, was to say it as quietly as possible to make it more threatening. He looked at me in a truly horrified fashion. 'But I don't know,' he replied.

'You fucking lying bastard.' I raised my fist, but then my badminton partner intervened. He had played so many games with me that he could anticipate my every move. I tried getting him off me but thankfully, God in all His wisdom made the upper classes (and I use the term loosely) substantially taller than the lower classes and I failed to push him off. I resorted to the sort of abuse I'd heard outside pubs in Belfast, but he didn't take any notice. I suspect he couldn't make out what I was saying anyway, by this stage, since my accent during the course of the evening had become successively stronger and less decipherable.

I returned to my room that night, bloodied and scarred. I had lost my trophy, my dinner jacket (someone had also pinched that as a prank), my veneer of sophistication, but thankfully not my self-respect. It was obvious to me, even with all that alcohol inside me, that I could never become a fully fledged Trinity man. I could perhaps be a Trinity man in the lecture theatre or on the sports field, but not, unfortunately, in the college bar.

The exams, the competition, the work were within my grasp – the pranks, the laughter, the self-conscious, self-important poses were not. I resorted to violence only because it was a coherent alternative. From cultured Cambridge collegian to boorish Belfast brawler in one short step, but neither persona was really me. I wanted to be somewhere in between, but that was the most difficult position to maintain. It has no internal coherence or consistency. There were no models around, no one to imitate or copy. Or so I thought.

Young men can be amorphous, malleable things. With my secondhand Moss Brothers' dinner jacket (which cost a fiver) and my field colours ties, I almost started to look the part (even if I didn't always act the part) some of the time. But parents are less amorphous and less malleable. They are fixed in old familiar shapes which are obvious to anyone who glimpses them. I always feel for working-class students with their parents visiting them at university – you can see the mixture of emotions in some of their faces – pride and shame in equal measures. The strain visibly shows.

I only had one parent by the time I got to Cambridge, but she visited me with a very close aunt and uncle. Together they form this strange and completely unmanageable triumvirate. If they had felt the slightest hint of shame from me, they would

133

never have forgiven me and I would never have forgiven myself. And yet here I was, trying to acquire an education and assimilate some taste, and trying desperately to escape from my past. And here they were – spectres from my childhood coming to haunt me.

It was July – out of term, at my insistence. The twelfth week. They all wore sunglasses. My uncle made an effort – he wore a suit, but it was a thick woollen suit which had got crumpled on the drive. He looked to all the world like a big Irish farm labourer dressed for the local hop. My aunt was his alter ego and antithesis – small, grey, wizened, with a permanent cough from smoking sixty a day. The cough, once it started, bent her double. And my mother, dressed in her bargain clothes – nylon everywhere – slacks and top – and her hair teased up into a Gina Lollobrigida style circa 1962, but going thin.

I wanted to keep them out of sight and keep them sober. But the plan failed somewhere along the line. My uncle insisted on visiting a pub he had heard about in the east side of Cambridge, a part I had never been to, 'Laudate dei', but then he sank twelve pints quickly (with everyone else sinking the equivalent in whisky or Carlsberg Specials). They then as one insisted that we should go into the centre of Cambridge for lunch. We parked on Sydney Street. My mother kept up, she trotted along beside me, her sunglasses over the edge of her nose. My uncle trailed some distance behind before slumping up against the wall of Heffers Bookshop.

Now Cambridge likes to boast a few eccentric tramps and professors, but the sight of a large Irishman nailed to a wall with drink in the middle of the day turned more than a few heads. His big thick woollen suit was making him sweat. His face was red, his hair tousled. His words were short and to the point. 'Geoffrey, where the bloody hell are we going?' His words made me sweat – my aunt, bent double with her cough, remained at the end of Trinity Street shouting instructions all the way up it. She said she wasn't going to bloody well move until I found a proper place for us to eat. My uncle had lost his sunglasses.

We eventually got to the Whim in Trinity Street, which was a good choice because they sold sausages, which was all my

134

aunt ate. My mother kept her sunglasses on throughout the meal and asked the waitress if she sold Carlsberg Specials. Thankfully, they weren't licensed. My uncle ate his meal in silence before eating my aunt's. I didn't say a word, not even to practice my polite conversation.

As we left, I spotted my college tutor. He looked at me in his usual way and then at my guests. It was just a fleeting glance, but it said everything – contempt and pity intertwined – 'Never aspire, boy,' it screamed in my face. I hung my head. 'Who was that nice man?' my mother said as we walked back to the car. 'Your tutor? Why didn't you introduce us?'

12

The Comfortable Middle Class

Celebrating the twelfth

It was six a.m. Belfast was quiet. I was talking to two young girls in a quiet middle-class suburb of Belfast. They were getting ready for that day's festivities. 'The twelfth'. A stark name for any festivity, but it did its job. Nothing needed to be added. It's hard to think of any ordinal number standing alone like that without elaboration or explanation, from anywhere in the world, with so much symbolic significance. They had been counting down the days to 'the twelfth' for weeks now. They were even singing about it, and the singing had started weeks before as well. 'It's on the twelfth I love to wear the sash my father wore.' And sashes would be worn all over Northern Ireland that day as Ulster remembered good King Billy's defeat of the Catholic King James at the Boyne some three hundred years ago. Even though it seemed more like three weeks ago to some.

But this was also the morning after the night before, the morning after 'the eleventh night'. The singing hadn't stopped.

> 'Oh the Popey had a pimple on his bum
> And it nipped, nipped, nipped so sore
> So he sent for King Billy to rub it with a lily
> And it nipped, nipped, nipped no more.'

'Last night it was wicked,' said Alison.
Joanne, 'but we had to be in bed by eleven
day today.' All over Belfast, as Joanne an
bonfires had been lit, and effigies of all those tr
and folk-demons, who had tried to sell out the Prot
over the past three centuries, had been enthu
burned. There was Lundy, the governor of Londonde
had wanted to open the gates of the city to the Catholic
of King James. 'Up he went! Yoooooooooh,' as the flames
caused his papier mâché head to explode. A few streets away
was the Pope. 'He's a nice wee man,' said one old-age
pensioner almost apologetically. She had her grey hair dyed
black in streaks. 'He's from Poland, you know.' There was a
brief pause in the conversation as the flames licked his papal
robes, which had obviously been made out of some orange
dish cloth. 'But he's very afraid of flying,' said the pensioner,
as the charred remains of his paper head flew off into the
blackened sky. 'Otherwise why would he kiss the ground
every time the plane sets itself down?'

I was about to try to answer this when her companion
intervened. 'It's better him kissing the ground, than the Taigs
kissing his bloody arse, which is the kind of thing you might
expect from them.' I noticed that here was a man of approximately the same age as the old lady, but slightly the worse for
drink. 'Oh Jimmy, for goodness sake. Try to control yourself,'
said his friend. 'Control myself! Control myself! I always
control myself. That's my problem. That's our problem! We
always try to control ourselves. We've let those traitors live in
our midst for too long, far too long. What do you say, lads?'
And this rhetorical question caused that great primeval scream
to be issued again. 'Yoooooooooooh.' The roar banished me to
the next street. There, I witnessed the flames tickle Mrs
Thatcher, that Jezebel, that harlot responsible for the Anglo-
Irish agreement. There she was, complete with peroxide mop,
suddenly engulfed in fire. 'Yooooooooh.' They were roaring
again.

I stood picking out the faces in the flames. Transitory images
as the fire licked and curled. I made some comment about Mrs
Thatcher displacing the Pope and Lundy from the top of the

was not meant to be a provocative comment. 'She sold us out. Sold us down the river,' explained one young man with UVF tattooed on his knuckles. 'She's still better than Kinnock though. You can't trust him. He'd really shop us. If he ever got in, you'd be able to see the bonfires from as far away as Scotland. That's how strongly we feel about him here. And as for Ken Livingstone.' The young man's face contorted. His mouth was compressed into a strange and improbable shape. The sounds came out in a rapid sequence. 'Doo doo doo doo doo.' There was a long pause, as if he was waiting for the full significance of what he had just said to sink in. He looked very pleased with himself, as if he had just said something of great truth and importance. He had only really grunted. I stood there looking very confused. He followed up his very subtle verbal communication with an even more subtle wink. I didn't quite know what was going on.

I had to point out that despite all this multi-channel communication, I still wasn't sure what he was trying to tell me. The young man looked perplexed. He held up his knuckles for me to read. He slowly and deliberately pointed at each letter in turn, as if he was dealing with a very weak pupil, struggling to read this indelible message. I didn't want to tell him that I had read his knuckles already, as he was chucking wood onto the bonfire. His speech was becoming more elliptical, more covert, more partisan. 'The lads . . . the boys . . . the Organisation. You don't need me to spell it out for you, do you?' He started making those sounds again: 'Doo doo doo doo doo.' He was trying to use a slightly faster style of delivery now for this message. Faster and with a higher pitch. Slowly its significance was starting to dawn on me. 'Do you mean – rat a tat tat, rat a tat tat?' He smiled at me, like you might smile at some poor fool who nevertheless had been trying his hardest to follow some difficult lesson. 'You've been reading too many war comics, you have. Haven't you ever heard an automatic weapon in real life? They don't sound like that at all. It's more doo doo doo doo doo. But you've got the basic idea.'

Alison and Joanne had missed all the elliptical communication and veiled threats of the night before. They had been getting ready for the twelfth night in a slightly different way –

they had been busy cleaning their concert flutes the night before, so that they could play their own distinct role in just one of those processions of bands and Orange Lodges that make 'the twelfth' the day that it is. Their band coincidentally has won the Northern Ireland Flute Championship, which may appear a little incongruous to those who hold a very rigid view of the bands that march on this particular day. Alison herself put it very succinctly: 'Basically, we are not a kick-the-pope band. We play things like "Moore Street" and "Flag and Empire", although we also have to be able to perform "The Sash", of course.'

It was seven a.m., and this prize-winning band, which consisted entirely of young girls and older men, was marching up through Whiteabbey to the house of the Master of the Orange Lodge for breakfast. They breakfasted on sausage rolls. Their local Lodge joined them there. The Lodge, unlike the band, had men of different ages – older men like the band members, who seemed to be taking the whole thing very seriously indeed, and younger men who were slightly less serious in their approach. They appeared to be there for 'the crack' as much as anything. 'We always get a lot of banter,' explained Alison, as if anticipating the approach of one youth with a very severe skin complaint. 'Give us a go on your flute, love, and I'll see you later in the field.' 'Just look at Eddie, there, getting himself fixed up already,' was the riposte from his companion – a youth with the same basic skin complaint as his friend. The band moved off slowly, but not slowly enough for some. 'Slow down, Geordie, for goodness sake', came the plea to the band leader from the third flute from the back. 'We're having to trot to keep up with you.' 'You always get this kind of banter,' explained Joanne. 'It's all part of the fun of the day.'

The band with its lodge marched to the local Orange Hall. Band members from six other bands lined the road. Joanne pointed out the subtle distinctions present here: 'I think it is true to say that five of these bands are kick-the-pope bands, one is a more serious flute band like ourselves.' The different bands obviously attracted very different kinds of following. Nearly all the members of one of the kick-the-pope bands were

139

skinheads complete with earrings. I noticed that quite a few of these skinheads had UVF tattooed on their knuckles. This band seemed to attract a considerable female following. 'They're all wee mills,' said Alison, 'millies, you know, girls who are a little bit common. They'll carry the spare sticks for the drummers, spare cymbals and even spare bearskins for the big drum. The drum major for that particular band does tend to get through a few skins on the march. Last year he got so carried away he banged his own stomach. It was very badly bruised. The mills also carry the drink for the band. You'll see that they drink as they're marching. We don't have a following like them. In fact, nobody follows us. But the kick-the-pope bands generally have a lot of respect for us. They just play these little enamel flutes and they think our concert flutes are really rather special.'

It was time to move off. The bands marched for about half a mile before boarding some coaches to take them to Larne. 'There's always plenty of banter on these coaches,' explained Joanne. 'It's all pretty harmless really, but my father is a drummer in the band and he tries to keep an eye on us.' The banter seemed to consist entirely of young men of a certain type asking young ladies of a rather different type for a go on their concert flutes. The coaches got to Larne at about eleven o'clock. There was just time to get an ice cream, before the bands had to form up again at eleven-thirty. The crowds at the sides of the road were now four deep, with the youngest children sitting on the kerb itself waving their Union Jacks. 'This bit always makes me feel really proud,' said Alison, as her band produced another controlled rendition of 'Moore Street'. The next band along in the procession, however, were less controlled, some would have said totally out of control. The band leader was throwing his stick in the air, doing a ninety-degree turn, and still managing to catch it with his hand behind his back. Just. 'There might be a few accidents on the way back from the field, when he has had a bit more to drink,' whispered Joanne. There was something very familiar for both the bands and the audience about the whole thing. 'All right, Millie, what about ye. Long time no see. See ya at the field.'

At the field, a big banner across the entrance read 'Welcome'.

There were a whole series of stalls selling the various para-phernalia of the Protestant cause – Ian Paisley tapes, Union Jacks, and assorted T-shirts with Red Hand of Ulster logos, or 'Ulster Still Says No' written on them. There were also stalls selling cheap watches, as well as numerous chip, burger and ice cream vans. These vans competed for customers with a variety of church committees selling sandwiches. The Lodge lay down its banner, with the big drum just behind the banner. The band and the Lodge had to meet back there at three-thirty. The younger men went off in search of the bar; Alison and Joanne collected their ticket for lunch. 'I think that this bit is mainly for the men,' said Alison. Joanne nodded. What they really meant was that this section of the day's festivities was designed for men who like a drink. Their father George is teetotal, so he set off with three of his friends to buy a round of soft drinks. This may be 'the twelfth' in Ulster, but this is still Ireland, and people take the buying of rounds seriously. So it was soon time for the next round for George and his friends – four ice creams. Then the next – four apples. Then the last round – four more ice cream cornets.

Alison and Joanne sunbathed on the hot afternoon. The air smelt heavy of burgers and beer. Joanne and Alison don't eat burgers and they don't drink beer. Little pockets of individuals played the flute and drums badly now. Drunken Lodge mem-bers weaved their way slowly from bar to burger van and back. Some stopped on the way. 'Don't look behind you Joanne, there's some man going to do a pee. EEEEEK!'

So what is the attraction for two nice middle-class girls from the suburbs of this whole somewhat anachronistic spectacle? I remembered all the veiled threats of the night before. Did they know about them? What has all this marching go to do with anything in the modern world? Surely this celebration, and all celebration like it, was really just an opportunity to express the bigotry of centuries openly, publicly, communally.

It was as if they anticipated my question. 'I feel proud today,' said Joanne. 'I don't really think much about the history side of things. You don't have to think about the history to get a lot out of it. Everybody knows and understands the signifi-cance of today without even having to talk about it.'

'When the band starts up, you just feel something,' said Alison, 'and when you hear the crowds cheering, it's hard not to be deeply affected by the whole thing. We really are very different from most of the other bands marching today, but I suppose that really deep down inside we do have something in common with the other bands and their followers, and that comes out in the music no matter how well or badly it's played.'

I was going to suggest that all they really had in common was 'tired feet', when I spotted my friend with the tattooed knuckles from the night before. He was smiling broadly, or rather grinning broadly. Content, at last. Content and drunk. 'Rat a tat tat,' he said as he walked unsteadily past. 'Doo doo doo doo doo,' I replied.

'What was that all about?' asked Alison. 'Oh, men's talk,' I said, 'just men's talk.'

Writing condolence cards

She sat alone in this big detached house off the Antrim Road in Belfast, staring at the blank sheet. When she was young, they called her Goldilocks, it's not hard to see why. Slowly the lines started to build: 'Of all the little memories . . . I treasure in my mind . . . the ones we've shared together . . . are the very special kind.' Not bad, she thought, not bad. She could tell that she was in the mood. Today, she was most definitely in the mood. She never stops when it's going this well. 'You're always there to guide me . . . and lend a helping hand . . . whenever I've a problem . . . I know you'll understand.'

Jackie always wanted to be a writer. She also wanted to stay indoors in Belfast, so there she sat composing verses for greetings cards. She gets one pound a line for these verses – it can be quite lucrative, one day she managed to write 324 lines. 'But,' she said, 'I was exhausted for days after that.' Some days she doesn't manage to write any lines. Valentine's cards, greetings cards, sympathy cards – she said that she was particularly good at cards of condolence.

> May the Lord gently rock you
> in his everlasting arms

and the shadow of his mighty wings
protect you from all harms

She sold that one, but sometimes she's not so fortunate.

God is always near you
when he calls his loved ones home
He's there to guide and comfort us
so please don't feel alone

This last one was rejected. Jackie herself could see why it was not entirely suitable. 'The problem,' she said, 'is that God seems to be walking with the person that's dead, he's not there to comfort the ones left behind, and they were the ones that I was trying to comfort in the verse. Some days you can produce loads of verses that nobody will buy.'

Jackie was desperate to become a full-time writer. 'This is something you can do from your own house,' she explains. She started in a big way by going straight for *the* novel; it was a novel about two psychic sisters. She sent it to several publishers but it was rejected by all of them. Then it was time for her short-story phase; she wrote thirteen in all, it took her a day to do each one. 'I wanted to see what was going to happen to the characters that I had created – that's why I did them so quickly.' None was accepted. One magazine suggested that she should consult the *Writers' and Artists' Yearbook*. This was her salvation. It mentioned verse writing. So here she sits, verse after verse, at a pound a line.

She said that she liked writing verses because it meant that she could do it all from her front room. She stressed this a lot. When she was in the mood, it was very easy. 'Sometimes when I get drunk, the verses just pour out. In fact, sometimes I find it impossible to stop rhyming. If someone says something to me, I reply in verse and it just goes on and on.' Sometimes it was not so easy. She said that she didn't go out very often. 'Sometimes, you just have to sit and work at it, and some days the lines just won't come.'

She was twenty-five, and lived with her parents. When she was twenty-one she worked as a secretary for her father in his factory on the Ormeau Road. One day two men arrived, dressed in mechanics' overalls, and wearing balaclavas and carrying machine guns. She remembered that day very well. She and her sister were talking about a wedding at the exact time the two men barged in. She said that she remembered thinking that it was her brother dressed up, playing a practical joke. 'He was always fond of jokes,' she said. The men said that they wanted into the safe. The Ormeau Road is a predominantly Catholic area, but theirs was a Protestant firm. It was almost certainly a paramilitary robbery – the work of the IRA. 'I thought that they were going to murder us. My father was out at the time. I remember thinking that I hope that he doesn't come back, while they're here, or he'll get it too,' she said calmly.

One of the robbers walked into their large safe. Her sister was asked to get the money out of her handbag from beside the safe. Her sister nudged the door of the safe by accident, and managed to lock one of the robbers in the safe. 'I thought that they'd definitely shoot us for that,' she said. One of the men held a Stewart's carrier bag open for them to put the money in. Jackie said that all she could think of at the time was, 'How cheap, they're taking all our personal belongings and putting them into an old tatty carrier bag.' She said that she refused to put her purse into the bag. 'My driving licence was in there, with my address on it. I didn't want them coming round to our house and murdering my mother,' she explained.

The robber apparently hesitated. 'Well, just put your money in the carrier bag instead,' he said. The only money in her purse was a collection of two-pence coins. Her sister, in the meantime, was trying to give them everything, including the typewriter, and any other office equipment that happened to be lying about the place. Her sister was hysterical. Jackie said that she was in slow motion and the images have stayed with her. She can still play it back now, and watch it all unfold right in front of her.

She said that she didn't want to go back out to work in Belfast after that. She thought Belfast was just too dangerous a city to work in. She also reckoned that the robbery produced a complete personality change in her. Before the robbery, she was confident and an extrovert; after the robbery she was very different. She hasn't driven a car since the hold-up. On one occasion after the robbery, she applied for a job as a typist, but she got so anxious the night before, she was up all night worrying about it. She was supposed to be there at nine o'clock but rang in just beforehand to say she couldn't make it. She was depressed afterwards for three days. She applied to the Northern Ireland Office for compensation for the psychological effects of the robbery on her, and eventually she was awarded £1,500, which she says is the very minimum. 'It's not an obvious injury, like losing a limb or something, so I can understand why the compensation was so low, but the psychological effects of something like that can be more enduring. I'm just very anxious all the time, basically.'

So she retreated into the big house on the Antrim Road, and opted for the solitude and safety of writing. Her latest effort is a play called *Y-fronts and Petticoats*, which she sent to Ulster Television. She hasn't had any reply yet.

In the meantime she was sticking to her tried and tested formula of verse writing. 'It's quite easy really,' she said. 'There's a knack to it. For example, when you do a twenty-first birthday card, you wish the day first – "Hope your day is delightful" – then you wish the year – "and this year is just the start/ of finding all those special things/ you wish for in your heart" – and then the future – "May the future hold good fortune/ in everything you do/ and that's exactly what is wished for/ with lots of love for you."'

'It's a formula, you see, but sometimes you can find a great deal of comfort in sticking to a formula.'

The king of ladies' tights

We sat in a restaurant with great slabs of rare steak covering our plates. The steak was so large that you could discern the profile of the cow from which it had come. 'Great value for money in this restaurant, fantastic helpings,' said Tom. 'Give my compliments to Peter, the chef. I'm a regular at this joint, you see.' The potatoes rose in great mountains to the side of my plate. 'Would you like me to try to squeeze a few more on?' asked the waitress. This was Ulster cuisine at its finest, and Ulster hospitality at its most pronounced. 'Och, where would you put them? We've hardly room for anything else on our plates. We could hardly squeeze a wee pea on . . . Go on then. You've forced us.'

Tom and his wife Kathleen are regulars at this restaurant just below Napoleon in repose, and the zoo. Tom sported a dapper little moustache, and he had that confident air of the successful businessman. 'Put it this way. I've done all right, if you get my meaning.' He winked. A Jaguar XJ6 stood gleaming outside just behind the stubs of pillars in mottled concrete, artistically arranged to deter the bomber. 'I've always loved Jags – plenty of style, plenty of comfort, nice and roomy.' A status symbol for the Antrim Road, but he did not need to say it. A status symbol for the golf course. 'I play a bit of golf,' he added almost unnecessarily. 'All nineteen holes.' He winked again. Tom, you might say, has a zest for life. They still talk about his parties and his largesse. All of his staff were treated to Dickie Rock, the king of the Irish showband scene at Christmas. And the bar bill the night of one of his sons' weddings? That is the stuff of legend. And excess. 'Ulster people do tend to be very generous,' said Tom, almost apologetically.

'I'm in business. At this moment in time, I'm classed as a draper, I suppose. My business consists of mostly women's and children's wear. I've got eight shops right across the Province: Antrim, Craigavon, Ballymena, Rathcoole, Glengormley, and three based in Belfast – two on the main Shankill Road.'

Tom's shops – Kay's Corner, named after his wife Kathleen – consist of a chain of budget shops in the city, catering, in his words, 'for the masses'. The masses in Belfast are subject to religious and political division, this we all know, but the degree of division and segregation goes somewhat beyond religion and politics. It affects ordinary daily life to a large degree and, with it, commercial organisation and shopping habits. Tom Pierce knows all about that – his first shop was just off the Shankill, and as the song goes, 'If your name is Timothy or Pat . . . you'll never get up the Shankill with a Fenian name like

146

that' (sung to the tune of 'If you're Irish, Come into the Parlour'). This song pre-dates the Troubles by some considerable time.

Tom opened his first shop in Agnes Street just off the Shankill in 1969 just 'when things were hotting up, just when the present Troubles were starting. I was a printer in those days,' he said. 'I bought a little shop just off Agnes Street in 1969, from a jeweller. He couldn't get any insurance for his jewellery business any longer – he'd been robbed so many times. In fact, he had been robbed so often that he had to vacate the Shankill. This was nothing to do with the Troubles. This was just ordinary people trying to get money for nothing, which happens in any town in the country. But it was mostly youngish people who were doing the robbing. He knew that. It's a very localised people, you see. It's community in and of themselves. I presume that the Falls is likewise. He couldn't get insurance for his jewellery business. Every time that they took two or three hundred pounds of his gear, he was at a loss so he virtually just had to pack up and go.'

'The insurance on the Shankill was so prohibitive that most people didn't bother with it anyway. We never had any insurance on our shop. You just couldn't afford it. What you had to do was put up the best alarm system that was available to you and take your chances with the rest. Being a printer I hadn't any money anyway – I was earning twelve pounds a week and my mortgage was six pounds and fifteen shillings. I set up the business by buying stock with two hundred pounds borrowed from the bank, to build a garage is what I told them, and two hundred pounds borrowed from a friend. He told me not to pay him back until I could afford it – he waited two years for the money in the end.'

'Our first shop was very small. You couldn't have got more than three or four people in at a time. The rent was a pound and ten shillings a week. We sold mostly tights in those days, a whole selection of ladies' tights, nearly fifty brands in all. I was the King of Ladies' Tights. In those days we had a broader selection of the community in the shop. You would have had some people from the Falls in those days – the odd Seamus or Sean – which you couldn't get now. But most were locals of

147

course. My wife and sister worked in the shop – they knew all the locals and the locals knew them. I was still continuing then as a printer. So this was my first wee business and it lost money.'

He stabbed at his steak. 'Business is a tricky little game, you know. You shouldn't underestimate it.' Some blood ran across the plate. 'There's a lot of cut and thrust in business.'

'After about a year I got a shop on the Shankill Road itself. It was about a quarter of a mile from the first shop. Shankill Road people would have run past the shop in Agnes Street without looking in. I have a theory about this. People like to be where other people are. At least, that's what I've found. So the Shankill Road could have been heaving on a Saturday, and I would have done no trade on Agnes Street. When I first got the new shop I was in painting the ceiling for a couple of days and I took more money than they did in the Agnes Street shop during the same period. I took sixteen pounds one morning when I was painting the new shop, my wife Kathleen had only lifted about six pounds in that time. That was the difference in the two places. You had to be on the Shankill Road itself, there was no point in operating from one of those wee side streets. You had to be actually on the road.'

'The new shop on the Shankill itself did a roaring trade. It was a pleasant time on the Shankill then – the Troubles were just starting. The people of the Shankill were quite friendly. There was a mix of both communities in the shop. The road wasn't as good as it had been in the fifties though. In the fifties the Shankill was at its height – the Falls was such a poor shopping area in comparison. So naturally on a Saturday they'd all come across to shop on the Shankill from the Falls. On the eleventh night, the shops wouldn't close till midnight on the Shankill. They'd have their tea and open again. But that was before my time there.'

'That first Christmas in 1969 though, I was going to stock up my shop from the local wholesalers. I was carrying the cash on me. Another trader from across the way had said to me that it was very dangerous to be carrying all this cash around with me. He told me to hide it in the boot of my car, which I did, along with a chicken if I remember. When I got home, the

148

money was gone – something in the region of four hundred and fifty pounds. The police reckoned that it was just somebody trying my boot on the off-chance. But this happened in seconds, while I went into the shop to lock up. It could have wiped me out completely.'

'I was never going to find out who took the money. It was a proper community on the Shankill in them days. They protected their own. If boys stole out of my shop the local population would step in to protect them. I was an outsider – from Glengormley, travelling in each day. It didn't take them long to find out which foot I kicked with though. I knew one other chap who ran a shop and he had a Catholic wife – they managed to find that out very quickly indeed. How, I don't know. Everybody likes their own kind, basically. I was the right religion, of course, so things weren't that bad. There were, by the way, some Catholic-owned shops on the Shankill at that time – the last one closed in 1972. It was a wee ice-cream shop owned by an Italian – just opposite mine. He was shot – by his own side, would you believe. He was taking his granddaughter to school when he was hit by a stray bullet. His wife continued on with the shop for a short time after his death before she packed it in.'

'After a couple of years I decided to expand, so I opened another shop on the Newtownards Road this time. I fancied a change of venue. The Newtownards Road is a lot like the Shankill – working-class and Protestant. I wouldn't have moved into a Catholic district. My pedigree was better now – I was known as a Shankill trader. I sold goods at the cheaper end of the market – I undercut the other budget shops, I was dealing in clothes for the masses. I sold a lot of baby-wear and women's fashion wear. The shop on the Newtownards Road did fifty per cent less trade. I was never asked for protection money by the Organisation for any of my shops. Occasionally you'd be asked to contribute to the Loyalist Prisoners' Association collection at Christmas time, just for a party for old people or something like that. But never protection money. The problem of course in running a business on the Shankill is that if you ever sold it, word would quickly get out that someone had put the finger on you and forced you to leave

149

the road. People would say you'd been intimidated. I couldn't really sell up and move to another location – I was forced to expand,' he said with a laugh. 'The Troubles made me expand. They made me a success.

'There was a ready market for the goods I was selling. Belfast was now set in the Troubles – people didn't want to move too far from their homes to shop. There weren't any Seamuses or Seans in the shop now. I expanded again and got a shop on the Woodstock Road. I had a bigger outlet now, so I was starting to travel to Manchester to buy the goods wholesale. I was cutting out the local wholesaler who had a mark-up of between twenty and thirty per cent. I bought the goods from these cash-and-carry jobs run by the coloured fellas in Manchester – the kinds of places that used to be run by Jews. They could get the goods cheap because it was their aunts and brothers who were producing them. I always found the coloureds to be very partial to a bit of cash and I found the Pakistanis and Indians to be very trustworthy. I'd go across in a small van and fill it up with stuff. I'd perhaps carry a thousand pounds in cash on me. I never had any insurance. I was a born risk-taker. Other traders in the meantime had caught on to the fact that there was a fair turnover in tights. I was no longer the leader in the ladies' tights market, so I got more and more into baby-wear, the shops were small, you see. Always the cheaper end of the market – the gear would come from Sri Lanka and the Philippines.

'I expanded again. I got a second shop on the Shankill. This time I bought the property. My first shop was on the lower end near Aberdeen Street, the second was on the upper end. I found that people from the lower end of the Shankill hardly ever went up the road and vice versa. Villages within villages. There were two distinct markets. I also opened a ladies' fashion shop next to the Bayardo Bar on the Shankill. The premises had been a Wilton's Funeral Parlour. The Bayardo was frequented by the paramilitaries. There was no problem living next door to it, although unfortunately a man got shot just outside it. The Bayardo also got bombed – by whom or for what I don't know. It was at night luckily so no one got hurt, but it cracked the walls of my fashion shop.

150

'The men from the council assured me the walls were perfectly safe. But one day, when the girls were serving, the walls collapsed. Thankfully they fell outwards. It could have been much worse – they could have fallen in. The council secured the place, but not well enough. The shop was looted, I still wasn't insured. The Northern Ireland Office assessors arrived and I was allowed to sell off damaged stock. I got five thousand pounds for the damage to my stock, two thousand pounds as an interim award within four months and the rest within two years. You always have to wait for the compensation.'

'I had to consolidate now. Some drapers never make any money until they retire – all their money is in their stock. This wasn't my philosophy. I was in the business of quick turnover. I was in what I like to call the grocery end of the drapery trade – the demand end of the business. Grocers, as far as I understand it, try to turn their stock over every eight weeks. The average draper turns his stock three times a year. I endeavoured to turn my stock over every eight weeks. If a garment didn't sell, I slashed the price and sold it. In the communities I was working in, if you don't sell cheap, you don't sell. I had to trade across the water – to bring in goods at competitive prices.

'But I now went into partnership with a wholesaler who was also a friend. We opened P & W Supplies in Rathcoole, a Protestant area. My partner was more conservative than I was and this shop was insured to the hilt. Then with the same friend we entered the big league and bought a shop in the first shopping centre in Antrim. That was in 1981. It cost twenty grand to fit the shop out. I had to borrow from the bank to buy it. My philosophy has always been that you should borrow plenty and use as little as possible and keep the rest for emergencies. In Ulster there are usually plenty of those.

'Now I was in the bigger league my pattern of buying was different. I used to buy little and often – now I bought everything in bulk, in cartons. I could afford a few mistakes. In 1969 I'd go to a wholesaler's with a hundred quid, now I'd spend twenty grand at a time on buying from the coloureds in Manchester. I like to say "I've made more from the coloured gent than from the white gent." Coloured wholesalers will work on smaller profit margins than whites – that's why I go to them.

'We expanded again, to a new shopping centre in Ballymena. Twenty grand for fittings, fifteen grand rent, nine grand rates, six grand service charge, twelve grand wages. The premier league. But in my view, we weren't buying in enough stock to make money. My partner was very conservative – too conservative – he was always looking at the bank balance. The shop was understocked so we were missing opportunities to buy goods to sell. In Ballymena we needed a turnover of between two thousand pounds and two thousand eight hundred pounds a week to make money. We didn't have the stock for that – we were losing money.

'I went into business next with my son and a Mr McGeown. He had previously owned the Woodstock shop that I'd acquired. He was a Catholic, he had shops in Andersonstown and Ardoyne – the Catholic heartlands. We set up a company called Pricewise. At one stage Pricewise had thirty-one shops and a turnover of five million pounds. But this time I was the conservative one – they were building up too much stock. It frightened the living daylights out of me. Perhaps it was too strong a meat for me. It's all a question of balance. Too far in one direction and bang! I withdrew with five shops of my own and a third of the Pricewise empire.

'My philosophy in my shops is that I give a good-value product and I always employ locals. Belfast is really a collection of villages. Everybody knows everybody else. Your customers may come in for more of a yarn than to spend money but there's a good community spirit. To sell goods the secret is to get a woman to handle the merchandise. When she's handled it you're halfway to selling it. If you keep your stock in cellophane bags it stays cleaner but it doesn't sell so easily. I'm just like a grocer: I get the customers to handle the fruit, then they buy it. I feel I'm offering a good service to the public. There's no real problem about being in a partnership with a Catholic. He has his own problems. He has to cope with his own paramilitaries. He doesn't pay protection either, but he does give the odd tenner for the old people at Christmas to collectors, just like me.

152

'Funnily enough, I've never been to his Andersonstown shop. Mr McGeown used to come to my shop on the Shankill but I got a bit worried about this recently and advised him against it. People got to know him. There's a lot of tit-for-tat killing in this town. I was worried for his safety. We provide a good service to the public, but the yahoos on either side don't seem to care much about that. You have to keep a low profile and just be that extra bit careful. All the time you're watching and waiting. But if you're half sensible you can run a very successful business in this town.'

Now the Pavlova had arrived. Huge wedges lolling over the sides of the dishes. 'I'm off to the races in Dublin at the weekend in the Jag. This is a great wee country we're living in, if only people would stop killing each other. There are too many yahoos on both sides who want to spoil it for the rest of us.'

I nodded eagerly as the brandies arrived.

13

Little Palaces

Soaking it up

'Excuse me, love,' said the old lady in the black and white dress. She was nudging the shop assistant in the back. I couldn't help noticing that this old lady, in her late sixties, must dye her hair black. I was quite shocked – not by the hair, more by the noise. It was the kind of shop where everyone speaks in hushed tones, and this voice was far too loud. And then there was the accent on top of that. You've heard that voice on the news a thousand times. A strangely familiar voice, but nobody famous. Certainly nobody famous. But straight from the news summaries nonetheless – the old crow by the side of the road, the bystander, the victim.

I had a good chance to study her there in that posh shop, but the shop assistant stubbornly refused to even look around. 'Excuse me.' It was louder this time, louder and more insistent, irritating even. She was nudging the shop assistant now in the small of the back. The shop assistant made a forty-five degree turn. I could see the assistant's face for the first time – she looked irritated and bored simultaneously. 'How much is this nice bathroom set here?' said the old lady. The shop assistant picked the set up and made a great show of turning the price tag, the very visible price tag, around for everyone to see. This was a moment of great dramatic tension – the movement preceded any speech. 'It's nine ninety-five, madam, it says so on the label, if madam would just care to read it. Did you wish to purchase it?' She spoke with an exaggerated accent, a telephone voice, an accent that can only be maintained for a few sentences. In Belfast, they are as fond of the telephone voice as anywhere else. 'Does madam wish to purchase it?'

There was a barely visible shake of the head from the old lady. The shop assistant made a great show of replacing the bathroom set with considerable deliberation. She did it by turning her back on the old lady. But the old lady was not that easily discouraged. 'I've got the loveliest wee bathroom in my new house, you know. It's gorgeous.'

She began to tell the shop assistant all about her bathroom at home, all about its colours, its patterns, even its layout, and why this particular set at nine pounds ninety-five might not *quite* be suitable. The old lady said the one word 'quite' in something approaching a telephone voice. The shop assistant sighed audibly several times.

I followed the old lady out of the shop. I asked her what she hadn't liked about the bathroom set. 'It was lovely, but they're only five ninety-five in this other wee shop I've found,' she explained. 'I'm doing up my bathroom at the moment. It's all in beige, you know. I've got a brown and beige carpet, brown and beige towels, now I'm going to have a beige bathroom set.' I had heard all of this once already, of course. Even I knew about her bathroom's colours and layout. But I was still intrigued.

'Have you had the bathroom long?' I asked. 'Funny you should ask,' she replied. It was the opening she required.

Elizabeth, it turned out, had got her bathroom seven years ago in that great slum clearance of West and North Belfast. But the novelty certainly had not worn off. Before this time, she made do with a zinc bath that was hung on the yard wall. The bath had leaked for three years before it was dumped. After the zinc bath, she stood in a basin and washed herself from a tap in the kitchen of her terraced house. 'I didn't have to do this for too long, because it wasn't that long before my sister's house got converted – got a bathroom put in that is, it was probably about four years ago. After her house got converted, I used to go to my sister's once a week for a bath. It's hard to explain how nice it was.'

155

But this experience had made her yearn for even more novel and more intense experiences: 'You know, I'd love a shower,' she said and then explained how she liked to visit the posh shops in Belfast and elsewhere checking the prices of shower attachments. 'But too dear for me,' she said. 'But there's nothing like a shower.' It turned out that Elizabeth had only experienced this sensation four times in her sixty-eight years, at the house near Dublin of the daughter of a friend.

Elizabeth uses her bath once a week. 'It's just habit, I suppose. When I was young, I used to go to the public baths once a week. Everybody did. My husband, who died twenty-three years ago, used to go to Falls Road baths. I thought that he meant the swimming baths, and it wasn't until we went away on holiday that I realised that he couldn't swim. It was the public baths he was talking about. Then when I used the zinc bath, it was once a week. The problem with the zinc bath was that you would have to have the bath in the front room. There was always the danger that someone would walk in on you, right in the middle of it. Of course, in the street where I lived you liked to keep the front door open, when you were in – it was a friendly street – before the Troubles. The bread man or the insurance man would just knock on the door and walk straight in. One night the bread man walked in while I was bathing my feet in the bath, just sitting in my underskirt. It could have been much worse, of course.' We both laughed.

Elizabeth moved into her new house with the bathroom seven years ago. She was still as proud as punch. 'I'd lived in the same house in Belfast for sixty-one years. It was cheap enough, the rent was still only a pound a week in 1982, before they were sold to the Housing Executive. The Housing Executive had them for eight years before they pulled them down. I was the last one in my street, all the houses were coming down. I was waiting for my house to be finished on the front of the road. On Saturday, all the houses in the next street were pulled down. There were a lot of rats about the place. I was moving in June, and I've always liked to sunbathe. I used to sit out in my backyard, but I only ever looked up, not down – I was too frightened of what I might see. On the Saturday night, there was no gas or electricity in the house. The RUC arrived, and I was just sitting there crying. The RUC contacted the Housing Executive for me, and they sent this electrician up, and he put all these new light fittings up for me, but the lights still wouldn't work. On the Sunday, I met this Clerk of Works from the Housing Executive at church, and he arranged to have me sent a gas cooker and a bottle of gas. It meant that I could have a Sunday dinner.

'The workmen helped me move from the old house. They told me that there wasn't much point in bringing the carpet from my old house, or most of my clothes. Everything was too damp, everything had mould all over it. It was a very damp old house. I left a lot in the old house, including a sewing machine, which I didn't mean to leave. I had to get out in such a hurry in the end. After sixty-one years, it was such a last minute rush. I'd been born in that house, but I never looked back when I left, not once.

'When I got to the new house, I went straight to the bathroom. I bought a new flannel and a sponge. A friend bought me a brand new back scrubber. I had some fancy Yardley soap and talcum powder that one of my sisters had bought me for Christmas a few years ago. I'd been keeping it for the new house. The only problem was that it had been sitting getting damp in the old house. I didn't want to unwrap it until I got a bathroom of my own. By the time, I got the packet open, I realised that the talcum power was damp right through. But I've still got it sitting out, even if it is a funny greeny-blue colour. It's an expensive make, you see – only the best for my little palace. It's lovely and warm in my new bathroom, there's a radiator in it. I love to sit in my new bath and think about all the good times that I've had.'

No matter what

My father was from the Shankill, and my mother never let us forget it. He wasn't an Orangeman, and he wasn't a bigot, and he didn't hate Catholics. But she was proud of his Shankill roots, even if she did only mention them by way of a joke.

He need not have been a Shankill Road man, he grew up on Upper Charleville Street just off Snugville Street, which ran from the Shankill to the Crumlin. He could have been a Crumlin Road man, if such a thing existed. But it didn't and he wasn't. 'He was secretly very proud of his background,' she says. 'He didn't boast about it, but then again he didn't have to.'

The Shankill was the loyalist backbone of Ulster. Staunch, God-fearing, true blue. For God and Ulster. But oh so negative. Action only through reaction for most of the time. 'Not an inch.' 'No surrender'. 'Ulster says no.' The gable walls were always spouting out words like 'no', 'never', 'not', 'nowhere'. Nothing was more negative. But when the Troubles were raging, I never felt safe until I passed Unity Flats and got onto that long winding road home.

But that was then. Now the Shankill has been decimated. Some say deliberately. 'If you want to destroy Ulster, you start with the Shankill,' said one loyalist, 'that makes perfect sense. The loyalist people of Ulster are going to be sold down the river. They knew we'd fight to maintain our heritage, so they started attacking the very heart of Protestantism – the Road itself.' 'It's not what it was,' said my mother, 'let's face it.'

The Greater Shankill Development Agency has been set up to do something about the decline. Its brief is to set about regenerating the area. As one of its employees, Jackie Redpath, explained to me: 'Twenty years of so-called redevelopment have radically altered the community of the Shankill. Many of the social problems that are now being seen in the area go back to that redevelopment, which was extremely traumatic for the community. The redevelopment did more damage to the Shankill than the Troubles ever could have done. The Troubles were just a series of incidents in effect – they impinged on life in the Province but then they went away again. Redevelopment was here twenty-four hours a day. Redevelopment took away the band halls, the boxing clubs, the shops. It attacked the very fabric of the community on the Shankill by destroying the support systems which allowed the people to live through poverty. The bulldozers also wiped away street after street. The new building programme couldn't keep pace with the devastation. For example, between 1973 and 1977, four thousand houses were demolished in this area and only two hundred and thirty-nine houses were built. The people of the

Shankill were rehoused in Glencairn, Springmartin, Ballyduff, Rathcoole, even Antrim. They were shunted away to a life where there was no social structure. There were better houses in these far away places, but there was no life. Or no life that they would recognise.'

Jackie himself is a product of the Shankill. Tenacious and determined, a wee man somewhat wary. He eyed me suspiciously, when I went to visit him at his office in the centre of the road itself. 'You've been away from Belfast for a very long time,' he said, 'you can get out of touch very easily when you go across the water. It's easy to lose your roots.'

I wanted him to articulate my roots to me. I felt my roots, now I wanted somebody to explain them to me. They say that Ulster and Ireland and the struggle is all rooted in the past. So what was there back there in the mists of time which made the Shankill what it was, and me, the son of a Shankill Road Hero, what I was? Was there, in fact, anything distinctive about any of it?

'There are ways in which the Shankill is typical of any working-class community, to be honest, but there are also ways in which it is quite distinctive. It is distinctive, because of a whole series of events from both outside and inside. If you had to identify one primary influence on the Shankill, then I would say that it's a community shaped by a history of struggle. The Shankill in one form or another has been around for a very long time. It was the route from County Down to County Antrim. Legend has it that St Patrick went up the Shankill from Downpatrick to Slemish. Shankill comes from Sean Cill meaning Old Church in Gaelic, and it is said that the first church in Belfast was founded on the Shankill by St Patrick himself. The Shankill Graveyard is, they say, Druid in origin. The Shankill is referred to in papal documents down the centuries. The Shankill has been around for a very long time.

'But some of this is going back to mythology. One hundred and forty years ago, our ancestors were driven into this area through poverty to take up jobs in the mills. They came to Belfast in search of work and shelter. The same thing happened with the Falls as well. The Falls was populated with Catholics because that was the route to the west of the Province – the

Catholic parts. But it was the same in both cases – the mill owners wanted the workers right beside them, so that they could start at six in the morning. The conditions that these workers came from were incredible, the conditions they came to were incredible. These people lived in hovels, a third of all children died before their second birthday. The Shankill developed out of that to be the industrial heart of Belfast, one of the premier cities of Europe in industrial terms. It was a remarkable success story – the way that the people turned the hovels into wee palaces held together by paint. Hard work made the place the great centre it was. Our forebears worked their way out of poverty. They transformed the place through their effort. They made their wee palaces for themselves.

'The other strand in the history of the Shankill is, of course, loyalism. It was probably to do with its proximity to the Falls. This led to more sectarian incidents over the years. It probably sharpened the concept of loyalism on the Shankill. East Belfast is Protestant but in East Belfast the sectarianism just isn't as fierce. The Shankill has always been surrounded. Over the years the image began to crystallise. Home Rule and the Somme were very formative influences in the history of the Shankill. The 36th Ulster Division was virtually annihilated at the Battle of the Somme. Every family from the Shankill was affected by it. This gave the Shankill a great sense of serving one's country, but also a great sensitivity to being betrayed. Those soldiers were betrayed at the Somme. In retrospect it's not clear whether that battle was even necessary, or what the generals were hoping to achieve by sacrificing so many young men. The life blood of the Shankill was spilled at the Somme – for what?

'The next great period of struggle was in the thirties with the hunger riots where the people of the Shankill and Falls fought side by side. But that didn't last. Along came the Second World War, and another call to arms. The Shankill responded again magnificently. And when the blitz came, if anywhere in Northern Ireland was going to be hit, it was going to be the Shankill. Belfast was left defenceless because it was reckoned that the German bombers wouldn't be able to penetrate this far. So again, you find this great duty to one's country coupled with a feeling of betrayal – this sense of being left to fend for yourselves – when the chips are down.

'But the redevelopment of the Shankill is the greatest challenge this community has ever faced. It left only thirty per cent of the people still in the area for a start. The rest were shipped away – sometimes back where they came from – back to the country. There was some grand economic plan behind the whole thing. The idea was that you create new towns like Craigavon, in green field sites, then you construct major road links – the M1 for Antrim, the M2 for Craigavon. The Shankill, the Crumlin and the Falls were now to be seen as radial roads – access roads – nothing more. Oh yes, and you also need some flats to be built to block the noise – noise barrier flats – the Weetabix flats that they started to put up. The plan for the Shankill was to have a district centre for leisure and a district centre for shopping connected by some footbridge so that you need never set foot on the good old Shankill Road ever again. The plan was to get rid of all the shops on the road. That, at least, was the planner's dream. A whole new way of life was envisaged, with 1.5 car parking spaces per family. 1.5 mind you. It was all pie in the sky. It was never going to work from the beginning.

'Twenty-five per cent of this plan was actually implemented, but then in the 1980s the government started to pull back. The whole thing was proving too costly. It just wasn't realistic. The area was just left, and to be honest it's a right mess. So this is what you find today. Those young people with any initiative leave. On one estate on the Lower Shankill there is sixty per cent unemployment, fifty per cent of the incomes on the Lower Shankill are £60 or less per week. In terms of all of the conventional indices of social deprivation, of the six worse wards in Belfast, four are in the Greater Shankill area. And the Protestants are meant to be the ones with all the money in Northern Ireland. The Catholics are meant to be the ones suffering social deprivation. There's an ageing population on this road struggling to get by in the face of unemployment, deprivation, the Troubles and an area that was started to be redeveloped and then left.

'Of course, no matter where you go in the world, people will

161

have heard of the Shankill. It's like the Falls – world famous. Mention loyalism, or the Orange Order, or the UDA strike which brought the Province to its knees and where do people think of? It certainly is loyalism that has made the name of this place, but what made its people was the struggle against poverty. Poverty has made and modelled this community. The people of this community are used to pulling together to survive and they will now. No matter what. Do you understand that? No matter what.'

I left that grey concrete slab of a building where the Shankill Development Agency is housed, thinking not just about what Jackie Redpath had said, but how he had said it. His were the politics of conviction. These were my roots which he confronted me with. Not St Patrick coming down off Slemish driving the snakes before him, but the mill workers at the dawn, in the grim grey, smoky half-light of a Belfast morning, half remembering golden mornings somewhere in the Glens of Antrim from those far off days of their childhood, or their parents' childhood. Told and retold, as they counted their blessings with their promise of prosperity. Just round the corner. When you're prepared to work, that is, the way all Prods do.

A child had taunted me that morning, 'What's always in front of you, but you cannot see it? The future.' The future had driven them here, and here they now were. Abandoned. Fighting to get back to the time when there was something, even something intangible, still in front of them.

The wall at the corner of the street was unsullied and unmarked. It cried out for some familiar message. Not an inch, No surrender, Ulster says no. That which you cannot see.

I understood the syntax of desperation, so I got out my chalk and scrawled 'No matter what' in letters a yard tall. Visible from the concrete bunker of the Shankill Development Agency, and visible from the street corner where the hard men passed their day, with only their noses in front of them.

The backroom

There was a front room and a backroom. This was the backroom. It overlooked the yard. I was seven years old before I managed to climb over the yard wall for the first time. My older brother taught me how to do it. You had to open the toilet door until it was level with Donaghy's wall. Then you put your left foot on the top of the middle panel in the door, then your right foot in this little cleft in the middle of Donaghy's wall then you swung your left leg onto the corrugated iron roof. It was always slippy, especially in winter, so you had to scramble along the roof, using both your hands and your feet. The motion always looked a little frenzied.

But it was worth it. You could see right into Ella Gordon's yard, and the Donaghys' yard from up there. Yards were private. There was no back door onto the entry. You carried your bin out through the front room. It was a sign of maturity when you could carry the full bin outstretched in front of you, out through the front room without hitting the furniture. I liked sitting on the yard wall. It was the only glimpse of those other yards that you ever had.

The yards of Limepark Street backed onto ours. My mother always told us that young girls lived in the house directly opposite ours. She used to tell us that they had 'a quare view'. In winter instead of running to the toilet my brother and I would sometimes piss in this great gleaming, golden arc out onto the frosty paving stones. According to my mother these young girls of indeterminate number and age would watch diligently as we did this. I never saw them, and it didn't stop me melting the slugs with my scalding piss.

The backroom had a dresser, a chest of drawers and a bed with three legs. The other leg had buckled at some time in the past. It was still there, according to my mother, it just needed fixing. My brother said that if it was somewhere in that dark hole below the bed, then it was beyond repair. It was all right for him, I had to sleep in that dip. You had to try to level yourself with your shoulder until sleep came. The bed was always damp.

We had a paraffin stove. We called it 'the heater'. We used to buy the paraffin out the back of the Post Office. The stove gave off fumes, but I loved that smell. It was always warm and inviting. But the fumes quickly gave you a headache. One of my mother's 'friends' had given me this little yellow table which I would carry around with me. The friend also gave me a set of *The Modern Encyclopaedia Illustrated*, Volumes 1–8 in a nice wooden stand. My brother Bill said that this man was trying to buy my affection. But the table was dead handy. The sides were adjustable so you could sit on the bed and do your 'eccers'.

It is the first time that I have ever tried to write this word. Looking at it now, I can only assume that it is some derivative of 'exercises'. I had never thought about it before. I had a lot of exercises at night. Hours of exercises in that fuggy damp room. The Encyclopaedias weren't that useful, although I did learn about Aachen, Aalborg and A-arc, before I realised that this was no knowledge at all.

My granny had died in that room. She lived there with my Aunt Agnes before Agnes was married. Bill and I lived in the front room with my mother and father. That room was even damper than the backroom. One Saturday morning, Bill was asked to waken my granny. He was six at the time. 'I can't,' he said, ''cause she's dead.' Agnes went up those stairs laughing at the fantasies of a young boy. My granny lay quite still. She had died in her sleep. We never thought about that. But Bill did like to frighten me with tales of death and morbid ghosts who wanted to inhabit our house against all odds and reason. I would be lying in that damp dip in the bed, and he would say that he saw a hand coming through the wall. 'It must be Ella Gordon's,' I said quite spontaneously. This became part of a repertoire. He would make a ghostly sound and I would say, 'Oh look, it's Ella Gordon's hand coming through the wall.' Ella got blamed on a lot of things in that backroom.

I got ready for my wedding in that room. It was in the Christmas vacation from university. My mother wasn't speaking to either of us. Bill and I were both at university picking up cosmopolitan ways. Leaving our working-class habits behind us. Bill's fondue set had leaked all over the kitchen table. The oil had taken the varnish off. We had left that house by then, and given that the wallpaper was hanging off the wall, and that the light in the outside toilet didn't work, and given that the bed seemed to have been reduced from three legs to two and a half legs, we thought that the varnish off the table would never have been noticed, at least not until the honeymoon was over. We were wrong. When you have got very little, every detail is picked up. We went to the church in silence. Bill was going to loan me his Triumph Spitfire for my honeymoon, but he couldn't stand the atmosphere anymore, and anyway he was bored. So he left. He had spent the week climbing around the yard wall, practising his rock climbing skills. But the attractions of the yard wall had dimmed, so he did not stay.

He was always good at leaving. When he was eighteen, he left for the Alps and Chamonix. I rehearsed how I should say goodbye to him, but I got more and more anxious about this particular ritual. Should I shake his hand, or clasp his shoulder? Should I pat him on the back? Should we embrace? In the end I did nothing. I didn't even come downstairs. But I watched him walk down Barginnis Street for the bus. I heard him swear before he left. 'That little shite couldn't even be bothered to come down the stairs to say goodbye to me. He's an ignorant little shite.' I watched him walk in that peculiarly vulnerable way of his, from the front room. But he had forgiven me by now. The honeymoon was one night in a hotel somewhere outside Belfast. I can't remember where. It was dark.

I dressed for Bill's funeral in the backroom. His friends all came back. They would have walked with him all the way, but there was nowhere to walk to. His spirit was elsewhere. His body was elsewhere as well. One friend was a fireman, one worked in insurance. Few had continued with their trade, although one still was a spark. Bill had served his time as an electrician. Some of his friends had even managed to move to their bungalow in Bangor. My mother's dream. Neither Bill nor I ever managed to fulfil that dream. My mother's greatest regret was that he didn't continue with his trade. 'But he always knew best. At least he would be alive today.' But maybe not. She sat in that front room looking down Barginnis Street dreaming of the sea wall in Bangor, and the sea and the ocean and the ship which would take her away. 'I would love to go on a foreign cruise – just the one. Anywhere in the world. Anywhere.' He dreamt of climbing – over that wall, out of that yard, over the next wall and the next. Higher and higher. Up and up. Until you could look down and see Ella

165

Gordon's yard, and Joey Donaghy's yard, and the heater in the backroom. Higher and higher, further and further, until it would all look quite cozy.

Images of home

The taxi driver was early again. Every taxi driver had been early since I arrived back in Belfast, and I was getting sick of it. He looked impatient as I made my way slowly out of the house. I wanted to make the point that he was ten minutes early. He tapped on the steering wheel. We had not got off to a great start.

'Where did you say you were going again?' he enquired. It was almost belligerent.

'Maghaberry,' I replied.

'Maghaberry?' He looked me up and down inquisitively. 'Maghaberry jail?'

'Yes that's right,' I replied as I sat in the front seat beside him, 'Maghaberry prison.' There was a long silence. He looked at me again this time from very close quarters. It was quite disconcerting. He looked at the house out of which I had emerged, my mother's house as it turns out, part of that great redevelopment in North Belfast courtesy of the Northern Ireland Housing Executive. It lay close enough to one of those imaginary lines in the road which divide Protestant and Catholic Belfast. His was a Protestant taxi firm. He looked at the road again, as if searching for the exact position of the line. There was another long silence.

'Are you visiting someone in Maghaberry then?' he asked in as innocent a sounding voice as he could muster in those circumstances. I was fully aware of the potency of my reply. I knew that this was my moment. So I cleared my throat and let the silence build expectantly. 'Indeed I am – it's someone I've known for a very long time – his name is Jim Watt.'

The taxi driver nearly choked. 'Jim Watt, you mean *Tonto* Watt. *You* know Tonto Watt, the UVF bomber.' The taxi driver was clearly impressed. He continued, 'I've never met him personally, but I've got a friend who once met him in some bar or other on the Shankill. How is he? He's been away for a long

166

time, I know that. I'm from the Shankill and down there Tonto's still a hero. They haven't forgotten him. Tell him that from me. Out of sight but not out of mind. Away but never forgotten.'

I had read similar sentiments on a thousand gable walls about all the heroes from both sides. Heroes whose names had been scrawled in bright blue letters or bright green letters – depending, but to be honest I couldn't remember a thing about them. These names did admittedly produce some kind of mild shiver down the spine – you knew that the name meant something and usually something horrible, you just couldn't remember what. 'Tonto Watt' was probably out there somewhere on some gable wall, or perhaps it was now just 'Tonto' – alone and rapidly fading. Memories of the Troubles or memories of some old TV series about a man in a mask and his faithful Indian friend. Who could tell? After all it had been over fourteen years since Jim had been given eight life sentences for his part in six murders and two attempted murders and a further twenty years for a series of thirteen bombings, and possession of explosives, guns and ammunition. He has always said that at the time he thought that he was fighting a war against the IRA. But that was all a lifetime ago.

'Tonto Watt,' repeated the taxi driver still obviously impressed. It was impossible not to notice that the mood in the taxi had changed. No understanding of any conflict where two sides do terrible things to each other will ever be complete without some analysis of the positive feeling that develops when you are with one of your own. That day it had been touch and go, but now as we drove out of Belfast on a bright sunny winter's morning, all seemed right in the world. It was as if Bobby the taxi driver had known me all of his life. I explained to Bobby the purpose of my trip to Maghaberry – Jim had recently been allowed out for two visits – once last August for four days, and then for a week over Christmas. Indeed, he was one of 434 prisoners allowed out for Christmas, 144 of them like Jim serving life sentences. All of the lifers had returned on time, although five of the others hadn't. I told Bobby that I wanted to talk to Jim about what it had been like, to go back to a city where the Troubles still continued. What

167

had he noticed after all those years coming back to a town that he had once known so well?

Bobby could see why it might be interesting. He himself had recently picked up a friend from the Maze, who had been let out for six hours' compassionate leave, after spending twelve years inside. 'He didn't know how to put on his seat belt. He was looking everywhere for the wee hole. He'd only ever seen the M1 motorway on the telly. He was terrified by the speed of the car. And when we eventually got to the Shankill, he hardly recognised any of it apart from the road itself. To be honest he wasn't too sure where he was most of the time. And to cap it all, he spent the whole time while he was out talking in a whisper out of the side of his mouth. I had to tell him that in the outside world there's nobody trying to listen to your every conversation. He still couldn't stop it though. He spent the whole time talking like this – ' and Bobby squeezed his lips around and out of the side of his mouth and contorted his whole face. And we both laughed at what a long time inside can do to someone. 'You have to have a laugh if you're from Belfast, otherwise you'd go daft, let's face it,' added Bobby.

We were now at Maghaberry, where Protestant and Catholic, IRA, INLA, UDA, UVF and all combinations thereof live together and are all led into the same big visiting room. Jim seemed to arrive last. We ordered two Kit Kats and two coffees off one of the inmates who acted as a waiter. Jim left one half of his Kit Kat at the side of the table, and it was promptly lifted by some friend on his way back to the cells, who gave a cheery wave as he turned the corner. He could have been IRA or UVF or even the FTP graffiti brigade, but in here it didn't seem to matter. At last. There were now deep-seated similarities between people from different sections of the community, who had spent substantial proportions of their adult life locked up with more than enough time to reflect and regret. Jim said that he had cried when his mother gave him his watch and the key to the house at the gates of the prison. 'I also cried when I saw the cows in the field. You're overcome by the emotion and what you've missed. You get butterflies in your stomach and a lot of prisoners can't eat when they're out. That's only to be expected. My niece drove me home from Maghaberry and she

168

had her child in the back. When I went inside my niece was just a little girl. Our house was a lot smaller than I had imagined it, and Silverstream itself looked really run down. You carry this image of your home all the time you're inside, and you're shocked when you see the reality of it.'

Many things had changed since he had gone into prison: 'I couldn't get used to money on the outside. I got this taxi one day and the fare was one pound sixty. I couldn't recognise the notes – they'd all changed. I was fiddling with these notes, and I could see this taxi driver looking at me. He must have thought that he had a real space cadet in the back. I apologised and told him that I'd been locked up for fourteen years, but when he heard that he didn't want to take any money off me. I told him, "No way, I'm paying the fare like anybody else." But I got through money like water. My daddy had been saving up for me since I went to prison, so I had a few quid in my pocket, but I didn't know what it was worth any longer. One person would tell me that twenty quid was a lot these days, and another would tell me it was worth hardly anything. I didn't know where I was.

'There was a lot to get used to. When I went into my bedroom I thought that my mother had put curtains round the bed. I was really shocked. She told me that it was a duvet with frilly bits around the edges. When I was sentenced all beds, at least in Silverstream, just had blankets on them. I walked everywhere – I wanted to take everything in. Belfast wasn't disappointing. I thought that Belfast was the most beautiful place on earth. I thought all the women were beautiful, and I must have been staring at them. The smell of perfume was overwhelming. In prison your senses get starved. It was lovely just to walk up the stairs and feel the carpet under your feet, or to stroke a dog. It's beautiful. It was also lovely to have a bath in private and just lie there without interruption.

'Of course, when I went out with my brother to one of the local clubs, there were all these people who wanted to shake my hand. They said that they'd never forgotten me, but they'd never been to see me in all the time I was inside. I was some kind of hero to a lot of these young guys. They all wanted to meet me, but they must have been very disappointed. I've stopped drinking, and I spent a lot of time in church when I was out. These young guys wanted to meet the old Tonto Watt, the head-bin, the drinker, not some Christian sitting there with an orange juice. Some of the others who were let out for the week spent the whole time drunk. When they got back, they couldn't remember a thing about their visit. I wanted to savour every minute of my freedom.

'The one thing that did disappoint me about being out was how superficial people seemed. In here we have time to talk. There they want to argue or storm off. But, of course, if you're only out for a week, you're treated as the centre of attention. Everyone's saying, "Are you all right, Jim? Is there anything I can get you?" They're tripping over themselves to be nice to you. You only see the nice side of people. The next time I get a visit out I'd like it to be more normal.'

It was getting towards the end of my visit, but there was one question that I was dying to ask him. Although I had known Jim since I was a boy, I had never come across the nickname 'Tonto' until all the publicity surrounding his arrest and conviction. Where had it come from? Jim shuffled uneasily. 'Well, when I was in my teens I tried to use a sunlamp, but it made my face go all red. All the lads at the corner were taking the mickey out of me, and started calling me "Tan-o". Then a few years later I was introduced to one of the big UVF commanders on the Shankill, "Frenchie" Marchant, who was later killed by the IRA. Anyway, I was introduced to him as "Tano", but he misheard it as "Tonto". To be honest I was too embarrassed to correct him, so Tonto stuck. Belfast knows me as Tonto Watt, or thinks it knows me.' And on that note Jim was led back to his cell.

Meanwhile Bobby, the taxi driver, had been waiting patiently throughout my visit. He looked genuinely pleased to see me. 'How's Tonto?' he shouted from his cab.

'*Tano*'s fine,' I replied, as I jumped into the back. He looked quite puzzled all the way back to Belfast.

14

Two Wee Bus Runs in Troubled Times

My bus ground its way through the suburbs. The suburbs of Belfast, with the trees still in bloom, and the green leaves still firm on the branch, despite the gusting wind reminding us all that autumn would soon be with us. The leaves were defiant and for a second you couldn't help wondering if this summer might not just last forever. I sat on the back seat, the hard back seat towards the rear of the bus. The soft cushioned seats of the buses in Belfast have been replaced by something altogether more functional and distinctly less comfortable towards the back of the bus, presumably to thwart the vandal and the bomber both. The bomber who might otherwise by tempted to force something down that yielding gap between the bottom and back of the luxuriant soft black vinyl seats. But it would take more than hard seats to make me sit towards the front. I've spent a lifetime at the back. That's what you do when you get on the bus. You head for the back and let your shoulders swing this way and that on the way there. Hard seats are not a sufficient deterrent. We've got hard asses anyway. We're not moving forward. No surrender. The sun burned my neck through the back window.

It was the middle of a glorious afternoon. Glencairn, the estate at the bottom of Divis, almost looked picturesque in the haze. A sun-kissed village on the foothills of one of the mountains that surround Belfast. Schools everywhere were just getting out, and the roads were getting busy. Time to look around and appreciate Belfast. I noticed them out of the side window of the bus. There they stood in a long, snaking line patiently waiting their turn to board the bus. The school blazers were blue, the shirts blue, the ties blue and white stripes. Traditional school uniforms from maybe twenty years ago, binding them together. Many of them wore matching blue ribbons in their hair. Six-year-olds as pretty as a picture on a warm September day. They were waiting to board the buses to take them to other parts of town – the Catholic parts. Their school was stranded in a Protestant area, so they had to be bused out. It was part of a daily ritual, which seemed a little ridiculous on that glorious day in autumn with the leaves still on the trees. Some had already boarded the bus, and they were bouncing up and down in anticipation. They sat in little sociable groups on the bus, talking about the events of the day, chatting, chattering away. They carried satchels in various bright colours. Most of the satchels had pink straps.

Our bus, the Balmoral bus heading from Silverstream down past the school had pulled in abruptly just opposite. The bus had nicked the front wing of a white Ford Escort driven by one of the mothers picking her child up from school. The bus driver was now out collecting insurance details of the mother who was dressed in a bright pink tracksuit. The driver smiled benevolently and somewhat patronisingly at the woman, as she skipped onto the road then onto the pavement then onto the road again to evaluate the full extent of the damage to her pristine vehicle.

Our bus was growing impatient. 'Fuck's sake, get a move on. You can hardly see the fucking dent. You'd need a magnifying glass to see the fucking thing.' I looked back towards the children boarding the bus opposite. I noticed that a little girl with the face of an angel with bright, bubbly golden hair was making faces at our bus. She was sitting about half-way down the bus, on her own. She alone oriented our way. She poked her eyes up this way and that. Her lips protruded right away from her otherwise perfect features. She had spent many hours practising this in front of a mirror – that was for sure. I assumed at first that she was putting on this show for a young girl on our bus about three seats ahead of me. Perhaps this slightly older girl had provoked her in the past. Perhaps she had seen her before. She must have done. I just sat there and watched the young Catholic girl transform her angelic looks for perhaps five minutes before I realised that she wasn't making faces at anyone in particular on our bus. No, it was the bus that she was making faces at – our bus – the Balmoral bus – the one that goes down the Shankill from Silverstream. The bus down the Protestant Road – the bus full of Prods. I was the only person on our bus to sit and watch the display. The others ignored her.

Suddenly a school bus full of eleven-year-old boys started to squeeze down the centre of the road between our bus and theirs. The boys wore a uniform that I recognised. That meant that it had to be a school from my part of town. As the bus squeezed itself down that narrow ravine between our bus and the bus full of the angels in blue, the boys started shouting and giving the fingers at the young girls. The ravine was very narrow, so it took quite a time for this bus to squeeze through. The boys heaved and pushed, gesticulated and swore – silently – through several layers of thick Belfast Corporation glass. Their mouths too were contorted this way and that – opening wide and quickly closing. Their eyes swore too. Straining, slit-eyed gestures as the lids were pulled down tight, tight in public displays of hate. Terse movements of the lips and tongue as great guttural sounds ripped out and were lost in the glinting glass, reflecting those warm luxuriant rays in which we all bathed. Protestant and Catholic alike.

The girls appeared not to see them. They didn't look, and they didn't look away. There was no response, let alone no contingent response. They just continued. But one young girl sucked her bright blue purse as if it was a pacifier. She sucked and sucked and gnawed at that purse for security and comfort. The boys hissed and spat, with the hissing and the spitting increasing in desperation as their bus started eventually to navigate out of this social ravine in which it had found itself.

This left us and the angels still facing each other in a silence, filled I thought by a kind of shame. I asked a boy opposite the name of the Catholic school. He shook his head. 'No fucking idea. Our Lady of something probably. Or Our Blessed Virgin

173

Primary. How the fucking hell should I know. Why do you want to know anyway? Do you want to put your name down for it or something?' His two friends, sitting across the aisle on the bus, though that this response was very funny. They too were the sort that head automatically for the back of the bus. This was a school that they passed every day in life. Eventually, our driver was satisfied that he had got enough details of the female motorist and we were off down towards town. The day already ruined.

Two generations later, I was back in the north of the city. She had had a great day. 'But it could have been even better. We had our wee bus run to Newcastle, but I didn't want to go to Newcastle. The club secretary asked us where we fancied going, and I suggested the Ards Peninsula. It's lovely down there – I used to go down there with Billy, when he was still alive. I love Greyabbey. It's beautiful. But most of the members of the Senior Citizens' club are Catholic – thirty-eight of them are Catholic to be exact, there are only eighteen Protestant.'

I said I was struck by her way with figures. There were no mere approximations here. Everyone was paraded and accounted for, before the final figures came in. There was no ambiguity and no uncertainty. Nobody was in the middle. Everyone was one thing or the other. Prod or Taig, even in that bright, unseasonable sunlight.

'That's the way it is around here. Everybody knows who everybody else is. It's as simple as that. But we were outvoted. The Catholics fancied Newcastle, it's a Republican area after all. You can't blame them. So that's where we had our wee bus run to.'

'But perhaps they like the way that the Mountains of Mourne sweep down to the sea in Newcastle. Perhaps that's why they wanted to go to Newcastle? To view again that formidable natural beauty. To look at those mountains.'

I said all of this before I noticed that she was looking at me as if I was daft. 'Look, I understand their point of view. I wouldn't try to criticise them for it. But it was obvious why they wanted to go to Newcastle.' This time I said nothing.

'Normally, the bus would stop at Ballynahinch on the way here, but Ballynahinch had all the bunting out. The red, white and blue was still flying from July, so we went straight through the town. But I still enjoyed the trip. If they were going to hell on a wee bus run, I'd still go with them.

'But it's a great wee club. We meet once a week and have a cup of tea. Then we have a ballot.' I suggested that she might mean a 'raffle'. 'We're not English. We call them "ballots". Then we have a wee game of bingo for 20p. First prize is one pound. We have a big meeting every month where they tell us how much is in the kitty. They also tell us who has died in the past month so we can put a notice in the *Belfast Telegraph*. With what's in the kitty we have two dinners – one at Hallowe'en and one at Christmas and two wee bus runs. We went to Coleraine – a very loyalist town – in June. But it was miserable weather. I wanted the bus to go on to Portrush, because I haven't been there for years. But some of the members of the club said that it would freeze ye in Portrush. It's always windy in Portrush, that's what they said. I know what they meant. It's too bloody loyalist for them up there.

'The argument was settled anyway. The secretary of the club just said that it was too expensive for the bus to go on to Portrush. He also said that it was too expensive to stop in Ballymena, so he said that we would stop in Antrim instead. The only problem was that we couldn't afford an Ulsterbus, we had a cheaper bus from Lurgan. The driver from Lurgan didn't know Antrim – he couldn't find his way about, so we went straight through Antrim without stopping. But we had a lovely dinner in Coleraine – turkey and ham, new potatoes, followed by Pavlova. Then we went out and walked round the shops in the rain.

'It's a very integrated club, and that's why I like it. It's only been going for a few years, and it was an attempt to get both sides together. It does that very well. There's never any trouble. The secret is that nobody ever talks about religion. The Troubles are never mentioned. There was a lad gunned down outside his house the other day. You can see his house from my front door, but you couldn't talk about this at the club. You can say things like "Did you hear about that terrible shooting?" but that's about it. You can't really comment on it, in case people think that you're taking sides. Both sides are at

175

it anyway. One side's as bad as the other. We never talk about anything sectarian. You couldn't talk about these things in a mixed club. You wouldn't dare to, even though I know all the members. I've always known them all my life. There are no strangers in the club. These are people who have lived in this area all their life.

'We had a great wee sing-song on the bus on the way back from Newcastle. We had "Pack up your Troubles", "It's a long, long way to Tipperary" and the old favourite "When Irish eyes are smiling." My neighbour whispered to me that I should sing "The Sash", but that was only a wee joke. You can't sing songs like that in mixed company. Everybody knows that. Everybody knows the score.'

_____

15

The Unnatural Conclusion

The butchers

The taxi driver was crouched over the front of the seat reading something. I explained that I wasn't quite ready. 'Don't worry boss. Take your time. No probs. I'll get you to the airport in time. It'll be wee buns.' He continued reading. The book was concealed inside a newspaper. It wasn't until I got back into the cab that I glimpsed the title as he hastily closed the book and returned it to the glove compartment of his car. It was *The Shankill Butchers – A Case Study of Mass Murder* by Martin Dillon. As the blurb on the cover says, 'Between 1972 and 1977 the Shankill Butchers killed more people than any other mass murderers in British criminal history.'

I asked him what he thought of the book. 'Incredible. Lenny Murphy was fuckin' wild. He hated them basically. Let's face it.'

'Wild' can be a funny adjective in Belfast. It can be peculiarly positive. 'Wild' isn't like being a 'moonman' or a 'spacer' or a 'space cadet'. It doesn't imply that the person referred to is deranged or out of control or unrestrained or undisciplined. Oh no, you can be very disciplined and still be wild there. Lenny Murphy, the leader of the Shankill Butchers, was certainly disciplined, orderly, systematic even.

My driver flicked through the book: 'Have you read this? It's wild.' Here we go again, I thought. 'Did you know any of these boys? You must have done. You're the guy who knows Tonto Watt.' I had never met this taxi driver before, and I was certainly finding it disconcerting the way everyone seemed to know my business. The bush telegraph travels fast over there. 'There's a photo of Tonto in a white polo on page 140.' And sure enough, there below a photograph of Big Sam McAllister, stripped to the waist – all six foot of him and sixteen stone, stood Tano. About five feet six inches. A white polo, covered in a dark pullover. Not smiling. Only Lenny Murphy was smiling. A slightly eerie smile. I had talked to Jim Watt about the book. Perhaps not surprisingly he resented his inclusion in the book. The Shankill Butchers quite literally butchered people – and not just Catholics. Jim was a bomb maker. The Brown Bear team normally led by Murphy planted a bomb that Jim Watt had made, but that was in 1977, when Murphy was in prison. That was his only connection with the gang.

The taxi driver wanted to discuss it. 'Did you know Lenny? What was he like? He once helped my granny get her new fridge into the kitchen. She says that he was a lovely wee lad, but a bit wild. And he hated Taigs.' He added this as something of an afterthought. It wasn't just my driver's granny that thought he was a lovely wee lad. There were eighty-seven death notices in the *Belfast Telegraph*. Lenny's Aunt Agnes wrote, 'Nothing could be more beautiful than the memories we have of you; to us you were very special and God must have thought so too.' There were other notices from friends and associates including one 'From old friends, Dinks, Harper, Hacksaw, Fox, Dick, Basher, Noel, Head-Monkey, Artie and Stewartie, B-Wing, H-Block, the Maze prison.' His mother Joyce Murphy had said, 'My Lenny would not have hurt a fly.' But Peter McKenna writing in the *Irish Independent* quoted a UDA leader as saying that 'Lenny was a typical psychopath.'

Dillon's book is an extraordinary document. He was granted access to the confessions which the group made when arrested and to coroners' reports. These in combination make chilling reading. The arbitrariness of the selection of victims is horrific. They butchered Catholics, and any Protestants that happened to cross them. 'The Butchers did make the odd mistake,' admitted my driver. 'They did their own kind by mistake

178

sometimes. But sometimes you have to have boys like that on your side. You have to fight fire with fire.'

The odd mistake? They butchered anybody who got in their way. They were ruthless, barbaric and arbitrary in their execution.

In 1976 Stephen McCann and Frances Tohill were returning home from a party in Jerusalem Street near Queen's University. They were cutting through Millfield, close to the Shankill. Murphy was in the Maze at the time. Mr A, one of the shadowy godfathers of the Organisation, told William Moore that he should run the Brown Bear unit in Murphy's absence. Moore was out cruising the streets looking for Taigs – any Taig would do. McCann and Tohill were in the wrong place at the wrong time. It was after two a.m. Stephen McCann was abducted and beaten. He admitted that he was a Catholic. Martin Dillon himself uses that expression 'admitted he was a Catholic'. McCann was driven to Brookmount Street on the Shankill. Moore collected a butchery knife and a .22 pistol from Mr A. William Moore's confession read as follows:

'I want to tell you the whole story. I want to get it off my chest. It was Lenny Murphy who first got me involved in killings. One of the ones I did was the wee lad we picked up in Millfield and dumped him in Glencairn. I was drinking that night in one of the clubs, I think it was the Lawnbrook. I was along with Sam McAllister, John Townsley and Artie McKay. I know Artie well and I think his second name is McKay. He used to live in Winchester Street and he now lives in Antrim town. After the club finished the four of us had a chat and decided to go out and get a *Taig*. My motor was outside. At that time I had a beige Mark 2 Cortina. Mr A. owns it now. The four of us got into my car and I drove down the Shankill and turned into Millfield. I turned into the first street on my right, Brown Street beside the car park. I parked the car a few yards up in Brown Street from Millfield. Artie and Sam and me got out of the motor, John Townsley stayed in the motor a while. Artie, Sam and me stood against the wall at the corner of Brown Street. We seen a fellow and a

179

girl walking along Millfield towards the Shankill. That's why we stopped there. We were standing at the corner a couple of minutes when the fellow and girl reached us. The fellow was on the outside and the girl was walking on the inside taking his arm. They were on the same side of the street as me. We waited until they walked past and when they were about ten or twenty yards up the street we ran after them. I grabbed hold of the girl and pushed her onto the ground. I knelt beside her and held her down. Sam and Artie grabbed hold of the fellow and pulled him round the corner and put him in the motor. I let the girl go and ran back round and got into the motor. I drove up Brown Street, along Townsend Street and up the Shankill. The fellow was between Artie and Sam in the back seat and while I was driving along they hit him a couple of times. He wasn't unconscious but he wasn't shouting or anything. I drove to Brookmount Street and went to Mr A.'s house which is—. I told him we had a *Taig* in the motor and he gave me a .22 pistol and a knife to do him with. I drove up into Glencairn. I drove up Forthriver Road and turned at the car park where Morrissey was found facing the community centre. Me and Artie and John Townsley took the fellow out of the motor and walked him across to the back of the community centre. I told the fellow to sit down. He sat down. I shot him once in the head just at the top. When I shot him he fell sideways on the ground. When he was lying on the ground I cut his throat. It was a butcher's knife I had, sharp as a lance and it just slits his throat right open. We left him lying there. Sam had stayed in the motor and he drove it over beside us. I got into the driver's seat and drove back to Mr A.'s house and gave him the gun and knife. I dropped the other three off and went home.'

The pathologist's report concluded that death was due principally to the bullet wound to the head. However, the major wounds to the throat were not made by a single action as Moore claimed in the statement. There were multiple cuts as

Moore cut his throat right back to the spine in full view of the others. There were other injuries to the body consistent with a beating. As Dillon notes Moore's confession is full of careful understatement.

The butchery continued. The pathologist's report on another victim, Joseph Morrissey, reported that:

'He had sustained numerous blunt force injuries. There were eight separate lacerations scattered all over the scalp and another on the left side of the forehead. There were linear, V-shaped, cruciate and arcuate and they could have been caused by a hatchet. One of the wounds to the scalp, above the right side of the forehead, was associated with a subjacent fracture of the left side of the skull. Two more lacerations were situated under the right lower jaw and there were a further two lacerations on the left side of the neck, below the left angle of the jaw. These four lacerations were transverse and the two on the left were associated with fractures of the left side of the lower jaw with teeth torn out. These injuries could also have been caused by a hatchet. There were numerous injuries on the back of the left upper limb obviously sustained in an attempt to defend himself and some of these could have been caused by the blade of a sharp hatchet.'

The butchery only stopped when one victim, Gerard McLaverty, survived. His written statement of his ordeal read as follows:

'As I walked past the Belfast Royal Academy I saw a yellow Cortina car. It was parked on the opposite side of the road with its lights out. It was facing up the Clifton-ville Road. I could see two men in the front of this car and at the same time two men walked towards me on the same footpath on which I was standing. I had seen this car draw up while I was walking and had seen these two men get out. I then saw them cross the road and walk towards me. I was the only person on the street at the time. I would describe one of these men as large and

181

fat. The two men stopped me and the large, fat man told me they were from the CID Tennent Street. They then asked me for my identification. I showed my diary with my name on it to the fat man. I then felt the fat man put a gun in my back. He ordered me to go to the yellow Cortina across the road. As I was getting into the back of the car I could see the gun in his hand. I got into the back seat of the car and the fat man got in also and sat on my right. The other man got into the car and sat on my left. There were already two men in the car. I said to the fat man, "I've done nothing to be picked up." He said: "We are taking you to Tennent Street to check you out and then we will drive you home again." He then put the gun in his inside jacket pocket. None of the others spoke. The car did a U-turn on the Cliftonville Road, drove down the Antrim Road to Carlisle Circus, up the Crumlin Road to Cambrai Street and along Cambrai Street to the Shankill Road. The car then turned left into a street off the Shankill Road and stopped on the right-hand side of that street. No one spoke to me during the journey. I was stopped at the side door of a building which fronted onto the Shankill Road. The man sitting on my left got out of the car and I saw him opening this side door with a key. It appeared to me to be a steel- or metal-covered door because it rattled when it opened. While this was going on the fat man told me that I would be going into the building and would be kept there to get more details. We all got out of the car. The two men in front of the car took one of my arms each and marched me into the building. The fat man came behind.

When I got into the room, the fat man said: "You're staying here." I saw a dining room chair and two electric heaters in the room. They made me sit on the chair. There was what looked like a shop counter in the room. The fat man said: "We're gonna check up on you and we won't be back till the morning." They did not go out. The fat man and the car driver went behind the counter and came back with sticks. The stick that the fat man had had a nail driven through the end of it. They both started beating me round the head with the sticks. I put up my hands to protect my eyes. I was afraid of the nail in the fat man's stick piercing my eyes. The fat man said: "Get your fuckin' hands down or we'll give you more." I started to squeal with fear and pain and they stopped beating me. They had a teapot and a kettle and the driver of the car went and made some tea. The fat man asked me if I wanted tea and I refused. I said: "I want to go home." The fat man said: "You are not going home. There is no way you are getting out of this." They all sat and drank their tea. I was sitting in the corner and they were all sitting watching me. When they had finished their tea, they put their cups away and came back to me. The driver punched me on the side of the face and eye with his fist. I was knocked onto the floor and he took his heel and drove it into the side of my face. They set me down on the chair again and the driver of the car took the lace out of his right boot. He gave it to the fat man and then they held my hands behind my back. The fat man held me and tied the lace loosely round my neck. Throughout this the other men did not touch me but they stayed at one of the two doors in the room. When the lace had been tied loosely round my neck, the other two men left and locked the door from the outside. The fat man and the car driver had broken open the other door before the first two left. When I was alone with the fat man and the car driver they took me out of this open door into an entry. The yellow Cortina was in the street at the end of that entry. At this time the fat man had a large clasp knife. The driver tightened the lace around my neck and the fat man started slashing at my clothes with the knife. With the tightening of the lace around my neck I lost consciousness.

When I regained consciousness I was lying in the entry. There was a crowd of people around me and I was taken by ambulance to the Royal Victoria Hospital. Both my wrists were severely slashed and my neck was sore and swollen. I would describe the fat man as being twenty-four years old, tall and fat. He was wearing a black

183

leather jacket and black trousers. I think he was wearing a jumper. At one time I saw his right arm and he seemed to have a scar inside opposite his elbow. I would describe the driver as being about twenty-five to twenty-six years old, tall, of medium build and longish hair. He was wearing a brown leather jacket and blue trousers. It was the fat man and the car driver who attacked me. I would describe one of the other two men as small, of light build and about twenty-two years old. He was wearing a white jacket.'

Gerard McLaverty survived. He identified Big Sam McAllister and Benny Edwards standing on the streets of the Shankill during the second general strike. The strike that brought the UDA and the UVF onto the streets in an attempt to close the Province down yet again. It turned out to be an impromptu line-up. The Butchers were arrested and convicted. Lenny Murphy himself was gunned down in Glencairn in Forthriver Park. There was RUC speculation that Loyalists might have been involved in his assassination. It would have been imposs-ible, so the argument goes, for the IRA to track Murphy on his own territory. Murphy's stomping ground was the Shankill and Glencairn – both Protestant heartlands. The argument goes that there was collusion at the time between the IRA and the UDA and UVF in racketeering. Lenny Murphy may have been too 'wild', even for the Organisation.

Dillon's book is disturbing. Not least because the whole thing seems so extreme, so irrational, so beyond our normal experience. Not a single mass killer but a gang of them. In court, all of the defendants were found to be technically sane and therefore criminally responsible, and dealt with accord-ingly. To date all of those convicted, including Jim Watt, identified on prison office files as part of the gang, have served a minimum of fourteen years four months. One William Townsley has been released on licence.

Dillon hunts around for some psychological explanation for this collective insanity. He considers that Lenny Murphy and some of the other gang members may have been psychopaths: 'That represents the difference between the offender in North-

184

ern Ireland who, had it not been for the terrorist war, would have stayed out of trouble, and offenders who were on a collision course anyway and would have offended even had there been no civil unrest.'

He seems to be implying that the Troubles were just a convenient excuse for some people, already on some collision course. They were already hurtling along, dangerously out of control, on the road to nowhere. The Troubles gave them a motive which they didn't need and an excuse – in the eyes of others – which they did. But what was the collision course and why couldn't someone have applied the brakes sooner?

The road to nowhere

I balanced in the plastic basin on the floor. The geyser heated by gas coughed and spluttered, occasionally ejecting small concentrated globules of boiling water. The knack was in trying to direct these boiling globules through the cold tap below and then onto your bare skin. Otherwise you got burned. There was no hot water in the house, just boiling water and freezing cold water. No in between. This was how we washed – in the kitchen by the back door. Balancing with one foot in the basin, trying to shield yourself from the frosted door to the living room, with the neighbours sitting watching the flesh-coloured shape beyond twist and turn as he tried to get the soap off his back with a handful of boiling water. There wasn't much privacy. There had been a bath – once. In some far off half-remembered days we used to get the bath into the front room, right in front of the coal fire. We boiled water for the bath in the kettle. It was something which occurred on a Saturday night. But now the bath had rusted, and I ran every day – crisscrossing Divis and Cavehill. I came back caked with mud, and faced the geyser. The bath remained pinned to one wall of the yard with a rusty nail.

You always felt a little defenceless standing there naked balancing in the basin, with just a glass door to protect you from the prying eyes. 'Oh, your Geoffrey is getting big, Eileen.' But there was no alternative. You were defenceless. And then I heard his voice. 'Oh, hello, John, my Geoffrey's just having a bath.' She always called that process of trying to wash yourself by standing in a basin and allowing water – either too hot or too cold to trickle down your back – having a bath. 'Oh, it's okay, Mrs Beattie, I can wait.' He was always so polite, and she could never see through that. 'Would you like a cup of tea, John, while you're waiting?' 'That would be very nice, Mrs Beattie. Thank you very much.' 'We'll have to wait until he's finished though. GEOFFREY! John's out here. Could you get a move on.' I rubbed and rubbed at the back of my leg with the other foot, but all this rubbing with the trickle of water from the geyser couldn't dislodge that mud. I didn't want him in the kitchen with me like that.

My mother continued to talk. 'He's been out running again. It can't be good for you – out running in all weathers. I don't know why he does that. GEOFFREY! John's here. Get a move on. I want to make him a cup of tea. Unless you want me to come in there while you're having a bath.'

She turned to John. 'I don't know what's he's afraid of me seeing. I saw it before he did. I am after all his mother. GEOFFREY! John's here. Sometimes I think that that boy is deaf. GEOFFREY!'

I put a towel around me and went out into the living room. John sat on the settee beside the stairs watching the TV just past my mother. He was grinning. He was wearing yet another new brown leather jacket and a pair of Wranglers, which were at exactly the right state of being washed out. The turn-ups were perfect. He wore a pink 'skinny' jumper under the jacket. Tight round his stocky frame. His brown brogues shone. My mother always liked to say how well turned out he was. I could never be that well turned out because I only owned one pair of Wranglers. 'You should be out working at your age. If you want trendy clothes, then you have go to out to work.' My jeans never really got dirty, but they often got limp after a few days' wear. His were always crisp. John was very careful about his appearance.

My mother went off to make the tea. We sat there in silence. I was waiting to find out where I was to go that night. It was never very democratic. 'I thought we'd go up to my sister's in Glencairn. There's something that I want to pick up.' That was it. There was to be no further discussion about where we would go, or what we would do. Glencairn it was.

'Where have you two boys decided to go tonight then?' said my mother returning with the tea. 'It's a Friday. I bet you'll be off to town. You boys will be down in the Starlite tonight. I know what you get up to. I wish I was your age again.' We were currently barred from the Starlite. A friend of John's from the Shankill had been involved in something. We had arrived at the disco, as it was finishing. Whatever it was. We saw none of it. The friend passed us on the stairs up to the club. He was being pushed down the stairs by the bouncers at the time, but not before they had punched or kicked him in the face. His lip was hanging off. We were guilty by mere association. He said that he would be back when he had found somebody to 'back him up'. He asked us but we were still hoping to go in as paying customers. The following week we discovered that we were barred. In the minds of the bouncers we were associated with the incident, so they barred us. We were barred from most clubs at that time, usually for very little reason.

We simply accepted being barred. We took it like men. There was always the odd drunk who would stand and argue. 'You're barred.' 'No way am I barred.' 'Look, mate, you're beat.' (Pronounced 'bate'.) 'I'm far from beat.' 'You're fuckin' beat.' 'I'm far from fuckin' beat.' 'Look would you mind not swearing.' And so it went on. We never argued, which probably reinforced the bouncers' belief that it was right to bar us in the first place.

So it may have been Friday, but it was unlikely to be the Starlite. Unless we wanted trouble. I went upstairs and dragged my Wranglers out of the corner of my bedroom. This was the room that nobody ever ventured into, except me. Pictures of Free and cobwebs hung from the ceiling. Pictures of Free and Rod Stewart covered every wall. 'I'm not going to clean that room until you take all that shite off the wall.' So it was never cleaned. My brother used to live with me in that room, but now he had gone to climb mountains, and I claimed the room with my photographs cut from *NME* and *Melody Maker*. The bed had only three legs and you always ended up in the dip at the far end, but now at least the bed was mine. Even if it was damp, with nylon sheets.

Admittedly, the room was also very untidy. Book prizes from Sunday School sat on top of the chest of drawers. Encyclopaedias lay everywhere. The drawers themselves were full of all sorts – a harmless plastic cosh which was a skittle full of sand, some 'drugs' of an unidentifiable kind stolen from our local chemist's, and coincidentally the place where my girl-friend's mother worked, a black enamel chain, which I had used once in a fight.

'They could do with a wash,' my mother said when I came back down the stairs. 'Why don't you leave them out some-time.' But if I had done this it would have meant that I would have had to go out at night with my grey flannels from school. The grey flannels with the regulation bottoms. Great BRA insisted that the regulation grey trousers be of a certain minimum width. I was once sent home because I had the temerity to wear socks with a black-and-white diamond pattern on them, rather than the regulation grey or black. My Aunt Agnes had bought me those socks, specifically for school wear. She couldn't understand it either. After school I had to rebel against such inane discipline. I had to. I would rather have walked through Hell in my Wranglers, and have them covered in the excrement of a thousand lost souls and still wear them, than abandon them for a pair of Academy trousers.

My mother was usually slightly suspicious of strangers, but she had taken to John right away. I had met him one fateful night at a pop concert, which was held at Dunmore greyhound stadium. I had heard about him before he came up our way, but that night he appeared. My friend, Bill, and I were with two girls. It was a big night for Bill and me. We had fancied these girls for ages. The concert was our ideal opportunity. John obviously liked them as well. I assumed that he wanted to make some kind of impression, in his own inimitable style. I remember how crisp his Wrangler denim jacket was. He had two friends with him from down the Shankill. He said that he knew us, because he was coming to live up our area. There was no argument, but suddenly he pulled a hatchet from inside his jacket and swept it towards the head of my friend.

Bill ducked and it glanced the side of his head, as he fell off this balcony. To this day, I can't remember why John should have done this. It all seemed so irrational. The girls shrieked and departed. This seemed to be the point as much as anything. We were left with him. He asked us about ourselves and he was most impressed by my educational achievement. 'Twelve O levels. I've never met anyone with that number before.' He asked me if I wanted to have a look at the hatchet. It was the first time I had ever seen anybody produce one in a fight, even though it wasn't exactly a fight. He said he would see us around.

He turned up the next night, as we hung about outside the chip shop. He had a friend with him – wee Hutchie. We all just stood there – watching, waiting. Not doing much – as usual. There was a bit of banter. The crack. The jokes stopped when John arrived. Everybody was slightly wary of him. It was Hutchie who broke the ice, unintentionally. He made some crack about Glencairn – about the fact that it always looked unfinished as an estate. I remember thinking that this was a fair comment. That was it. John got him in a headlock and dragged him around the pavement. Hutchie's body was forced over and down, as John led him around and around. This was like some kind of ritual degradation. A ritual degradation of someone who was evidently a very close friend. Hutchie had after all walked all the way up from the Shankill with John. I had seen this kind of horseplay before, but what struck me about that particular night was how long the whole thing went on for. For a full twenty minutes Hutchie was led this way and that. Every now and again, he would put up some kind of struggle and the two bodies would stumble onto the road and then back onto the pavement. It was the duration of the episode which turned the whole thing from horseplay into something different. I wasn't sure what this something different was. I had never come across it before. Eventually he released Hutchie whose face had gone red. But not before he could give him one last ritualistic kick up the backside.

I discovered later that John didn't even like Glencairn.

John then turned to face the rest of us. For approval. From that moment on, I was extremely wary of him. I wanted to melt into the group. He asked me if I fancied some chips. 'I know you don't have any money. You're still at school. I'll buy them.' I couldn't think of any way of refusing his hospitality. So I accepted his offer of queuing with him for the chips along with all the drunk men coming from the pub. I had been selected out of the group. I had been isolated. We stood there in silence. He despised those drunk men in the chip shop. These men who had turned to drink 'to drown their sorrows', 'to forget their woes'. You could see it on his face. They were weak.

He disappreared for a while, and when he reappeared he was at my house. He said he had something for me, and he unwrapped a brand new pair of Wranglers. He asked me if I fancied a trip into town. I explained that it was Sunday night, and on a Sunday I had usually about four hours of homework. 'Just this once. Everybody needs a break.' He had a pleading, insistent manner. He argued that it would only take an hour, and that I would learn something useful, something that books couldn't teach me. He said he wasn't going to leave unless I went with him. Twenty minutes later we were on the bus to town. He led me along Royal Avenue, and into the doorways of shops. 'The mail piles up in the letter boxes all over the weekend. You can fish the letters out, and find cheques in them.' He would pull out handfuls of mail and then disappear around the corner to open it. 'It's nearly all shite this week, but I've got a couple of things.' I was the anxious look-out, but he never showed me what he had managed to retrieve out of those letter boxes. I returned to Turgenev and Dostoevsky and tales of other lands that I also didn't understand.

Apart from cross-country running and hanging about the corner, my other big recreation was badminton. We played in a church hall, and a friend, Raymond, and I played for both the church Junior Badminton Club and the Senior Badminton Club. We did this all day Saturday. We would go along about one o'clock and put the nets up and play all afternoon. We would stay over at tea time, and play all night. We played a lot of matches and we would eat sandwiches and Paris buns after the games. If we were very lucky we got diamonds or 'curn' squares (currant squares). If we were very lucky we got

190

chocolate Paris. Raymond and I had a prodigious talent for eating buns. John felt excluded on Saturdays. One Saturday he said that he was coming with me. He tried to play and like many before him discovered that it was harder than it looked. He only tried it once.

One friend of mine from the badminton club, but one who did not hang about the corner, was called Maurice. He was overweight and was often called names because of this. John took an instant dislike to Maurice. Maurice, by the way, despite his weight problem was a fair badminton player. In full view of all the girls at the club, John grabbed him and pinned him down by sitting across his chest, with his knees on his shoulders. He did this on the stage of the church hall. There had been no real reason for John to grab him, but nevertheless I could see it coming. 'Look at the diddies on fat chops there. Imagine getting hold of those. Hey! Big diddies!'

He started questioning Maurice about the size of his diddies and about his masculinity. 'Come on fat chops. I bet you lie playing with your diddies at night. Does it turn you on to tweak them?' Maurice did not answer. Indeed the way that John was sitting over his chest, it was doubtful whether he could answer. John borrowed a lit cigarette from another friend who was smoking, and pulled up Maurice's badminton vest exposing the fat flesh. With careful precision John lowered the lit cigarette down towards his chest, just to the side of his nipple, until it was nearly touching it. Maurice writhed and gurgled. John held him there, and then touched his flesh with the lit cigarette. Maurice screamed. 'Come off it. That wasn't sore. Surely you couldn't feel that through those layers of fat. You're well protected, you fat bastard. You probably can't feel anything.'

John lifted the cigarette away. Maurice strained to see the position of it. Then John once more started to draw the lit cigarette down again towards his chest. Maurice frantically twisted and bucked. His head was right back at an angle. He couldn't see what John was going to do. The cigarette came lower and lower. At the very last minute John flipped the cigarette around so that the lit end was pointing back towards the palm of his hand. We, the audience, could all see that.

Maurice couldn't. So John touched his naked chest with the very tip of his bent index finger. Maurice screamed again. He thought that he was being burned again. The mind can play tricks like that, and John knew it. He screeched with laughter. 'What did I tell you? The big fat shite cries if you just touch him with your finger.'

But the humiliation did not stop there. Maurice lay on that stage, not knowing whether it was going to be the finger or the cigarette. It took many minutes before John decided that enough was enough. When he eventually got up, Maurice lay there. Crying and quivering. Full of shame and humiliation. In full display, in front of the girls he may have hoped to impress with his ability with a badminton racket. John was grinning. 'I've had enough of this fucking game,' he said. 'It's for wankers.'

John never wanted to feel excluded from anything. He would call mid-week in the middle of winter, when I sat alone in my house huddled over the electric fire, doing my homework. All three bars of the electric fire would be blazing away and there would be some heat for perhaps eighteen inches from the artificial burning coals. The rule in our house was that you were only allowed to have two bars on at any one time. But as soon as my mother went out, the three bars would be put on. It was the only form of heating in the whole house. John arrived one night with some acid. He wanted me to drop it there and then. We had been experimenting with this up at a house in Glencairn at weekends. But I was a strictly weekend drug taker. I would take a black bomber on Friday lunchtime, and talk my way through an afternoon at the Academy, before going to the Starlite on a Friday. Or not, now that we were barred. I might take the occasional half tab of acid on a Saturday in Glencairn. But never mid-week. I knew that discipline would be my salvation. John could never understand this. It was as if I was trying to exclude him from a major part of my life. He stood in the middle of the front room and threatened to kick the electric fire if I didn't drop some acid with him. He even threatened to tell my mother that I had been burning three bars all that night. That night I got away with it. Two nights later I didn't. He arrived in a car. He just

192

said 'get in'. That night there was no fooling. He drove badly out along the Horseshoe towards the airport. We saw an army patrol. I assumed that they would flag us down. They didn't. We dumped the car about fifty yards from my house down the side of the Ballysillan Arms. My prints were all over the vehicle. He wore gloves, but he never warned me to get a pair. 'You're clean,' he said. 'They'll never trace you. You'll be all right. You're a fucking Academy boy.'

I had to see him every weekend. The Academy had a Christmas disco. I kept this very quiet. Eventually, I had to explain that I couldn't see him one Friday, because I had decided to go to the disco in the school gym. He said that he wanted to come along. I thought I had convinced him that this was not possible. He acquiesced. I told him that it would be really boring, but he could still sense that I really wanted to go. The reason was that there were girls that I saw every day at school that I wanted to meet socially. Girls from my class who headed in a different direction when school was over.

I had only ever gone over towards the Cavehill and the Antrim Road socially just the once – to a disco in a scout hut way over in middle-class Belfast, and that had ended in disaster. All for one girl. I knew that she liked me. A friend had given me a black chain to carry with me. 'You'll feel safer with this. You won't know anybody over there.' It was useless trying to explain that I was going to mix with my class mates and that I would be perfectly safe. So I carried the chain in the pocket of my Wranglers. I walked to the scout hut and got there very late. Most people seemed drunk, but the girl was there. I can't remember her name. Many people recognised me and I really felt that this time I had broken out of the social chains binding me to Ligoniel and Silverstream and that little patch of no-man's-land in between. She smiled my way. I was talking to a friend from school – all six foot two of him – all skin and bones. He weighed less than nine stones. We called him 'Tubey'. Tubey was another badminton player, and we stood talking about badminton tournaments. It was that kind of night. Suddenly the door swung open and in swaggered a gang of Academy boys – all dressed up for a night out. They acted drunk. The crowds separated as they pushed our way.

193

Tubey didn't manage to get out of their way in time, so he was pushed over for good measure. He was so light, this was no achievement. I took one pace forward. This was more an act of defiance than an act of bravery. I thought that I had left all this behind for one night. I was angry that it had followed me here. Somebody hit me on the side of the face. I stumbled. From the moment I saw them coming in, I had been gripping the chain in the pocket of my jeans. As I got up off the floor, the leader of the gang – a rugby-playing member of the Academy – stepped forward. A forehand shot hit him square on the forehead, a backhand sent him reeling across the floor. He seemed to be bleeding rather badly. Many people screamed, including I suspect some of his gang. The lights went up. The organisers ran forward to search me. An unseen hand touched my back. I passed the chain to it. No chain was found on me. It was nevertheless suggested that I should leave immediately. I walked slowly towards the door and as I did so I felt someone slip the chain back into my pocket. This was like a dream. When I got to the door, the girl was waiting for me. She asked me if I wanted to walk her home. The rugby player who had started all this still lay on the floor. 'Did you see Beats?' I heard them say. That was my nickname. It always had a slightly different ring to it after that night.

I was enchanted. Even when I kissed her outside some large detached house off the Antrim Road and I discovered that her lips were tight and unyielding. And very, very dry. 'It was probably her lipstick,' explained one of my friends, Raymond, later. Raymond knew more about these matters than me. 'Expensive lipstick is dry. It's got nothing to do with her lips.'

She wanted to see me again, but I said that I wasn't sure. She said that she understood. 'They'll be after you. You'll be a hunted man.' The truth was that I didn't know if I could face that walk again. Or those dry lips.

But the Christmas disco was my only way of finding out if tight lips still liked me, and if I still liked her. I drank a half bottle of Mundies full-strength South African wine on the bus down the Cliftonville. The disco was packed. Mundies gave you a rush to the brain. 'I wanna tell you about my baby.' This was me singing. 'You know she comes around. She's about

194

five feet four – from her head to the ground.' 'Gloria' was the Belfast anthem. The lights dazzled me. I scanned that crowded gym and I saw her immediately. She was there. 'And her name was G L O R I A.'

Even then I never knew the name of dry lipstick but, because she was an Academy girl, I could probably have made a stab at her surname and her initials.

But she was about five feet four, so that was okay. Tonight there would be no mistakes. Suddenly, a prefect came up to me. 'Do you know two people called John and Jinxie because they're outside waiting for you. I told them that they couldn't come in but they asked me if I'd got too many teeth. You've got some charming friends.' I pleaded with him to say that he couldn't find me, but he looked terrified. 'I'm not talking to them again. They're not reasonable people. You can try to talk to them if you like.'

I walked out into the cold December air. The effects of the Mundies had all but gone. John and Jinxie stood shivering in their short denim jackets. 'Fuckin' about time. You didn't tell us this fuckin' school of yours was so far down the Cliftonville. It's nearly in Tiger's Bay, for fuck's sake. Get us in.'

We stood there on that snowy night, and I explained that there was no possibility – none whatsoever – of the two of them passing themselves off as Academy boys. I could just about manage it some of the time. We stood in that snow arguing and I could feel the frustration and tension mounting in the two of them.

At that moment three boys from the disco came down to greet them. They had heard all about the reputation of these two from up at the turn-of-the-road, and they came down to shake their hand – to say that they had met them. To say that they knew them. I could feel that this was a grave mistake. One of these boys was 'Orbs' – reputedly one of the best fighters in the school, but this was a reputation based on a few punches thrown one wet afternoon in the third form. In other words, a reputation based on nothing. John and Jinxie were in a different league.

John enjoyed the temporary adulation from his new admirers, but this was just a temporary distraction from the frustration and the resentment building up inside him. He then asked their names. He said he had heard the name 'Orbs' before. 'Beats tells me you fancy yourself as a bit of a hard man.' I knew what was coming next. Jinxie took one step back and kicked Orbs with a flying kick full in the face. John picked up a milk bottle and tried to smash it over the head of one of the others. It missed and hit his shoulder. Incredibly, it didn't break. Orbs and his two friends fled. John and Jinxie were in hysterics. 'Fuckin' hard men. You could beat them with your fuckin' cap.'

'Who'd want to go into a place like that? You can't go back in now, Beats. You're going to have to leave with us.'

We walked home through the snow – up the Cliftonville, up the Oldpark, and then across the Ballysillan. The snow was deeper and thicker up our way. I was being taken home. The horizons were narrowing. The next disco that we were allowed into was in our local church hall. Catholics from Ligoniel were invited to mix with us Protestants. It was a chance to get the two sides together. All I remember is how strange they looked. 'Yokels,' said one of my friends. Their denims didn't even have turn-ups. We had seen them passing the turn-of-the-road many times on the tops of the Ligoniel buses. Hunched over, puffing at their cigarettes. Eyeing us suspiciously. And here they were. 'Oh, sugar . . .' It was the Archies.

I saw one of our lads carry a hammer in with him. He had it up inside his little Wrangler jacket. You could see the bump. For one awful moment I thought it might be a hatchet. But the bump was rounded. The bouncers at this disco were two churchwardens, not used to looking out for those sort of things. Twenty minutes after the disco started he used it. The victim was just one random Catholic standing in exactly the wrong spot – near the door. The boy who hit him with the hammer was fifteen. The lights went up and we stood about waiting to see what was going to happen next. One of the churchwardens examined the boy's head. John did not want to be outdone. He boasted that he could knock one of the Taigs over with one punch. The person he picked was not suspecting anything. John punched him from the side and fell on top of him on the way down. That did not impress his peers. 'He

196

only fucking went over because you fell on him. That was fucking useless.'

Later that night John cornered one of them by the hedge on Ligoniel Road. He waited until we were all in position before he 'weighed' into him. It was as if he wanted to smell the fear. It was as if he wanted to humiliate him. I always thought that John's reputation depended on the fear he could engender. Palpable fear, tangible fear. It was all in his timing. It was this more than any athleticism or natural fighting ability. Jinxie could stand holding a conversation with someone, take one short step back and kick them full frontal in the face. Linkie could cause great indentations on cars with one punch. John could do none of this, but he could make them sweat.

I can remember that boy's face to this day. Nobody did anything to stop John. But then again we never did. We stuck together. We backed each other up. You never knew when you would have to rely on your friends. But the point was that you could. I would have trusted some of those lads with my life. It was John though who threatened the cohesion of the group. He seemed to be playing to slightly different rules.

It was a strange night. Nobody ever talked about reconciliation between Protestants and Catholics after that. The Ligoniel lads got their own back and that night Jim Watt, who was generally very quiet and very well behaved the whole evening, got stabbed in the knee. He was stabbed whilst trying to reconcile the two factions. He had to hijack a bus to get him to the hospital. I'm not saying that this made him bitter or played any causal role in any of his subsequent actions, but it didn't help. Nothing that night helped.

But I knew that sooner or later, I was going to leave this behind and I did. John did not prosper. Despite his ways with a hatchet, he never became a Shankill Butcher. In the mid-1970s he was found in an entry over in the east of the city – he had been viciously beaten and severely kicked. His throat had been cut. He bled to death in the entry. He had been drinking heavily. He was never a butcher in the end, he was butchered. He was twenty-two years old when he died.

It was February and I was probably cycling up Trinity Street

197

in Cambridge as the mist crept in from the Fens. The mist probably chilled my bones and I never knew why.

I sit with some old yellow cuttings from the *Belfast Telegraph* in front of me. John was sent to the Maze on a theft charge, where the *Telegraph* explains 'he sought and obtained political status'. He fell out with those in charge of the Organisation in the Maze, and was then sent to Magilligan prison to serve out the remainder of his sentence. There he was beaten up. He was always too much his own man to take orders.

Four men were subsequently charged with his murder. The one who was sentenced to life imprisonment for his murder was himself a former inmate of the Maze. The three others got relatively short sentences after pleading guilty to causing grievous bodily harm.

The one who cut his throat was twenty years old and a Protestant.

Postscript

I often thought of John. He had a natural intelligence about him. Like me, and unlike many Academy boys, he liked numbers and words. He always felt that he never got a fair deal in terms of education. Those boys from the Antrim Road got it all. This undoubtedly played some role in his anger. Or this is what I like to think when I am trying to remember him in a favourable light. There was a poem that I showed him once which he liked. It was 'The Combat' by Edwin Muir. The last verse reads:

> And now, while the trees stand watching still
> The unequal battle rages there,
> And the killing beast that cannot kill
> Swells and swells in his fury till
> You well might think it was despair.

16

Territoriality

In the street

I hadn't been to the Falls Road for years. I'd been up the Shankill a hundred times in the meantime, and the Shankill is only a few hundred yards from the Falls, but I'd never made it as far as the Falls. In Belfast, you see, you have to be of one religion or the other, on one side or the other, a Protestant or a Catholic, a Prod or a Taig. There can be no middle ground. This was hammered home to me one day when I was still at school. I was walking on the lower Shankill with a schoolfriend who just happened to be Jewish. We were 'pulled', as they say in Belfast, by four youths. 'Are you Protestant or Catholic?' they asked menacingly. All the signs told me that those who had stopped us were themselves Protestant, so I answered 'Protestant', truthfully and enthusiastically. They turned to my friend, 'What about you fat chops?' There was a long pause. 'Jewish,' he replied nervously. There was an even longer pause – 'Well then are you a Protestant or a Catholic Jew?' 'Protestant Jew, of course,' said my friend, and we were allowed to go on our way, just. Despite this incident, I feel safe on the Shankill, on the Falls I assumed I wouldn't.

But this was my big chance – a walk up the Falls. For some reason the people that I know always say they're going 'up the Falls', never 'into the Falls', or 'down the Falls'. Perhaps the people I know never get out of it, perhaps they never return, perhaps Prods aren't allowed to.

The morning of the walk was a typical Belfast winter morning – thick fog with a strong smell of smoke hanging in it. A bit like how I imagine a 'peasouper' in London to be, around the turn of the century, but 'peasouper' sounds too homely and too cozy for the Belfast variety. The smell of smoke clings to your clothing. You can't shake it off. Belfast was relatively 'quiet', as they say in that resigned way. That morning, at two-thirty a.m., a twenty-nine-year-old UDR captain was shot dead as he walked his fiancée home off the Ormeau Road. The night before at around six p.m. a twenty-year-old Roman Catholic man was shot dead in his home by two masked gunmen. It happened in front of his mother and two sisters. 'Did you shoot him right?' one of the gunmen asked as they left, and the other turned back and fired one more shot into the victim's body, for good measure. The victim's mother described how the gunman 'took up a stance like something out of *Starsky and Hutch*. I was sitting squealing at him: "Don't, please don't."' But none of this had happened on the Falls, it happened miles away – two miles away.

I always think the Falls really starts in Castle Street right in the centre of Belfast, because it is in Castle Street that the so-called 'black' taxis line up, with the overflow in Chapel Lane. The black taxis are cheaper than the buses and more regular. They run on the Shankill as well, a proportion of the profits of both going to the Organisation, the IRA in one case, the UDA in the other. Up past the taxi ranks in Castle Street, up past Divis Flats now in the process of being emptied, you come across the unmistakable message on the gable wall: 'PROVO LAND'. At this point my little Prody heart beats faster. I hum when I'm nervous, and the first tune that comes to mind is an old Linfield supporters tune, Linfield being the most Protestant of Belfast football teams: 'Follow, follow, we will follow Linfield, up the Falls, Derry's walls, we will follow on.' I hum it anyway because it's the only tune that I can think of, but I take the precaution of leaving out the words.

On the left is a doctor's surgery in what looks like a metal cage, on the right a community clothes shop with a statue of

Jesus pointing at his blood-red heart in the window, with a 'Not for sale' sign just below it. Graffiti is everywhere, and it keeps you informed of all recent developments: 'Seawright got a hole in his head for Christmas'. And then is added by way of an up-date: 'McMichael got one too'. Seawright was the Unionist politician, and McMichael the UDA commander, murdered the previous month. On the next gable wall there are inducements to 'Vote Adams X' and 'Vote Sinn Fein', and then the curiously ambiguous 'Give them their rights – not their last rites'. But who is it referring to? Clearly not Seawright and McMichael, that's for sure.

Then it's up past Dunville Park, where there had been a punishment shooting the night before – a teenager was found lying with gunshot wounds to the knee and both ankles. A popular form of punishment for the IRA. But this morning the park is quiet, it's dominated by the Dunville Day Centre for Senior Citizens. Presumably many of the senior citizens remember the last Troubles and the Troubles before that. My Uncle Jack, who is eighty-three and born in Shield Street on the Falls, was driven out of the area in 1922. Nothing surprises him, and certainly not the current Troubles. 'It's always been like this,' he says. The graffiti on the wall puts it slightly differently – '7 years is enough, 700 is too much'. The Protestants get the best jobs, they say, my Uncle Jack ended up as a lollipop man showing kids across the road. Then it's up past the Royal Victoria Hospital, world famous for the skill of its surgeons, and the pioneering of new surgical techniques, out of sheer necessity. It's barely recognisable as a hospital from the outside – more like a run-down block of flats, until you see the sign 'Eye and Ear Clinic', with the 'Y' from 'Eye' missing. My father died there during what was meant to be a routine operation. Nobody ever explained what went wrong. We were just another routine working-class bereaved family. Then it's back to the graffiti 'IRA 1 UDA 0', and a bit further up 'IRA 2 Liverpool 0. And one hit the bar'. An army patrol makes its way warily past, it's the first one I've seen on the Falls that morning. The soldiers all look ridiculously young, most of them are small, ordinary working-class youths from another, but not too distant, culture. The patrol is accompanied by a young RUC officer. A soldier crouches on the greasy pavement, and a big black dog sniffs around him. The Falls, and indeed all of Belfast, is full of big black dogs, usually half Alsatian half Collie, out wandering alone, looking for someone to sniff. I suppose the soldiers are as good as anyone else.

Further up the Falls, the graffiti gives way to wall murals, and the football-type slogans give way to political slogans. On the corner of Beechmount Avenue there is a mural of a Provo crouching complete with grenade launcher. The name of the avenue has been painted over and replaced with 'RPG Avenue'. I asked one woman what it stood for. She said she didn't know, but she said that she wished that 'the army would leave the murials [sic] alone'. A pot of paint had been splattered all over the crouching Provo. 'The army do it in the middle of the night you know, and they're such beautiful murials,' said my informant before she left. I wished her well, so friendly and cheerful, so resilient, despite everything, like all ordinary Belfast people, Protestant, Catholic or Jew. I later discovered that RPG Avenue stood for 'Rocket Propelled Grenade Avenue'.

Further up are other murals linking the IRA and the ANC, with the message 'We aim to be free', and 'Victory to the Armed Struggle'. This is just before you get to the top of the road, with the City Cemetery on the right and, just past it, Milltown Cemetery on the left. Both doing excellent business. Protestants in one, Catholics in the other, with the main thoroughfare right up the middle, separating them, it seems, for ever.

The Falls is a few miles from my mother's home, but it seemed like another town that I was never allowed to visit. It could have been another country. The men had moustaches. They don't up our way. I spent hours in the City Cemetery at the grave of my grandparents trying to think why. To any of it.

In the head

They had been killed on their way home from work on a Friday. Pay day. They were all Protestant. Their lunch boxes were all over the road. Slaughtered because they worked for a construction company, which served the security forces. It was said that they were singing about the massacre in a bar in the Republican village of Pomeroy that night. 'It's dangerous being a construction worker in the North.' I never heard the tune, but it was probably jaunty enough, once they found something to rhyme with the word 'slaughter'.

It was the worst civilian atrocity since the Enniskillen Remembrance Day Massacre in 1987. Then Gordon Wilson forgave his daughter's killers, just hours after her murder, when the emotion was still raw. But this time there was to be no forgiveness. Nobody was going to forgive and forget the slaughter at the Teebane crossroads. The killing would go on. Since 1989 thirty people have been killed in a struggle between the IRA and loyalist paramilitaries in a small circle within a twenty mile radius of Cookstown. The killing fields of Tyrone, with its neat hedges. 'Not like the South. You always know when you're back in Northern Ireland,' said the man by the side of the road. And the long luxuriant grass all white on the stalk. In that cold unforgiving winter light.

I always knew Cookstown because of its sausages. There was a little jingle on Ulster TV, years back. 'Cookstown sausages . . .' I don't remember the refrain, or the message. Probably no more memorable than the wee song from Pomeroy about brickies and chippies with their heads mashed in. But Omagh, the county town of Tyrone, and just down the road from Cookstown, I didn't know. 'You've heard of Cookstown sausages, but you've never heard of Omagh glass? That's typical for a Protestant.' She sat in the bus shelter. Slim and slight. Not much over five foot. Blue grey eyes, but a pointed face. Thin. You could imagine it hollow. Ireland's long struggle was in that face, or could be. Pretty, innocent even, waiting for time and destiny to write its indelible message. I could imagine her with a black shawl pulled down over her head. Jesus, there's a lot to feel guilty about, and I'm not even English.

She had started the talking. 'You're quite chatty yourself . . . for a Protestant.' I asked her how she knew. 'I don't look out for specific features. I can just tell. Catholics are a lot more talkative and friendly than Protestants. But then again, I wouldn't say that you're not. I don't know how I knew. At university in Jordanstown, there are plenty who you could say for definite were one thing or the other. But there are some who would be in the middle. You might have been in the middle, but you weren't, if you know what I mean. I could just tell.'

I sat in silence. A dour Protestant sort of silence. She was twenty and a student. 'You're not Church of Ireland, by any chance, are you?' I nodded mournfully. Her eyes sparkled. 'That explains it. I always think that the Church of Ireland is as close to Catholicism as you can get. You're not like Presbyterians. You're more like us, even if you're not prepared to admit it. I do have some Protestant friends, you see. Some of them are very Catholic orientated. They mix a lot with Catholics, and so they become more like us – more outgoing, more friendly. I've been out with some Protestant boys. They always say that they prefer Catholic girls – they say that we've got better morals. I've heard all about what some Protestant girls get up to at parties. It's unbelievable.'

I'd heard the stories as well. I spent my youth hoping that they were true. I nodded silently.

'I've even been asked out by a RUC man, you know. He was searching my car at this wee tin shed in Strabane. He started chatting away to me. I knew that he was chatting me up really. He asked me out, and he said that he would meet me at this club in Strabane. I didn't go in the end. But it was for his own sake. I thought that he was being a bit silly, and taking an awful risk by asking me out. He must have known that I was a Catholic.

'My brother knows a lot of Protestants as well. He went to a Protestant school – Omagh Academy – so he had some Protestant friends. He only went to that school because he failed his Eleven Plus. My mother works in the grammar school in Omagh, but my brother couldn't get in there. My parents didn't want him to go the local secondary school, because it's pretty awful, so they paid for him to go to Omagh Academy. Protestant schools are all right. I always think they place a lot of emphasis on sport, too much emphasis really. Catholic schools are a lot more academic in my opinion. Also

204

Protestant schools are a lot less strict. The pupils are on a level with their teacher. They could just say that they didn't agree with what the teacher was saying. You couldn't do that in a Catholic school. Teachers are on a higher level from you. They're there to be respected. The thing that always gets me about Protestant schools is that the pupils are taught that Catholics are really, really bad. At least, that's what I've heard. We would never be taught anything like that about Protestants.'

Omagh was relaxed. A haven of calm in a troubled Tyrone sea. I wanted to feel calm again. I wanted to escape red, raw emotion, and grieving widows who couldn't catch a breath, and fatherless children waiting for daddy to come home with the pocket money on a Friday. Waiting, waiting still. She caught my eye again. 'Omagh is a very prosperous town, you know. We haven't had any bombs here for ages. They say it's because of our Sinn Fein-led council. The IRA leave us alone. We're all very anti-violence in this town. We don't agree with the IRA at all. The girls from the country at my school were very Republican, very pro-IRA, but they had good reason for it. They had experienced soldiers ransacking their houses. At least, that's what I'd heard. One girl at school knew a fella who had been shot. One time I was going to Coleraine and I had a friend with me. Some soldiers stopped us and my friend was giving them a bit of lip. Not much lip mind, it's just that he wasn't falling over himself to be friendly with them. So they warned him that he had better watch himself or they could make his life hell. There can be a lot of tension sometimes.

'It's more of a political war anyway than a religious war. In my opinion, if there had been a war in the first place when it all broke out in 1969, then it would have been the best thing that could have happened. My grannie's aunt used to be in the old IRA, when it was a respectable organisation.'

'My grandfather used to be in the old UVF when it was still a respectable organisation,' I replied. So here we were sworn enemies, from several generations back, sitting side-by-side, blinking into the winter's sun, waiting for a bus.

'My father and mother are both fluent in Irish. My father goes to Irish lessons run by the Gaelic Association. At the end

205

of the night, they're all giving these 'V' signs – for peace. But come to think of it – it could be the 'V' for victory. I went to Irish dancing for twelve years. My family are very into Irish culture. My father's from Donegal, my mother's from Cavan. All our relatives live in the South of Ireland, except us. If anyone ever asks me, I'd rather say that I'm from Ireland, than from Northern Ireland. I'm Irish basically. I don't have any sort of identity problem. The funny thing is that I was born in London, my parents lived there for a short while, so when any Protestants have a go at me, I say that I'm more British than the lot of you. But I'm Irish although that's not the same as being a Republican. I don't feel comfortable with the extremes on either side. I wouldn't feel very comfortable going up the Falls Road in Belfast. A friend once invited me up to a Republican club up the Falls. But I wouldn't go. I wouldn't know half the Republican songs anyway. I didn't realise until very recently that the Falls and the Shankill are right beside each other. Not a bit of wonder there's so much trouble in Belfast. But I'm proud to be Irish. It's great when you're abroad and they ask you where you're from, and you say Irish. They hate the English abroad. Where do you say you're from?'

So I sat there, in the throes of an identity crisis. What was I? She could be born in London and still not have the slightest anxiety about her Irish identity. And yet there was me. Born and bred in Belfast, and yet what? Waiting still.

'I always think that Ulster Protestants are a lot like the English. The English aren't very friendly. The real difference between Protestants and Catholics is that Protestants are very tight with their money. When I studied history at school we learned all about the Protestant work ethic and the rise of capitalism. I think that this is where it all comes from. For Protestants wealth is a sign from God that they are doing well. It is a sign from God that they are in favour. Catholics have a very different view. The Catholic attitude is, 'what's the good in hanging on to money? You can't bring it with you when you're dead.' If a Catholic goes out with forty pounds in his pocket for a night out, he'll spend it. A Protestant would come back with some money in his pocket. I have some Protestant friends and although they're very different sorts of people, they're very similar in some respects. They would both remind you if you owed them thirty pence. They would never forget about the money you owe them. They always have little ways of reminding you. But if they owe you money, it's a different story. I went out with this Protestant fella to this Van Morrison concert. I paid for the tickets by cheque. He said that he would write me a cheque afterwards, but he never did. He took me for a meal after the concert, and he was acting the big man. He ordered a bottle of wine each, and everything, then he asked me to pay half. Protestants seem awful stingy to me.'

The bus was late. The winter sun was setting over the horizon, casting long shadows over those killing fields, with their nice, neat hedges. 'You know, sitting here talking to you there's one thing I often wonder about. They always say that Protestants are the majority in Northern Ireland, but everybody I end up talking to is a Catholic. I don't purposefully look for them. Do you know what I think? I don't think the majority in Northern Ireland is Protestant anymore. I think those in charge are deliberately falsifying the census. I think that Northern Ireland has more Catholics than Protestants but they're trying to keep this secret. They've done worse things in the past. I wouldn't put this past them.'

The winter sun was expiring. Gone, dead, extinguished. The cold crept in. Through your bones, until you felt vulnerable and alone. You wrapped yourself against the elements. You comforted yourself. The talk was dying too.

'The other big difference between Protestants and Catholics is that Catholics can talk the hind legs off a donkey. Protestants tend to be a bit quiet, a bit too quiet for me. Except when they're ranting and raving that is. Only kidding. You're not all like the big fella, big Ian, after all.

'Now are you?'

In the heart

My Uncle Terence and Aunt Agnes really were an odd couple. He was big and fat, she was small and thin, painfully thin. He ate enough for two, she didn't eat enough for one; and he ate hers. Meal times involved a prolonged ritual. He would get stuck into his grub, she would pick at hers. She always left the meat. Then she would complain about not being hungry and he would shovel the remains on to his plate and he would complain too – about having to eat hers.

Their complaints weren't really complaints at all of course, just background noise – music for fluorescent suppers. It was a way of organising talk, of organising conversation (their complaints always meshed) whilst they ate. And they did share what they had – even if the end result was hardly equitable. He grew and she contracted: he was fifteen stone to her seven.

I knew them all my life. She was my mother's sister, he was my father's best friend. They were more than aunt and uncle – more like a second set of parents. They lived at the top of Ligoniel in Belfast, we lived at the bottom. I would be allowed to go to their house on a Saturday night and sleep between the two of them. My aunt worked in the carding room at Ewarts, the linen mill in Ligoniel. This was one of the dirtiest jobs in the place. The air was thick with dust from the flax. My mother ended up in the twisting room – one of the cleaner jobs.

'Your mother was always fond of style,' my uncle would say, 'she could go to work dressed – your aunt couldn't.' She would come to our house for lunch: it was always banana sandwiches. I would get her groceries – forty Woodbines for her (and later, Embassy for the coupons) and a half pound of steak for grilling for him. The butcher didn't sell much steak for grilling so he always gave me a bone for the dog. The dog, like my uncle, was always on a diet.

My father died in the sixties and soon after that my aunt and uncle moved to Bath, just before the Troubles started. My uncle worked for the Royal Naval Stores and he got a transfer. I never understood why they wanted to leave home like that. There was something else I didn't understand. Why they were never at my Aunt May's and Uncle Jack's after my father was buried.

May and Jack's house was one better than ours. They had a tiny front garden. That made all the difference. When my father died, all the relatives were invited to their house for the cold ham sandwiches after his cold body had been lain to rest.

I knew that it was cold. 'Go on touch it. Stroke his hair,' my mother had cajoled me. So I did. We sat that day eating those limp ham sandwiches. Not saying much. 'I bet you had a proper Irish wake.' They still say this to me now. But we're Protestants, I say. We don't go in for all that singing and dancing and drinking, or whatever it is that they do. We just sit there in our suits eating cold ham sandwiches. Nobody says much. It isn't a wake, in fact, it isn't much of anything.

There was one strange thing though. My Uncle Terence wasn't there, and he was my father's best friend. He had been there earlier that day, and he had been at the graveside, but now he was gone.

I had caught him crying earlier in the back bedroom in my house. He had obviously sneaked up there to cry, and looked embarrassed that I had seen him. He was always too much of a man to cry in public so he hides himself and cries. He cried that day when my father died, he cried when my brother died, he cried when his wife died. Three times in a lifetime isn't bad.

I didn't realise at my father's 'wake' that my uncle wasn't invited, that he had never been in that house, that house with the tiny garden and the cold limp ham sandwiches on the polished mahogany table. Terence was a Catholic. My Aunt May and my Uncle Jack were staunch loyalists. Jack was in the Orange Order and in the Black. My Aunt May was in the Orange Order as well. 'Your Uncle Terence just wasn't welcome,' explained my mother long afterwards. 'There was no point in arguing about it in those days.'

I would spend all of my long school holidays with my Aunt Agnes and Uncle Terence in Wiltshire and Somerset. My aunt was fifty-three and looked out of place in Bath among the foreign students, French schoolchildren, and the middle-class matrons who invaded the Pump Room. While my uncle worked, she would wander about Bath – the shops mainly. Woolworths and Littlewoods. She didn't think much of the Georgian terraces and, anyway, most of them were at the top of a hill. All those Woodbine and Embassy for the coupons made that hill unscalable.

They eventually got a house in Chippenham which was more to their liking. A huge council estate full of, well, ordinary people, and pubs, just like Belfast. Their friends were from Wales or second generation Irish. They found a local about five miles from their house, or rather it found them. 'We went into this little pub and people just started chatting,' my uncle would say. In a county of quaint little pubs with brass kick-knacks and imitation Charles II spaniels, they found a pub not unlike a Belfast drinking club. Plain, functional, unpretentious, dreary, and it stayed open until the small hours.

Their accents never changed – although they started saying 'cheers' when you bought them a drink (I'd never heard that before in Belfast) and my mother would comment on how English they'd become (although she's no expert, as she thinks that 'ta-ra' from Coronation Street is a typical and widespread form of English farewell). They said they'd never return to Belfast. 'Not bloody likely,' my aunt would say. They'd watch the Troubles on the television. 'Each side's as bad as the other,' my aunt would say carefully. 'I saw it coming,' my uncle would add. She never said she had. She was the Protestant, he was the Catholic. I'm not sure if that was relevant here or not.

They had met during the war in 1940, whilst out walking. Agnes was in the ARP. The relationship had to be kept totally secret, except from my mother. They used to meet in town for a drink or go for walks in the country. 'On Sundays we used to pass each other in the park,' my uncle said, 'Your aunt would be coming from church and I'd be going home with the lads after playing football. She couldn't even look at me, let alone speak to me. Her mother would have killed her.'

My uncle loves singing and sang in the choir at St Vincent de Paul in Ligoniel. 'My mother told the priest whom I was going out with so he had a long talk with me,' my uncle said. 'Then he threatened to make me leave the choir. I didn't give him the pleasure, I left.'

Terence didn't visit Agnes at home until after her father had died. It was 1955. She was now forty, he was thirty-four. They'd been going out for fifteen years.

My mother said that everybody knew that Terence was a Catholic right from the start because he came from Ligoniel.

'Jean, that was her chum, also went with one, but she didn't marry him. Nobody thought anything of it,' said my mother, 'because she was a good deal older than him. Nobody thought that it would be serious because of the age difference. She had a lovely fella run after her. He was a lovely big fella, he was in the Irish Guards. After the war this fella from the Irish Guards was on the buses as a driver, and he used to ask me about her an' all. But it just hadn't to be with the fella from the Irish Guards. She'd fallen for Terry. Years ago, she never went in for a drink or anything like that. They used to go to the Classic picture house, just where the British Home Stores is now. When they came out, he would have gone in for one drink, just the one, and she would have waited outside. She was afraid of anybody seeing her with him. They were going out for years before anybody in the family knew, except me.

'When my mother did eventually find out, I made sure that I was out of the house that particular night. My mother got the Minister down. It was the Reverend Craig and he talked to Agnes about the problems of having a relationship with a Roman Catholic. She was crying an' all, you know. I was glad that I wasn't there. My mother said that the Minister was very, very nice about it all. He just made her promise that she wouldn't turn with him. Neither she did. She never turned.

'But she didn't get married until our mother died. She got married in a registry office in Great Victoria Street. Your father and me stood for her. There was no guests invited to the wedding, there were just the four of us. Then the four of us just went and had dinner and that was it.'

'I have a Catholic friend from Ligoniel who used to say over and over again that they weren't married. Roman Catholics don't believe that you're married if you're married in a registry office. Then Agnes went to live up in his house up in Ligoniel with him and his mother. She didn't really get on with her mother-in-law because his mother was a bit of a bossy woman, but very kind-hearted with it.

'But I'll tell you something, Terry made her a very, very good man, because our Agnes didn't know what it was to pay a bill. So she could throw her money around her.

211

'My brother-in-law Jack never spoke to Agnes for years, but now he thinks Terry is a great fella. I got the shock of my life about him. I was angry at him, because it was none of his business. Agnes was only his sister-in-law. Our May wouldn't have been as bad. She didn't stop talking to her or anything, but Jack was terrible. Agnes didn't go into their house for years and years and years. When I was in their house we never talked about Agnes. It wasn't a forbidden topic or anything. I just didn't want to talk about her to them. Your Aunt May only saw her if the two of them were in my house at the same time. May would never have visited her up in her house in Ligoniel. In fact, I didn't go up much myself. But then again, I didn't need to because she was down every night. Agnes was never very close to May's children because she didn't see them very much.

'If they'd ever had children there would have been problems. She was pregnant, but she miscarried on the Liverpool boat, then there was no more. She couldn't have any more children. It just hadn't to be. It's not that she didn't want them. She would have made a very good mother. It's all a terrible pity.'

My uncle said that he had to leave Belfast in the end. He had worked in armaments during the war, before getting a job in the Royal Naval Stores. 'I was fed up with the Civil Service. I did everything right but my promotion was always blocked. It was like a brick wall. I was the trade union convener, but I was asked to resign. All the names on the list were Protestants, except for one Catholic – Paddy O'Hara – and everybody knew he never looked at what he was signing. I tried to get out to Singapore but they said I'd failed the medical. My own doctor said I was right as rain.

When they moved to England my aunt got a job in the Naval Stores in Copenacre, after twenty-eight years of inhaling flax dust. 'She couldn't believe her new job,' my uncle said. 'You could go to the toilet whenever you wanted to – and have a cigarette if you wanted one. If you'd done that in the mill, you'd have been out on your arse.'

In England, my uncle found a choir and practised his religion. My aunt gave hers up. They hardly ever went back to Belfast, and they only did so in the first place for a funeral –

212

my brother's. And a funny funeral it was, because there was no body – it lay on Nanda Devi in the Himalayas. His fellow climbers couldn't get it down.

In the time-honoured tradition after the funeral, my uncle and I went to the pub, but by then all the pubs where we live had gone and all that was left was a series of drinking clubs. And drinking clubs are sectarian in a way that pubs never could have been. No soft light, no carpets, no strangers. And when we went, he was the only Catholic in the bar, and the barman was the brother of one of the notorious Shankill butchers.

But no one bothered him, except to buy him a drink. It was as if those ten years away had never been, except he still said 'cheers' when they bought him a drink. Just the slightest hint of a foreign culture. They even visited my Aunt May's house for the first time. Her husband, Jack, was the staunch loyalist – it had taken him thirty-eight years to invite the Catholic home.

It was obvious this was where their hearts lay, and there were tears when they were leaving. There had been none the first time round. My aunt and uncle vowed to spend their holidays back home.

But there weren't many holidays left. My aunt's health deteriorated. For two years she couldn't walk more than a few yards at a time. When she inhaled, her chest made a loud whistle. The carding room and the saving for the Embassy gifts (always given to others) had taken their toll.

She died in Bath, cardiac arrest, respiratory failure, pneumonia; the grim reaper had made no mistake with this one. But at the time of her death, one strange thing had occurred. My aunt and uncle had come to resemble each other quite closely. They'd both gone grey, and old age had bent and shortened my uncle and made him thinner (in a way that the steak for grilling never could); infirmity had made my aunt fatter – her body had filled with fluid, and her abdomen had expanded. She had the same skinny legs but a massive torso. She resembled a sparrow at the time of her death. A grim house sparrow.

The funeral was very English. In Ireland, the relatives and

friends shoulder the coffin to the grave and fill it in, at least in part. In England, it is left to others. My aunt was cremated at her request; she wanted her ashes taken home – to be scattered like she'd been. This made the whole thing more English: clean and crisp; vaporised, and released into the ether instead of being dug into the heavy peat. The thick clay of history.

After the service, we went to the pub and my uncle told anybody who was prepared to listen that 'he had just buried his wife today'. Even though, I suppose, that what he really meant was that she had just been incinerated for him that day. 'Cremation is more civilised,' he said with a face heavily laden with emotion.

And I suppose that one couldn't help agreeing with him. After all, it had all been frightfully English.

My mother was very impressed with my uncle's treatment of her sister in life, and in death.

'Your Aunt Agnes stopped going to church after she married him. But he didn't give up practising his religion. He stuck by it. His only problem was that he couldn't take Communion because he had married a Protestant. But I'm telling you, there's not many would have done what he done. Your Aunt Agnes didn't know that she was going to die, and he could have buried her anyway he wanted to. He could have buried her in a Roman Catholic church, if he'd wanted to, but he didn't. He gave her a full Protestant service. He picked the hymns himself out of our hymn book, and he had the full service with the Minister preaching. Although she died in Wiltshire, that minister was Church of Ireland from Banbridge in Northern Ireland. That was a special touch. Then Terry brought her ashes over to Carnmoney to my mother's grave, and scattered them there. She was brought back to her own people. It was as if she was coming home.'

He did all that for a Protestant.

And a wife.

17

Gone But Not Forgotten

It was a beautiful morning. It had rained overnight, but the sun was already warm, and the streets were drying out. A row of small gardens, courtesy of the Housing Executive, backed onto the road. The gardens were crammed with flowers of every sort. Pansies jostled with dahlias, tulips with orange lilies. 'Love your pansies, Maisie, they're gorgeous. Any chance of a wee cutting, to stick in between my orange lilies. Flowers planted and maintained by generations reared on yards and window boxes. And good neighbourliness. You breathed deep in the mountain air, the fresh air off the hills that surround Belfast – Divis and Black Mountain and Wolfhill and Cavehill. The hills that you can see from any street, any yard, any dark corner, anywhere in Belfast. *They* were nature for the inhabitants of West and North Belfast for years. You could lie in your back bedroom and peer over your yard wall, and over your entry, and over the rows of yards and entries and over all the cold damp houses with the peeling wallpaper, and see those hills in the distance. Always there – comforting and reassuring.

I was somewhat taken aback on my first visit to West Belfast to notice that these hills could change. I was six years old at the time and my mother had taken me to the Falls Road bus depot to get the key to our house off my father who was a motor mechanic for Belfast Corporation, and based at that depot. I was always very proud of him, especially when he obtained for me the Belfast Corporation emblem, bearing the famous motto, off the side of a bus. We had discussed the motto in primary school, you see, but I was the only one to turn up at school with one in bright red enamel the very next day. *'Pro tanto quid retribuamus?'* it said – 'What shall we give for so much?' I always wondered what the answer was supposed to be. I thought that it was perhaps some sick joke. So here we were at the home of those buses all bearing this same enigmatic question, when I gazed out at those hills that I knew so well. To my dismay , the perfect symmetry of Divis and the Black Mountain seemed to have been broken from the perspective of West Belfast. They looked different from that angle, but they still looked imposing. Nature was always on the horizon in Belfast, but never closer.

But Belfast had moved on since then, and nature had now been pulled down from those hills and laid out in front of your wee house, and behind your wee house, and all the way down the street as well. The Housing Executive had worked wonders replacing Limepark Street with Limepark Mews, and bright wild orange flowers from the hills had been replaced with bright orange lilies in front of your house in Limepark *Mews*. 'Yes, Mews, Maisie, you heard me right. Mews.'

It felt good to be alive that day, just standing on that street corner surrounded by flowers, a few yards down from Limepark Mews. The friend whom I was going to visit had spent fourteen years in prison for terrorist offences, thirteen of those years in the Maze and not quite one in the new technological miracle, which is called Maghaberry. A new high-tech prison, with a difference. He had felt grass in Maghaberry for the first time in thirteen years, or so I had been told. Apparently, he couldn't get over how sensual it had felt. How sensual and how comforting. So there I stood at the corner, waiting for his father for the weekly visit. Or rather waiting and watching. A peculiarly Belfast form of recreation. Men in their thirties, forties and fifties will go down to the corner to spend a few hours to see what's what.

So there I stood. It was pension day, and as usual all the pensioners were out early. There were even couples out and about on their way to the post office on this beautiful morning. They greeted me, despite an absence of many years. I felt belonging. Some blossoms reached out of one of the small but perfectly maintained Housing Executive houses and lightly brushed the pensioners on the way past. A bee flitted from flower to flower collecting pollen. It buzzed ever so quietly. Everything was right in the world that day. But this was Belfast, and the sound of the bee was drowned out moments later by a noisier insect somewhere far above it in the sky. Somewhere up there in the heavens, where it was too bright to look. A helicopter circling and circling, reconnoitring and collecting God knows what.

A small neat-looking man approached. This had to be Jimmy. He was wearing a dark suit with a blue shirt with a long pointed collar, the kind that was all the rage in the 1970s, with no tie. A little enamel red, white and blue badge stood out on his lapel. This, after all, was North Belfast. He saw me staring up at the helicopter. He could sense my puzzlement. 'You know, I've often wondered what they can see from up there. Perhaps they could charge us for a wee ride over Belfast – panoramic views of your city guaranteed.' We both laughed and shook hands. This was the man's father. We stood together, as the pensioners passed. They all knew him. He recognised me, even though I had never met him before. 'You're the spittin' image of your mother.' He fiddled nervously with his badge. 'They'll probably ask me to take this off, before I get in to see him. Maghaberry after all is an integrated prison. Everything is divided up into houses, not like the H-blocks in the Maze. There are IRA men in the same house as my son – men he would have killed on the outside. But they have to learn to live together in there. They're all in the same boat. All away for a very long time indeed. You can't stay bitter for that long. One day you have to see sense. And because it's integrated the organisations can't take over and persuade them to do certain things.'

He returned to fiddling with the badge. 'But the officers at the prison will probably think that this badge might cause offence to certain sections of the community. I'll have to remember to take it off.'

217

It was the way this time that he said 'certain sections'. I wanted to side with him, but I couldn't. I opted for neutrality, I opted for platitude. 'Better safe than sorry, eh?' 'I volunteered. I had after all seen all those little sectarian badges of one hue or another that they wear in Belfast. And even without reading the fine print around the edge of the badge I could tell the type. You can spot it a mile off. Probably a Linfield supporter's badge. Or a UVF badge or maybe even a UFF badge, or perhaps a badge telling you that its owner actively supports the Red Hand Commandos or even the good old-fashioned UDA. He was just wearing it sort of accidentally on purpose, to show his true colours on his way to this new prison. Lest there be any mistake about where his particular allegiances lay at this new integrated prison.

We were waiting for the bus laid on by his son's former organisation, the UVF – a proscribed organisation on the Loyalist side. It had been explained to me the previous day by an official from the Northern Ireland Prison service that all passengers have to pay for transport to the prisons when the person they are visiting has elected to live in integrated rather than segregated conditions. The relatives of those prisoners who remain segregated travel free. The official had argued that this was just one kind of pressure that the various sectarian organisations can exert on prisoners to stay segregated. I fiddled nervously with my change, and asked how much the fare would be. 'It's free, he replied, 'but you can give a couple of bob to the driver if you want.' The bus may have been free, but since the prisoner we were going to visit had elected to live in integrated conditions, the ten pounds a week from the organisation which previously went to his family has stopped. There were still some sources of influence operating.

A blue minibus drew up. We clambered into the back. Apart from the driver, there were only women and children on the bus. 'We're a bit late today,' said one blowsy looking blonde on the seat nearest the door. She looked as if she had been an Elvis fan in her younger days, and she looked as if she was clinging onto as much of that style as possible through the intervening three decades. 'Like your badge though, Jimmy.' That badge again. Pride in sectarian belonging. I reminded myself that you can only bask in the positive glow of an in-group when you have an out-group to castigate. You can only have allies when you have an enemy. I ignored the badge, and concentrated on the Elvis fan's hairstyle instead. Her hair looked as if it had been dyed blonde weekly or twice weekly for the past twenty-five years. It looked worn out, not unlike herself. Her eyes were tired, and sad. Who was she going to visit that day? A husband? An Elvis fan just like her perhaps forced into a certain kind of macho role in the conflict? Elvis in *Jailhouse Rock*? Legs akimbo as he fired off his automatic weapon? Or a son? Perhaps a punk that just went that bit too far to prove himself. Surely not a father? Surely not some old Jim Reeves fan, soaked in sentimentality with some maudlin desire to affect change for the better? To return to the good old days that really never were. The good old days of entries and yards with enamel baths hung up on rusty nails on one wall. The good old days when we constantly told the world that 'we are the people'. For all the bloody good it did any of us.

That badge was winking at me again. Red, white and blue, on a kind of orange background. The words started coming back to me. It's not that they had ever been away, it's just that I haven't got much call to remember them these days. 'Sure it's old but it is beautiful and its colours they are fine.' When I sing this tune to myself, it is never my voice which actually sings the words. It's always somebody else's. I realised then why the Elvis fan seemed so familiar. It was her voice running through those words in my head. I had seen her before and hundreds like her – they were the ones swaying as they followed the bands on the twelfth of July. They were the ones singing at the tops of their voices, while I hummed 'The Sash' quietly to myself. They were the ones who managed just that little extra bit of volume as we passed every chapel, as I just threw embarrassed glances in the direction of those imposing and feared edifices. I could hear her now, singing and dancing and laughing and shouting on that very bus, despite the fact that she had not moved a muscle or a vocal chord, except to let us in. And greet us.

She was singing still: 'And it's on the twelfth I love to wear the sash my father wore', with 'sash' having an onomatopoeic quality like 'slash' or 'gash'. Ripping, tearing, slashing. Old

219

rhetorical questions seemed to be coming out of her mouth, and then providing their own answers. And what did your father wear on the twelfth? He was never a bloody Orange man. And they were right, he wasn't. He always said that he had better things to do.

The voices in my head stopped. The blowsy blonde had been silenced for once on the bus to Maghaberry, on the road to nowhere. The engine of the van sounded knackered and we slowed to a crawl, as we climbed over those hills that lock Belfast in to the Lough. Over the hill, past the green, green fields. Past nature. Past fields of a greenness that you find only in Ireland, with long lush spring grass, which the blonde's husband or son or father hadn't seen for thirteen or fourteen, or maybe even fifteen years.

A blond-haired child of about four with an angelic face and hacking cough climbed onto the seats for a better view of the fields and the lambs. His lips were stained with blackcurrant. His cough continued. 'That poor child's had a lot of operations on his bowels,' said Jimmy. I couldn't work out how this could be connected with the cough. 'He's not very well basically,' he said by way of explanation. The child was clearly excited: 'We're going to see my daddy.' he said. My companion recalled his own son at that age, and reflected on how things had turned out. You could see the lump in his throat. 'I never suspected him of being in any of the organisations, especially because he had a good job at the time as fitter in the shipyard. When the police and the army came to the house I was devastated. His mother couldn't believe it. She was English, you see, and he had always been reared with Catholics. My only way of understanding it is to recognise that it was a war situation when he got involved. Now, it's different, it's all about gangsters and you know something politicians here are the biggest gangsters of the lot. A major in the army told him that he was in the wrong job, that he should have been in the army with them. He knew that much about explosives, you see. But that's the past. All those lads on both sides have been taught a terrible lesson. They've all lost their youth.'

We were now pulling up to Maghaberry prison. I reminded my companion about the red, white and blue badge. I wanted to avoid confrontation, especially at Maghaberry of all places. 'Oh, yes,' he said as he fumbled for the pin. I had a chance to read the inscription on the badge for the very first time.

It read 'Dunkirk Veterans'.

Living in Harmony

He had the face of an angel and the behaviour of a little devil. He had spent most of the time on the bus clambering across the other passengers, particularly the children, who were easier and softer to climb on. He had eventually been placated with a large bag of M & M's. There was a certain serenity in the way that he ate them. His blue eyes were deep and still, his mouth was in perpetual motion. M & M's are Treets relaunched, and if I remember the advertising copy for Treets correctly, these were the sweets which were supposed to melt in your mouth, not in your hand. It was nearly correct. They were melting all over his mouth, and his lips and his chin and the bits at the side of his mouth were now stained brown. But the chocolates were running out.

It was now time for some more climbing. 'Billy, sit down. Sit and behave.' Billy's mother was looking harassed once more. Harrassed and very, very tired. But Billy knew that it was now time to look out of the window. It was all like clockwork. A bit of climbing, then the Treets, then you climbed into a good position, then you arrived. You could set your clock by it. And he did. He was now standing on tip-toes to see out of the window of the minibus. His muddy shoes were leaving marks all over the seat. His mother kept cleaning the marks surreptitiously. 'Come on sit down, Billy, we're not there yet.' But little Billy knew that his timing was perfect. 'That's where my daddy lives,' he said, pointing at this huge edifice on the horizon. Billy was not yet four years old, but he already knew that drive very well. He would know it even better in the years to come. That was the tragedy for Billy.

His mother preferred to look on the bright side of things. 'He likes this drive much better than the one that we used to have to take, when his daddy was in the Maze. It was as if he could sense the different atmosphere then. It got to you the

221

moment that you boarded the bus. Nobody liked going to the Maze. It was a very depressing place. The whole family was affected by it, even little Billy, But this place is really different. It's beautiful in there, such an improvement over the Maze. His dad can hardly believe it The cells I hear are really lovely. All the cells have integrated sanitation, you know.'

There was a loud roar of laughter from the back of the bus, 'Integral sanitation, Betty, integral sanitation.

Maghaberry may not have integrated sanitation, but it does have an integrated prison population. Loyalists and Republican prisoners are not segregated. Prisoners must volunteer to be transferred to Maghaberry. It is a big step for either Loyalists or Republicans from the segregated blocks of the Maze. They move outside their organisation's normal command structure. They leave the fight for freedom, or the war, or the campaign of terror, behind them. Their family loses any support or family benefits from their respective organisations. And as an official from the Northern Ireland Prison service put it 'the prisoners have to learn to rub shoulders with men that they would have shot on the outside. But, nevertheless, 160 segregated prisoners from the Maze have voted with their feet for transfer to Maghaberry. Obviously it increases the possibility of an earlier release, but it's a big step for them, and one shouldn't underestimate it.'

From the Northern Ireland Prison Service's point of view integrated conditions are a goal well worth striving for. At the time it was resisting all attempts by prisoners at Crumlin Road prison in Belfast to move away from integrated to segregated conditions. It hardly needs to be said that most of the major problems that the Northern Ireland Prison service have in the management of prisoners occur in segregated wings. Their current annual report speaks volumes on this matter. 'The difficulties in maintaining that balance [between the wishes of prisoners and the aims of the prison management] are seen most clearly at the Maze Prison which contains a large number of long-term prisoners, many of whom are serving indeterminate sentences and living in wings housing exclusively prisoners associated with one paramilitary faction or another. While the provision of improved facilities . . . was welcomed by many prisoners, it did not deflect the more committed paramilitary prisoners, and in particular those associated with the Provisional IRA, from their determination to challenge authority on a range of issues. The most serious challenge centred on a demand for the removal of an essential feature of the security measures associated with the management of the small number of prisoners in the highest security category. Such prisoners are moved between wings and blocks at frequent intervals. In the summer these prisoners insisted that they would not comply with orders to move. Their insistence was matched by a determined response by Prison Service Headquarters and local management not to concede to an unacceptable demand.'

The report finishes this particular section rather ominously: 'By the end of the period under report the Maze had returned to an uneasy calm with management anxious to ensure that the overt challenge to staff was not replaced by the more subtle conditioning of officers in wings.'

This conditioning process is sometimes not that subtle. As one serving prison official explained to me: 'You can go in one morning, and one prisoner will whisper to you that they know the name and address of your wife, or the name of the school that your daughter attends. You have to take this kind of thing seriously. Last year there were 100 threats against officers reported, and these threats were, unfortunately, given an added edge by the brutal murder of officer Brian Armour and the unsuccessful attempt to murder a senior Governor and his wife. So what do you do when a prisoner makes this kind of veiled threat. Do you ignore it? Or do you report him? If you do report him, it's your word against his. And that's only the start of the psychological pressure. In the segregated wings in the Maze, Republican prisoners will surround you and sometimes start shouting in Gaelic or pidgin Gaelic. You can't make out a word that they're saying, and they know that. Then they'll drop your name into the conversation, so that you know that they're talking about you. And that's all you know. It can be very worrying when this kind of thing occurs. In segregated wings they can coordinate their strategy to apply maximum psychological pressure to the prison officers. They have some

223

neat psychological tricks up their sleeves. Say, for example, you have two wings. One week, Wing A will be very co-operative and easy to work with and Wing B will just not co-operate. An officer will go into Wing B wearing his hat with a Crown on it, and the Republican prisoners will ask him to remove it. They'll say that they object to seeing the Crown. But the officer still has to try to work with these men, so he may take his hat off. Then one of the deputy Governors will object and tell him to keep it on. This creates frictions between staff, and allows allegiances to build up between staff and prisoners. This is exactly what the prisoners want. It's basically an attempt to subvert the system. Meanwhile the prisoners in Wing A are being very co-operative and building up a relation-ship with the officer, and then they'll suddenly turn. The officer ends up not knowing where he stands. In segregated wings with a unified strategy the paramilitaries can really work on the staff. And we all know where that can lead.'

Indeed in Belfast at that time, most of the population knew exactly where it could lead. This prison official was alluding to the case which had just been heard at Belfast Crown Court of John Hanna, a former principal warder at the Maze, who had been accused of setting up a former colleague at the Maze, Brian Armour, for IRA assassination. Hanna had denied a total of eight charges, including the aiding and abetting of this murder in October 1988, as well as the passing on of infor-mation about him and other senior prison staff to alleged IRA spy, Rosena Brown. The judge, Mr Justice Campbell, reserved his judgment in May on this particular case. But the lesson was clearly there for all to see. No one is immune to pressure when it is expertly and coherently applied. Segregated wings allow such coherence. Hence the desire for integrated wings, and the normalisation of Northern Ireland prisons.

But integrated prisons provide their own unique challenges for the prisoners themselves. Now for the very first time, they have to live in close proximity with the enemy, which can be unnerving for those reared in the segregated streets of Belfast. I had already read an excellent psychological study carried out by one of the prisoners themselves as part of his Open University Psychology degree, which addressed this very

224

issue. 'A question which has often given me cause for thought during my eight years in prison is, how come prisoners from very different political and cultural backgrounds can, in the main, get on very well together and even become friends? Remember these are men, who, only a few short years ago, would literally have been trying to kill each other. When thinking about this paradox I also noticed that even though they all seemed to talk quite freely together, one important topic never seemed to come up for discussion in "mixed" company, this was politics and the legitimacy of Northern Ireland. This suggested to me that even in this unnatural and in many ways regimented environment (where most of us share similar problems and where in many ways preconceived ideas about the 'other side' are broken down), there are still areas of "our world" which we construe completely differently from other people.'

This prisoner then used a particular psychological technique called Kelly's Repertory Grid technique to explore how he and a Republican prisoner, both sentenced to life imprisonment, construed certain core elements connected with the Troubles. This technique not surprisingly revealed that their views did differ pretty fundamentally, but their differing views did not prevent them from living peacefully together in this most unnatural of contexts. But they had learned to keep their views to themselves. As this prisoner wrote in his report, certain topics never seemed to come up for discussion in 'mixed' company.

So there I was in the visitors' room in Maghaberry in very mixed company, surveying the scene. We had already negotiated the usual round of security checks, and now we sat in a large brightly coloured room waiting for the prisoners to appear. On one wall was a very bright mural depicting various cartoon characters. This mural had been painted by one of the prisoners. A prisoner who presumably had practised his art on the sectarian gable walls of Belfast. Now the wall painting had to be neutral – cartoon characters fitted the bill perfectly. The prisoners filed in along one corridor.

In Belfast they say that you can tell Protestants and Catholics apart on the basis of their facial features. Protestants say that

225

Catholics have eyes that are very close together, Catholics unfortunately say exactly the same thing about Protestants. I watched all those pairs of eyes emerging in a huge snaking chain from the side corridor. Out to see their families. Out to see your son with his great big brown mouth and those deep blue eyes, who will change from child to boy from boy to youth from youth to God knows what without your influence or help. I watched those eyes. The eyes of the terrorist, the eyes of the freedom fighters fighting to make Ireland free, the eyes of the volunteers who had joined up to fight the IRA, the eyes of the ordinary foot soldier following orders – forever. And I prepared myself to do some quick mental calculations of size and distance, and shape and direction.

So there I sat, watching these men stream past, quite prepared to make allowances for thickness of eyebrow, width of nose and overall circumference of head. This was a unique opportunity for just such a test – a part of Northern Ireland, which is truly integrated. I suppose that I wanted to find some difference. I suppose that I really wanted to believe that there was something in it after all. I wanted to believe that these Ulstermen, these Irishmen were not just slaughtering their own kind, but killing the enemy. Whoever or whatever it was. The enemy with the eyes set so very close together. The enemy who stands out a mile. So I did my calculations. My reasoning was impeccable. Our bus was Loyalist, the bus behind ours was Republican. Where would the prisoners with the narrow band separating the eyes actually go? To us or to them? Left or right? Front or back of the room?

I watched and I calculated, and here for the very first time I can reveal the outcome of this critical empirical test from the integrated prison of Maghaberry. The answer was all over. The men with the eyes so very close together went left and right and front and back. Their eyes, unfortunately for bigots every-where, revealed nothing, except perhaps that one or two of them would undoubtedly cry when they got back to the privacy of their cells.

Along with little Billy, of course. 'He's very hard to settle after he's seen his daddy. Very hard to settle,' said his mother on the bus back.

18

Repairing the Damage

The other side of town

This was the posh end of Belfast. The place where the vowels are rounded and soft, the place where the trees on the streets shield the houses, the place where the university sits in all its Gothic splendour.

The far end of town.

Van Morrison, another Ulster Prod from the poor end of town, used to go up there to gaze at the houses and the tree-lined streets. And wonder. 'I may go crazy before that mansion on the hill.' Cyprus Avenue became world famous. And it's nothing special. Now. I saw it for the first time that day. But if this had been then, it would have been different. What were all those rooms for?

I felt it within. The fury. It had taken me all this time to get there. *Pro Tanto Quid Retribuamus*. Now, I understood. Some of them had got it all. We had got the same as the Taigs, and that wasn't much. And it was our lot who were trying to kill them. Jim Watt had been sitting in those prisons for fourteen years, dreaming of Silverstream, and the golden ponds of youth, before he was let out for a few days and realised that Silverstream wasn't quite how he remembered it. In reality it was just one big shite heap. Although he did recognise his chum's name scrawled over the name Silverstream on the road sign. I suppose that was some consolation in the end.

You have to get two buses up there from North Belfast, and with the Troubles it's an uncertain journey. Better to leave them to it. So this was Cyprus Avenue. I walked back down towards the university. There were trees everywhere. Trees, plants and shrubbery. Our little park is barren in comparison. I walked through the Botanical Gardens. It started spitting with rain again. This was my last day. It had been spitting with rain when I arrived, and now it was at it again. I sat down on a bench, before I noticed that someone was sitting at the far end. Pensive, in contemplation. It looked like a Queen's tie. An old boy of that famous university. Glasses almost off the end of his nose, with a young looking face underneath. A studied serious look on a face that you could imagine would be full of humour and fun. A medical man. I looked his way, and his face lit up. 'A touch of rain.' He spoke with that confidence and warmth and roundness of sound of middle-class Ulster. Those soft plump vowels. The Malone Road. heaven forbid. I've been trying to imitate that accent for years. 'Oh, yes, I'm from the Malone Road actually.' I can't do it. I can't even do this one sentence in that soft melodious tone. 'Beautiful, isn't it,' he said.

What the fuck was he talking about? That thought echoed through my head. It came out just like that. I had no control over it anymore. It came out in that very form. I was now the wee hard man, full of wee hard consonants from North Belfast. You can't give the slip to your speech in Belfast, and I wasn't even trying any longer. 'My tongue gets tied every, every, every time I try to speak.' That was Ivan Morrison just up the road on his day out to the big houses. I sat in silence with harsh sounds and harsh words in my head.

You are what you say, and I said fuck all. And anyway, what the fuck was beautiful about this park in the rain?

'I love this palmhouse here. The history behind it is something else. Do you know that this palmhouse is the finest example of curvilinear glass to be found anywhere in Britain?'

I sniffed loudly and narrowed my eyes, as if concentrating on what he was saying. My arse was wet and I wanted to go home. But this stranger was still talking to me. 'This palmhouse is the best preserved example of its kind. It's well worth looking at. I remember watching them rebuild it and thinking how wonderful it was.'

I hadn't even noticed it up to that point.

'There's not a lot of really superduper little bits in heritage terms in Ulster. You've got to go and rake around to look for them. There are some lovely bits if you're prepared to look, other than the lovely countryside itself, of course.'

I nodded as if I too had had that inclination.

'But I've got a lot of time for the Botanical Gardens, especially the palmhouse. There are some beautiful spots around here. Wouldn't you agree?'

I shifted my position on the wet seat.

'The quad in Queen's is still a lovely place. I was a student there, a medical student, but they have knocked our old medical building down, and put up a big new administration block.'

I just wanted to know one thing. I asked if he was from the Malone Road. 'I used to live in the Malone area, more the Lisburn Road side though. Strictly speaking, I'm not really an Ulsterman anyway, I was born in Manchester – that sounds funny but at three months I was taken to Belfast. But in my heart I'm an Ulsterman. In fact, I feel passionately about being an Ulsterman. The warmest people on this earth. I'm not a Protestant Ulsterman or a Catholic Ulsterman, I'm just some-body that was blessed to be brought up in Ulster.'

So here was the man in the middle. Neither heads nor tails. The coin resting temporarily on its side. 'You're not a betting man, then?' I enquired. He looked confused. 'Only a wee joke,' I told him. But then what would he know? The man in the middle from the Malone. The man with all the rooms in which to hide. So there we sat that day, sheltering from the rain in the shade of the trees and he told me a bit about himself.

The other side of the coin

'My heritage is actually quite confusing. My parents come originally from Glasgow. My father was a Protestant, my mother was a Catholic. I was brought up as a Protestant. At that time, if you crossed the pale as a Catholic, you were out. There was much wringing of hands about this, of course. She was cut off dead and they went to Manchester for the war years and my father worked as a baker there. He was a production manager in a bakery there, although he had come up through a working-class background. In Glasgow, he had been from one of those big families. There were five of them and his father had been a steel worker in the foundries and in the recession he had gone to Belfast. Now I don't know all the ins and outs of this but the story told in the family was that my grandfather came back a very bitter man. He was really resentful about the Ulster people. He died young, in his early forties, and left the mother to bring up the kids. That is all that was ever said to me, that he hated the Ulster people. There was something there he didn't like. I was never told what it was, I myself have no specific recollection of it. I was too young at the time. I think he may have seen me in a crib but that was about it. He was supposed to have died of cancer of the stomach or something, be it true or not true. He left my grandmother to bring up the boys, there were four boys and a girl in the family. I think he just came back from Ulster; as to whether he hadn't gelled with the situation, I couldn't really say. It wouldn't have been anything to do with religion because religion was never a big thing in our family. They went to their churches, but they weren't Wee Frees [Free Presbyterians] or anything like that. Religion was just a fact of life.

'The four brothers all did very well in their own odd ways in terms of career. My father, as I said, started off as apprentice baker, he did all the City and Guilds and got all his medals and things. He did very very well as a working-class lad, he educated himself by going to night classes. When he moved to Belfast he became production manager in Inglis's in Belfast and left Inglis's – oh, in the sixties and went into business with a friend. They had baker's shops all around Belfast, and then they sold out and he retired at fifty-eight years of age.

'All of the brothers on my father's side did well. One was in the Post Office. He started off as a telegraph boy but he ended up in a very senior position in the Post Office in Scotland. Another brother was a messenger boy in a grocery business, he ended up as a director of a chain store and the other one was the youngest manager of a tram depot ever in Glasgow. He was the oldest and brightest – I don't know if I dare say brightest, but he was always revered in the family. The sister married a guy who had a very successful confectionery business. The family were all very successful in their own particular ways.

'My folks in Manchester were very happy. My mother says that they were the happiest days of her life, in the war. The camaraderie was brilliant. My father was production manager with, I think, Beattie's, a bakery in Manchester. I've read articles about my father in a magazine called *The British Baker*, in the fifties. When I say they enjoyed it, those were good years for them, my brother was born there and I was born at the very end of the war. We came to Belfast in 1946, my dad went to Inglis's, the largest family bakery in the United Kingdom. It was probably a golden job opportunity for my father. I mean in terms of the money of those days, this was big business. My grandfather had been to Ulster as I've said, although he didn't seem to like the place, and there were no other contacts with Northern Ireland on the maternal side. My father and mother just moved there because it was a good job opportunity – nothing else, and I know my mother felt very isolated at first, when they had moved to Ulster. In Belfast we went first to Ravenhill Park which is just off the Ravenhill Road and we were living in a detached house there. We'd had a semi-detached house in Manchester. I took my mum back to Manchester a few years ago and we actually went to the old house, in fact they had been in a few of them because they had been bombed out of a couple of them. The detached house in Belfast was a wee step up for them. It was a nice area so it was, Ravenhill Park.

'My brother and I were sent to Downey House which was one of the prep schools of Methody. The prep school was very convenient – it was a 300- or 400-yard walk from our front door. Downey and Fullerton House were the two prep schools for Methody, and you know, we just went through a very ordinary education. We played with local kids and we got sent to Sunday School, just like everybody else. Oddly enough, it was my mother who was the one who shoved us out to Sunday School every Sunday, even though she herself did not pursue her own religion. As far as she was concerned she had been excommunicated, and that was the finish of that. I think that was probably a source of great sorrow to her. My mother never went to church with us, but my father always tootled back and forwards over the years, you know three or four times a year, maybe a lot more sometimes. He had been in the Boys' Brigade in Glasgow, you see, the family would have been brought up as regular church-goers. To this day he has books that were given to him as Sunday School prizes. That would have been very much the working-class Glasgow thing, being brought to the local Sunday Schools etc. But religion was never discussed in the house, certainly my mother never heard any derogatory comments about her being a Catholic. Justice would have been brought to bear upon us, if there had been any such comments. There wasn't any bitterness in those days. Downey and Methody must have been Protestant establishments, but there was no climate of sectarianism or antagonism to Catholics at the schools. I went to the local Presbyterian Sunday School. I was going to one up at the end of the Ravenhill Road, then we went to one up the other end of the Ravenhill Road. I never quite worked out why. One of my own kids was recently explaining to someone about my roots, and he implied that I went to Big Ian's establishment. I nearly died. Of course, at that time, Big Ian had something that looked like a little hut at the very far end of Ravenhill Road. I can remember that from when I was a kid. Well, I mean that's where they had been originally and then, of course, they moved down to the Martyr's Memorial, which was the all singing, all dancing establishment with parking for seventy-nine buses or what have you.

'The Troubles didn't really start in 1969. I remember the Troubles in the 1950s. We used to have these little trips over the border to Dundalk. I can remember going across there on a few occasions with sausages stuffed in the back of the car and that sort of thing. There was a border post burnt out, and I can remember people saying that it was the IRA who did it. But it didn't really dawn on me at the time who or what they

232

were. I think that would have been in the mid-1950s, I think I was about ten at the time. But I never ever saw any trouble. It was just some vague threat in the background.

'I remember that it was an annual pilgrimage for me with mother and father to go and watch the bands on the twelfth of July and my mother would wring her hands at the Glasgow bands and say what a dreadful embarrassment they were because they were always out of their heads, so they were. They were the scruffiest, roughest bunch of the lot, but it was the carnival element of the twelfth which appealed to the family. My mother always seemed very keen to go to watch the proceedings. She liked to watch, so that she could come home and tell us all that the dreadful Glasgow bands were such an embarrassment. It's funny, but all the days were sunny. You don't remember any wet ones. I assume that we went every year, but whether I'm right or wrong I don't know. Everybody went out to watch the bands on the twelfth. My father never teased her at all about it. Religion was never discussed in the family.

'Even though my parents were from Scotland, I never noticed their accents. It never dawned on me that they were any different. To this day I'm not aware of the fact that I speak in a somewhat different manner to any of my English medical colleagues. But remember the Scots in Ireland have probably had a much easier relationship with the Irish than the English in Ireland. You've got the Ards Peninsula with the Scottish Plantation element right through there and if you go up into Ballymena or Ballymoney, you could be in Scotland. I mean my dad was always known as a Scot. I'm sure, they would have called him "The wee Scottish man" but I was never aware that my parents were any different. They had no problem at all with the Ulster people. My father worked with them day in and day out. They were his bread and butter. They were a good work force. Ulster people have a tradition of being good workers. Against that, there are the problems that you have in any industry – the boys are out on a Friday night and they don't figure on Saturday morning. You've got to go and beat them out of their houses to get them in on a Saturday and get the plant rolling. In later years when my dad joined the other business, they had shops all over Belfast and they had a whole

233

hotch potch of people working for them. My father went in as a third partner to this firm. But I mean they had all sorts working in there. Of course the Troubles were just rumbling around the corner at this stage. The bakery of this new firm was on the Donegall Road. It was a good wee business. I mean it was very much a family business, so it was, there were no Jags sitting outside. They just weren't in that league.

'My brother and I were both sent to prep school – the reason I think was that the prep school was just over the road. My dad had obviously made every effort to educate himself through his night school and stuff and had done very well in his own sort of league, but education wasn't hammered in to us. There was no perception of the professions and how I got hooked was through my own GP. I used to play with his son and his books were there and I used to look through the books when I was about thirteen. That's really what started me off, and I got the bit between my teeth and obviously my parents looked after me and backed me all the way. I think when you go to grammar school, you know you've got to put some effort in. There was a lot of work and you worked hard without questioning it. I was no brilliant scholar but once I'd got the bit between my teeth, I made sure I got what I needed. I was always provided for – in sensible terms. If I needed a book at university, the old boy would say "go and get it".

'I went to the same university that everybody else went to – Queen's University in Belfast. I went up in 1964. Queen's was brilliant. This is an odd thing but I never wanted to go anywhere different. It had to be Queen's. I wanted to go to university desperately and I wanted to do medicine desperately. The day that my best friend and I got the acceptance letters we both zapped down into town, and got the medical school scarves. I mean scarves were still "in" in those days and it's the sort of thing you might go "yuck" at now. But it was a dream come true. It was a wonderful opportunity and I often feel sorry that other kids don't show the hunger and the longing to get there like we had. Queen's was wonderful, and it had a wonderful reputation for medicine. As far as I was concerned I was going to the best university in the world and I have no reason to alter my opinion now.

234

'Med school was a bit odd, so it was. The Dean ruled the Med School with a rod of iron. He had been a Professor of Pathology at something like the age of thirty-two and became Dean of the Medical School at the age of thirty-four and stayed there until he was sixty-five. He was a little man with a moustache. He had done some clever work in his earlier days in pathology, he was a brain pathologist, but I mean we revered him. To us he was like God almighty. The Dean was your bog standard Ulsterman, everybody was a bloody Ulsterman in those days. I understand that he died at about seventy-two or seventy-four years of age or thereabouts, on the steps of BMA House in England, still working. I mean that summed the Dean up. The Dean ran the Medical school. I mean he interviewed everybody personally, and you really got in on his blessing. The examination results were vaguely important but his impressions were crucial. If he didn't like you he wouldn't have had you in his school. The composition of the group was mainly Ulster people, not so many females, the rules and regulations read a fifty-fifty split nowadays but there were fewer females in those days, maybe a twenty-five–seventy-five split. That would be a vague guess. I mean I can remember lots of girls, I don't remember any dearth of them. In terms of religious composition, there was probably a real mix down the middle and I think I can really put my hand on my heart and say it didn't matter a bugger. We all went out boozing together.

'Do you know the only odd thing that I'll always remember? We always had a yearly dinner and these damn things always seemed to fall on a Friday and we had a guy who is a very successful surgeon in Belfast these days, and he would have to go up to the old Bish to get permission for the troops to eat meat on the Friday. I can't remember the name of the hotel we used to go to, we'd go to one of the hotels out on the Antrim Road there and have meat and two veg as the standard, for £5 10s or whatever it was. And I always remember that day, he would have to stand up and say that he had the authority from the Bish that those of other persuasions could have meat tonight. But even that was, you know, like someone saying "I'll have a pint of stout", or whatever. It was just part of the night and people would have been more surprised if he had

235

got up to say you could now start to smoke. Permission to smoke was a bigger surprise than announcing that the Bish says we don't have to have the fish tonight.

'At Med School, there was no sectarianism. We were very tightly integrated. We were the bad bunch and we would all troll off to the pubs and we stuck around together for years and years and years. We got thrown out of all the nice ones – we got thrown out of the Bot and then we got thrown out of the one across the road, the Egg, and we ended up drinking in our fifth and final year in 1969 at the bottom of the Falls Road in Divis Street. We drank in the pub beside the police station. The police station was on one corner and we were on the other corner. The Spanish Rooms was its name. It was rampantly Catholic down there. The justification for going there was the boys who had been to the Catholic St Mary's used to drink there before Med School, or so they said. There were some right clever buggers out of that school. A wonderful scatter of backgrounds. There were one or two nice people who had come through the right routes but an awful lot of very ordinary grammar school lads who had no great middle-class background. Ordinary lads from the lower middle class to lads from rock bottom backgrounds. These were wonderful years and we had some fun.

'In the Spanish Rooms, scrumpy was the big thing. You used to be able to take your bottle along and get it filled up. I'll tell you what, it was 11d for a pint of scrumpy and 1s 1d for a chicken roll. It was a really long roll, stuffed with chicken, and you had to hold the bugger to stop it springing open. There was the father and two sons behind the bar and they all had their sleeves rolled up and as I remember they all had forearms about nine inches across. As was the thing that you often find with working-class bars, the owners were very prim and proper and there was no nonsense. So you'd have all the wine victims downstairs drinking the scrumpy, then you'd have the locals, and you'd have these students coming trogging in and out. We would go upstairs and the landlady would light a fire for *her* boys and we would get the upstairs room and she would look after us up there. Now the girls would come along occasionally and they were not welcome. I remember one of

236

the lassies sitting with her feet up, she was a daughter of one of the eminent consultants in the city, and the landlady came in and said, "Get your feet down and cover your knees up!" She was a very prim and proper, Catholic type mother and if there were any breakages on the night, or the odd glass which got tipped over, the landlady would say, "Put the money in the charity box". You would never pay her, the charities did very well out of us medical students. So that's where we used to go on a Thursday night. The point I'm really trying to make is that I thought nothing of driving down Divis Street, for a drink just beside Hastings Street barracks, and there was no fear or intimidation or anything like that.

'The night things went wrong in August 1969, I was on the Falls Road in the accommodation owned by the hospital doing my Paediatrics. It was opposite the kids' hospital and of course Springfield Road was just round the corner. I was on the ground floor, front bedroom and there was a bus stop outside. How I remember this is the fact that you thought that these bloody buses were actually parking in your room with the noise they made. One night about three o'clock in the morning I heard "da de da de da" for the first time and thought, "That sounds like gunfire," having nothing other than the movies to base that statement on. I had no past experience of guns or shooting. I went over for breakfast to the Royal next morning and said, "Did you people hear anything last night?" just in case I was dreaming. They had all heard the gunfire. One of them told a lovely story. He said he heard the gunfire and he opened his window and he looked down the Falls and there was this auld fella coming up on a push bike. Suddenly, the gunfire goes off, so the auld fella jumps off the push bike. A taxi comes up the road as he flags the taxi down, throws the push bike in the back of the taxi, jumps in and they drive off. So obviously they had a little more insight to the potential problems of the situation than we had.

'Let's say for the sake of argument that this was a Thursday and my session finished on the Friday, Belfast had started to hum and lorry loads of lads were coming down the Falls Road, there were builders' lorries with guys in the back. I mean I've never seen anything like this before and there was obviously something not right and I packed my bag and I went home and that night it blew up. We had moved to Stranmillis, near the Malone Road, in 1968. I came in to the Royal the following night. It was a stupid thing to do. We knew there was something big going off and we wanted to be involved. The barriers were up. I came down off the Lisburn Road, a very steep road, and down at the bottom there's a very hard little Protestant enclave at the end of Donegall Road there. Once you got down there, you could see that the boys, the vigilantes, were out and finally there was a barricade across the road that went into the Royal and it was three cars high at that stage. Not three cars wide but three cars high. The boys behind the barricades were as pissed as newts. I just said that I was a doctor going into the hospital. I'd go spare if I thought that my son was doing something like that. That night I saw only one case come into casualty, and we had the old Professor of Surgery there who was an ex-military man, and to keep morale up he would set the chaps to clean the floor. We went up on the roof of the Out Patients and it was like the movies of the blitz. They were starting to burn out the mills to get the snipers down the Donegall Road. There was gunfire all over the city. There were all sorts of guns being used – shotguns, hand guns, the old Thompson sub-machine guns. The shooting was all over the place. In the morning when dawn broke, on the Grosvenor Road, you could have heard a pin drop, every side street had a barricade. Now I'm not talking about a few wee chairs, I am talking about things that looked like you'd brought in a team of engineers to build them. There was corrugated iron everywhere – there was no way you could get in, or out of the side streets. The road going up the side of Dunville Park had got a double decker in it and the bus was turned sideways. God knows how they ever got it back out again? But it was amazing. So the Troubles really started in my final year. We thought to ourselves: "Brilliant, we'll see all these injuries we've only heard about. It will probably last a few weeks." Then we saw the soldiers coming in and then we heard about all these different wounds. Then we started to see things we'd never dreamt of before. I was a Houseman at the Royal and then I went to the Department of Anatomy for nine months and then back into the Royal and I worked there for about another two years. I was in the Royal until 1974 and then I was sent out to a country hospital for a year and then I came back into the Royal and I more or less stayed in the Royal. I was Houseman there, then Senior House Officer, then I was a Registrar in surgery, then a Senior Registrar. Now a Consultant.

'In terms of the work that we do, obviously you've got your everyday bread-and-butter work that comes into any hospital, but against that we have had this war background, this military background. You remember all these odd experiences. I remember being in casualty one night, I would have been an SHO at that stage. It was the first night a petrol bomber was shot by the army and we had a guard in the hospital and we were told by him that there was a riot going on. But it was a terrible reality seeing that sort of thing. These are just flashes of memory from about that time. I had a youngster brought in. He had been murdered in a garage, he was in his overalls, and the thing that sticks with me is his hand was in his pocket, and it was still in his pocket when he got to us, and it meant that when this kid was shot he was actually leaning over the bonnet of a car looking at an engine. He was shot in the back of the head by some bugger whilst he was doing this and he was only a boy about seventeen or sixteen. It was the hand in the pocket that got me. It was the fact that here was a very ordinary guy shot with no knowledge of his impending death. He was shot up the Lisburn Road. Later I learned that this RUC officer was walking past the garage when he heard the gunshots. The officer saw this gunman running off, so he fired on him and he brought him down. So we got the dead youngster in and a little later in comes his killer who's been shot in the leg. I said, "That's bloody good shooting," and this RUC sergeant said to me: "That's just where he bloody hit him." You got the impression that the RUC guy had opened up on this gunman.

'I'll say another thing for the police, I never heard a sectarian comment once from them. You didn't know who you had lying in front of you – Protestant or Catholic, UVF or IRA. It's funny, this is another story. When people were shot, we used

239

to say, "Where were you shot?" Often they would be very cagey in their reply, but you weren't asking them where they were shot in terms of which area of Belfast did it happen. We were trying to ascertain where in their body they had been shot. We were trying to find out where they were sore. You never asked who anybody was or what their circumstances were. You would just never ever enquire, you just didn't know who they were. I used to listen to the news when I had been working to find out who I had been operating on and the circumstances of the shooting or whatever, but there was never any question of operating on a Catholic or a Protestant or a good guy or a bad guy. They were all guys who you were fighting to save.

'Casualty was a wonderful place to work in. The sister was a good Catholic lassie whose brother was a priest up in Clonard and she ruled with a rod of soft iron and I remember this Catholic lad being wheeled off to have his bullet taken out, and he turned round to Sister and called her a Protestant bitch. She laughed and said, "If my brother could only hear him saying that." And I can remember another thing in those very early days, helping hold a guy down – who was again pissed as a newt cursing us and telling us he would get us, he would fix us. Here we were trying to save this guy's life. That I remember from the early days. I can see him still, I mean it was just a combination of shock, and the fact that he had been shot and that he was a bit out of his head on drink. I don't remember whether he was a Protestant or a Catholic. What I can say is that the A&E folk in the Royal were the greatest on God's earth. You had the Consultant, the boss – for twenty years a missionary surgeon, a kinder man you wouldn't meet, a real Christian. I don't know how you'd define Christian, but you could not have got a nicer, finer man. Sister, a Catholic lass, and just this group in the middle. You didn't know who or what they were. I mean it never mattered. You know the old ploy in Northern Ireland was, "What school did you go to?" But there it just wasn't relevant. They were a totally mixed bunch, they worked as a super team. You know it was like *Mash*. There was the funny side you find in *Mash*, but everything you saw in *Mash* was happening in that unit. The

240

camaraderie, the stresses, the strains, the care. The number of times that I have been asked, "How did you cope?' But there's no problem coping when you're coping as a group. "Were you horrified at what you saw?" Of course you were horrified, but I mean it became second nature. Second nature's the wrong term for it. It implies that second nature's ordinary, but a nasty thing never becomes ordinary, but it becomes something you're dealing with. It becomes business, not business in any cold sense, but business nonetheless. But the care was wonderful.

'There were plenty of snipers in the early seventies who were hitting the police and the army in the head and neck with awful accuracy and one of the great myths from the movies is that the likes of Clint Eastwood, when he shoots you, he kills you straight away. But you don't fall dead like that. It just doesn't work like that in real life. You're not dead when you're shot. It takes time to die. And we'd get these boys brought in with half their head blown out with high velocity weapons and they're alive and they're kicking, they're gagging, trying to breathe and we would have a go and we would resuscitate them and then we would get to the stage where the brain surgeon or the neurosurgeon would come in and say, "Lads, there's nothing left in there. We can't do anything." So we would have to stop what we were doing, and Sister and the staff nurse would sit with that person until they died, and that could be for three or four hours. If anybody ever tries to say that there is sectarianism in a situation like that, then they're talking through their hat. Sister would hold the hand of a soldier or policeman, a member of the UVF or IRA. She didn't discriminate. It was brilliant. There was never a hint of any-thing like that. The quality of the care was infinite. It really was magic.

'Did I say a brilliant time? War can never be brilliant or horror can never be brilliant, but I have been privileged to work with some of those people in those days. It was great.

'It left you with many vivid memories. There was an incident where this kid was brought in. The supposed story was the kid was throwing a blast bomb. He was a fourteen-year-old. The account of the incident that we heard was that this soldier

241

sees him, steps round the window and shoots the kid with his SLR. He hit him in the groin and he blew out the femoral artery. So we had this fourteen-year-old brought in. You know, he was a child. Fourteen-year-olds like this are wee bony youngsters, they're not great hulking brutes of men. So here's this kid and we tried to resuscitate him and he died and when you lose a child or youngster you feel you've failed. When you come away your comment is that, "We've failed to resuscitate this kid", you cannot do the impossible but it does leave you with a feeling that you're still a failure. I mean there was a guy who was an eminent surgeon in Belfast who would be in tears at times like this. I remember that kid to this day. I remember the family of this kid coming in, and the abject despair and horror and the tears. I remember families coming in where the husband had been killed. The mother would come in with three or four kids and they all looked as if they could do with a damn good wash. They'd just been called out of the house and she had been doing the cleaning or whatever. The old mother or mother-in-law would be there and the kids would be going crazy, and you'd have a very inadequate room to break the news to them, and you were trying to tell them that their husband was dead. Of course they knew something awful had happened because they had been brought to hospital and herded into a wee room. The grannies were brilliant. So too were the priests. The priests were always around.

'I used to get the hospital priest to give the last rites to the soldiers, not knowing who they were or what religion they were. I reckoned that it was always better to go with something than nothing at all. It doesn't really matter at that stage. The priests have been really good. It doesn't matter a dicky bird when you're dying. Denomination is irrelevant at that stage. It all boils down to good and bad at the end of the day. It doesn't matter whether you go to mosque, chapel, church or just wander around your garden thinking good thoughts.

'There were plenty of murders and attempted murders to keep us occupied. A soldier walking past a lamp post with a bomb behind the metal plate in the side. The bomb would blow his leg off at the hip and we'd hear the Saracens coming up to Casualty, they had a very low whine, because of the

242

low gearing. At night you'd hear this banshee coming in, with this wailing sound, and it would stop suddenly in this low gear, and the back metal doors would open with a crash. It would be like the gates of hell opening with a bang. Whatever it is, is dropped in military fashion on you, full combat gear on – soldiers back off, clear away, I mean that's what they're there for and maybe an officer comes in. So you've got a guy with a leg blown off lying there in full battle gear. The first thing that you have to do is to try to get his flak jacket off. You can't cut a flak jacket off with a pair of scissors. Then you have to get stuck into resuscitating these people. They were brave men. They were all brave men. Very early on, I remember this wino being hysterical in Casualty, but in later years you never perceived any self-pity, any great fear, any cries for help or despair. That goes for them all no matter who they were.

'We had a very bad night when the IRA – the Provisionals and the Officials – fell out. The Provos went round shooting all the Officials, at least all the cell leaders that they could get hold of. We had a lot of these boys wheeled in, and some of them were very, very badly hurt. We triaged, that is we sorted out the living from the dying. We sorted out one client who was dying and somebody actually intervened and I ended up operating on the man and he was very, very badly injured. He had a lot of holes in him. But the good Lord was with him and we salvaged him. In the pecking order of things he was too near the bottom of the list to begin with. Triage is defined two ways, it has two definitions, one is that if the needs falls within your resources you take the most seriously injured and prioritise downwards. If the needs exceed your resources you take the least injured and prioritise upwards, i.e. the most seriously injured get set to one side to die. It's really a war classification and this night was so bad, we had so many come in, we would start with those we could salvage or were sure of salvaging. It's a straight decision, I mean you cannot devote teams to lost causes. It's not a cruel thing, it's a rational thing. This IRA man should have been put to one side. He should have been grateful for us saving his life, but he wasn't. He was a dour big bugger. Some of them could be wonderfully warm, I mean all

243

of them were basically warm. I only can remember him as the only miserable big bugger amongst them. The rest were great.

'We would see these punishment shootings on a regular basis. It was a bit like in a normal hospital on a frosty day you get broken wrists coming in at regular intervals. Somebody would just say, "By the way there's a kneecapping in reception." They used to shoot them through the calf or through the thigh, a lot of them weren't shot through the knee, thank goodness, because that really is a very nasty thing to do. We would just sort them out, and it would be a bit quiet, no talking, you'd never enter into any conversation over this as to who did this, or who did what. But I'll tell you a funny story. We got this boy brought in – he was squealing and very, very distraught. He'd been kneecapped. So I told him that I wanted to take a look at his leg. And he whispered, "I'm all right, doc." So I said, "What do you mean you're bloody all right, you've just been brought in the ambulance here, and here are the bullet holes in your trousers." So he whispered, "They haven't shot me," so I said, "What are you squealing about then?" So he whispered "They've missed." "What are you doing in the hospital then?" So he said, "Jesus don't tell them." The bullets had gone through the back of his trouser leg but missed his actual leg, so he lay there squealing on the floor. When he saw that the coast was clear, he got off like a shot. Boy, was he frightened.

'There were some very nasty punishments. We had kids brought in one day who had been thieving and the IRA held them on the ground and they dropped breeze blocks on their elbows from about four feet away. So you've got these rough youngsters of fifteen or sixteen years of age, who have been very badly punished.

'But they can be barbaric on both sides. I'll tell you a story that sticks in my mind. There was a lassie in my year, a Catholic lassie, her brother was a grammar school teacher at a good Catholic grammar school in Belfast, and he went to pick his sister up at the airport. Anyway he took a wrong turn somewhere near the Horseshoe Road and he ended up in a Protestant area near the Horseshoe bend. Well he got lost and he went into one of the streets up there and he got stopped by

244

these guys, and they twigged that he was a Taig. So they took him out and they interrogated him. They started to torture him, they burnt him with cigarettes – they gave him a really bad time. Finally they took him out into the country, put him on his knees, and cocked a gun at the back of his head. They pulled the trigger so he heard this gun going off. But there was no bullet in the chamber. So he cracked up. He got up and he ran, crying into the night. He was terrified. He had nothing to do with the Troubles, he just went to the wrong church. They had done all this to him for no other reason, other than the fact that he attended the wrong kind of church. I saw him at about ten o'clock the following morning and he had walked the streets of Belfast all that night. He just walked and walked and walked and his injuries in physical terms were not horrendous but to hear him talking, he had gone through hell. He was quite sure that he was going to be killed. Maybe it was an accident that he wasn't shot. Maybe they just let him go. Maybe somebody said that enough is enough. Or else it was a very cruel, sick form of humour. But he cracked up. I was seeing him just a few hours after it all happened, I mean, that's not even the start of the trouble. I'm just seeing him in that flat, shellshocked state just after the event. Just think what this incident must have done to him over the years.

'Working in casualty has taught me a lot about people. Not surprisingly, you end up thinking that the Troubles are bloody daft. Ulster folk are the warmest on God's earth, and yet they can do these insane things to each other in the name of religion. It's senseless. More than senseless when you've seen as much of death, as I have. Denomination doesn't matter a damn when it comes down to it.'

I left him gazing at the beauty of that curvilinear design of the palmhouse in the Botanical Gardens. He had earned his respite. His talk had brought me all the way from Scotland, right to that bit of Belfast that I had never known, but somehow resented anyway. They can't all be like him, I thought to myself. The swanks can't all be like that.

His talk had finally taken me back up to the Horseshoe Road, and that bit of Belfast that I knew best. The Horseshoe was our way out of Belfast. We used to walk to the Wee Shop up the Horseshoe every Sunday, then cut down into Ligoniel village. The Wee Shop had a large orange sign made out of cardboard, sitting outside it. It was a Fanta bottle. When you got to that cardboard sign, you knew that you had gone as far along the Horseshoe as you needed to, and that you would be starting to head back home. The Wee Shop was as far as you went. It was as far as you needed to go.

That Fanta bottle had seen some sights. Soldiers had been abducted and murdered out the back of the Wee Shop. Bodies had been dumped in the quarries nearby. Lone Catholics had been 'interrogated' and beaten under the gaze of that lone Fanta bottle. I wonder what they asked them and what other cruel games they played. I wonder how many other guns failed to go off.

I wonder how many other men were forced to walk and walk and walk the streets of Belfast. Without respite.

This was the bit of Belfast that I knew best, and yet I didn't know it at all. I had talked to some of the men of violence and they didn't know it either. Not surprising really, things change. The Fanta bottle has gone now, so too has the Wee Shop. It's a private house now. But then again, many of the landmarks had changed all over Belfast. You had to look a bit closer to read the signs, to see where you were. To see where you might be heading. To see where you might have been.

I decided to walk back into town. The winter sun made Belfast look radiant. I felt that glow inside like you do when you're home. I felt like starting all over again. I felt good.

Then, quite unexpectedly, the rain started. In earnest.